Erasing the

LIBERTY

THE BATTLE TO KEEP ALIVE
THE MEMORY OF ISRAEL'S
MASSACRE ON THE USS *LIBERTY*

PHILIP F. TOURNEY
WITH DAVID R. GAHARY

ROCKSTAR
PUBLISHING

Erasing the Liberty
The Battle to Keep Alive the Memory of Israel's Massacre on the
USS Liberty

First Edition 2018

ISBN 978-0-692-99228-9

Phillip F. Tourney with David R. Gahary

Rockstar Publishing · 6256 Bullet Drive · Crestview · Florida · 32536

Order more copies of *Erasing the* Liberty (softcover, 434 pages, 102 photographs and images, $25) from the above address.

Autographed and inscribed versions available upon request. Autographed copy: $50 Inscribed copy: $100 (please indicate inscription wording when ordering or email USSLiberty@ erasingtheliberty.com).

All checks and money orders should be made out to Rockstar Publishing

Printed in the United States of America

Table of Contents

PUBLISHER'S NOTE

Dozens of patriotic Americans availed themselves for this book—a labor of love for them, and us—including 15 survivors of the Israeli massacre and 15 others with a deep connection to the vicious assault. Their stories, and the stories of scores of others,* may be the final attempt—on such a grand scale—to get the terrible truth about the USS *Liberty* out to the world.

Marie Ward, whose brother Joe survived the massacre but sadly perished in a car crash a few years later, provided some never-before-published photos on the following pages, as well as Bob Hamel, who piloted the first rescue vehicle to reach the tattered *Liberty*. Also, John Lipscomb provided several documents related to the SOS messages his ship received from *Liberty*. All of these vital photos and documents will help shed more light on this dark page of U.S. history, and we are extremely grateful for them.

This book contains 50 chapters, to represent the 50 years since the massacre. As more information becomes available, more chapters may be added to future editions.

* All dialogue is indented to distinguish it from Phil Tourney's words, which tell the story.

Hauling caskets filled with the remains of my murdered shipmates
from the USS *Liberty*

Dedication

This is dedicated to my fallen shipmates and to all patriotic Americans and people everywhere, who, when they read this book, will come away shocked and dismayed as to how the U.S. government lied to the American people about the cold-blooded, premeditated murder of Americans on the high-seas, a cover-up perpetrated not just by them but by the government of Israel as well.

Fifty years is far too long. From LBJ to Donald Trump to all the congressmen and women who bow down to Israel first and couldn't care less about taking care of America—which they took an oath to the U.S. Constitution to do—all have become beholden to the Zionist state of Israel.

I would like to thank all who contributed to this book and those who are supporting making it into a full-length feature film.

Phillip F. Tourney

Naval Training Center San Diego (Boot Camp), Company 128, Outstanding Recruit Citation

Bronze Star Medal with Combat "V" for heroism or valor in combat

Purple Heart

Vietnam Service Medal with one bronze service star

National Defense Service Medal

Combat Action Ribbon

Presidential Unit Citation

Battle Efficiency Ribbon

Two honorable discharges from the United States Navy

They were sent there to finish us off. The aircraft were sent to make us incommunicado so we couldn't send an SOS out. The torpedo boats were sent to sink us. And the helicopters were sent to pick off survivors so there'd be no trace. It was a perfectly executed military operation.

—Commander David E. Lewis

There is no possibility at all that that could've been a case of mistaken identity. Our ensign was always flying, our ship was spotless, constantly being painted. The GTR-5 across the front of the ship is like in 10 or 15 foot letters. LIBERTY was across the fantail. This is one of the best air forces in the world at that time, and they couldn't recognize an American ship on a crystal-clear, beautiful day, with probably unlimited visibility? Anything other than that is bullshit. There is no question that they knew who we were.

—CTSN Robert A. Scarborough

They were trying to sink us and kill all survivors.

—CT2 Robert J. Schnell

There's nobody that can tell me that that was an accident, that was a case of mistaken identity, whatever you wanna call it, when you could shoot every antenna at least one time, some of them more than once. If you think that ship is somebody else, how do you hit all them antennas?

—DC3 James Clayton Smith

If anybody can look at what took place, and the damage, and buy into that it was a mistake, then their view of reality is just totally different than mine.

—CTSN Donald W. Pageler

If it was an accident, it was the best planned accident I've ever heard of.

—Commander David E. Lewis

All I want out of this is for the government to stand up and say, "Yeah, we screwed that up," and have the Israeli government stand up and say, "Yeah, we screwed that up." But that'll never happen. Not in my lifetime.

—DC3 James Clayton Smith

To all surviving members of the USS Liberty, *I say my love and prayers. You will never be forgotten for the sacrifice you made, and my heart goes out to the families who have lost their loved ones. Your shipmate,*

—SFM3 Dulio Demori

Foreword

When Phil contacted me in August of 2015 to discuss a new book project, I didn't know what to think.

I had interviewed the survivor of Israel's inhumane attack on his ship, USS *Liberty*, a few years earlier a couple of times, and had the honor of meeting him at a free speech conference in Texas as well. We got along but didn't really stay in touch. The call, as I was driving a moving truck across the mountains of Pennsylvania on my way to Florida from New Jersey, came from out of the blue.

I had read his first book, *What I Saw That Day: Israel's June 8, 1967 Holocaust of U.S. Servicemen Aboard the USS* Liberty *and its Aftermath*, and enjoyed it, but I wasn't quite clear about what Phil wanted to do: upgrade his book into a second edition or create a new one.

I would not find out too soon.

I read the book over and over again, until I knew it well. But it wasn't well enough.

Phil and I spent hours, almost every day over a year, talking over home phones, cell phones, Skype and email, digging through every detail of the book, revisiting old memories he surely had done hundreds of times. Despite this fact that I'm sure of, he was always gracious, always willing to explore each experience deeper than the time before, in the hopes that I would thoroughly understand what he—and others—had gone through.

As the new book evolved, we uncovered things about the *Liberty* that few knew, maybe no one knew. And we put it all together in this new book, *Erasing the* Liberty*: The Battle to Keep Alive the Memory of Israel's Massacre on the USS* Liberty, its sole purpose being to educate as many people as possible about this shameful chapter in U.S. and world history.

We chose the title *Erasing the* Liberty after Phil had used the word "erase" several times over a six-month period while we worked on the book. It was the perfect title, because that was exactly what "they" were trying to do, they being those people, who, through their ceaseless manipulation to drown out any attempt to introduce the story of the *Liberty*, had effectively erased the history of this ship from the pages of time. This had to end, we both agreed.

Along with the plan for a new book came a plan for a movie: a full-length feature film that will tell the accurate—as this book does—history of the ship, and much of what its crew has endured, for over 50 years.

We all know that if those in charge of the mainstream media—whether the print media, the big book publishing houses, the television networks, or the major movie studios—wanted you to know about the *Liberty*, you would already know.

They don't want this story told: not today, not tomorrow, and not ever.

But we do.

And we hope you do, too.

The last chapter of this book will show you how to help us get this story onto the big screen, whether it's the silver screen, HBO, Netflix, or even the lowly Internet.

Either way, let's get it done, if for nothing else than for the remaining *Liberty* survivors, who have been harassed, abused, accused, and berated, all for wanting to tell anyone they could about what happened that clear, sunny day in June, over a half-century ago.

—**David R. Gahary, USN (Ret.)**
December 2017

1

Navy

My name is Phillip Francis Tourney, born December 18, 1946, proud survivor of the USS *Liberty*, attacked by Israel, June 8, 1967, and this is my story, as well as many survivors and others.

There are some destinies that cannot be avoided. For me, joining the United States Navy (USN) was one of them. Both of my older brothers had joined, and so the thought of one day being part of that club was something as natural to me as breakfast in the morning.

The USN, founded October 13, 1775, traces its origins to the Continental Navy, and is the largest navy in the world, with almost 300 deployable combat vessels and over 3,700 operational aircraft, including the world's largest aircraft carrier fleet, manned by over 300,000 active duty personnel and over 100,000 in the Navy Reserve.

"The mission of the Navy is to maintain, train and equip combat-ready Naval forces capable of winning wars, deterring aggression and maintaining freedom of the seas."

Until my 17th birthday—when you could join with your parents' permission—I did my duty as a family member by working and helping Dad with his plastering business. Mom and Dad knew that as soon as I hit the big "1-7" I was gone, and they were fine with that. So literally, on my 17th birthday we headed down to the recruiting station where they signed the papers for me.

As soon as I put my John Hancock down, I was whisked away for some physical tests right there in the same building. The Navy doctor who examined me said I wouldn't make it through the physical; I was devastated to the point of tears. I got dressed and left the building.

Immediately after the test, Mom and Dad relocated to California, where, as Dad hoped, business would be better. I went with them to help Dad out for two months, but it was no use. I simply had to be in the Navy, no matter what it took. I talked Dad into signing the papers one more time so I could try again to enlist.

Thankfully, the U.S. government did not have computers back then, because I had to tell a little white lie when asked on the forms if I had ever enlisted in any other branch of the military previously but been denied. I was always scared to death that one day, out of the blue, some tough-as-nails Chief Petty Officer (CPO) would come up to me, yank me out of whatever training I was doing and send me home. (CPO is the seventh enlisted rate in the U.S. Navy.)

Phil Tourney on leave in 1964

Rate refers to an enlisted sailor's pay grade and rating refers to their area of occupational specialization within the enlisted USN. USN enlisted rates run from E-1—where "E" stands for "enlisted"— (the most junior enlisted sailor) to E-9 (the most senior enlisted sailor), which is used across all U.S. military branches.

E-1 to E-3 sailors are considered apprentices and are divided into five groups with colored marks designating the group to which they belong: Seaman, Fireman, Airman, Constructionman, and Hospitalman.

E-4 to E-6 sailors are non-commissioned officers (NCOs) and are called Petty Officers, who not only perform the duties specific to their rating, but must also assume a leadership role.

E-7 to E-9 are Petty Officers, but are distinct within the USN, with separate uniforms, berthing and dining facilities. Called Chiefs, these selectees are authorized by the U.S. Congress, leading CPOs to state, "it took an act of Congress to put these anchors here, it will take an act of Congress to take them off." The anchors they are referring to are their insignia, a gold anchor with "USN" over it.

For USN officers, rank, not rate, is used.

O-1—where "O" stands for "officer"—to O-4 are junior officers: ensign, lieutenant (junior grade), lieutenant, and lieutenant commander; O-5 and O-6 are senior officers: commander and captain; O-7 to O-10 are flag officers: rear admiral (lower half) (one star), rear admiral (two star), vice admiral (three star), and admiral (four star).

On September 19, 2016, Chief of Naval Personnel (CNP) Vice Admiral Robert P. Burke announced, "We're going to immediately do away with rating titles and address each other by just our rank [and rate] as the other services do."

The CNP—nominated by the President and confirmed by a majority vote in the Senate—is responsible for the overall manpower readiness for the USN.

The news shook the Navy community, where some ratings "dated back to the Continental Navy," reported the *Navy Times*. "The Navy has had nearly 700 different rating titles in that time," and are so ingrained in Navy culture, the saying "Choose your rate, choose your fate" is something every sailor has heard.

Three months later, the plan was scuttled.

"Navy leaders are reversing their controversial decision to eliminate sailors' ratings and will restore job titles across the fleet," reported the *Navy Times* on December 20.

Navy officials admitted that "the overwhelmingly negative reaction from the fleet was a key factor in the decision," said the *Times*.

I arrived at 7 A.M. on February 6, 1964, retook the written exam and again passed it like a champ, and this time, however, to my great relief, I passed the physical, no problem. I was sworn in and officially became the property of Uncle Sam as an E-1. I took the oath of enlistment at around 11 A.M., and 10 hours later boarded a bus from Los Angeles to San Diego.

I, Phillip Francis Tourney, do solemnly swear that I will support and defend the Constitution of the United States against all enemies, foreign and domestic; that I will bear true faith and allegiance to the same; and that I will obey the orders of the President of the United States and the orders of the officers appointed over me, according to regulations and the Uniform Code of Military Justice. So help me God.

Boot camp was only supposed to last two months, but with Vietnam going on and no one wanting to wind up as a "ground pounder," young men were joining the Navy in droves. As a result, there were thousands of enlistees, and boot camp was extended from two to more than three months. I went through boot at Naval Training Center San Diego (NTC San Diego), Company 128.

Official Navy photo of Phillip Francis Tourney (1966)

NTC San Diego operated from 1923 to 1997, and is listed on the National Register of Historic Places. Just 361 acres of the 435 acre site is now occupied by Liberty Station, which includes retail and commercial districts, a residential district, an educational district, a hotel district, an office district, a promenade, and a park and open space area along the boat channel. It's very curious to me that the name "Liberty" was chosen for "the largest historical preservation project in San Diego."

The hotel district contains the USS *Recruit* (TDE-1/TFFG-1), a two-thirds scale model of a USN *Dealey*-class destroyer escort—when I was there, but later refurbished to look like an Oliver Hazard Perry-class frigate)—and was commissioned on July 27, 1949, built right into the ground that I, and *millions* before and after, had trained on. The *Recruit* was actually a commissioned vessel, but classified as a "non-ship," and was also known as the USS *Neversail*, and assisted with the training of over 50,000 new recruits *per year*. *Recruit* served continuously as a training facility from 1949 until NTC San Diego was shuttered in 1997.

USS *Recruit* (TDE-1)

It's ironic that *Recruit* was decommissioned while I served aboard the *Liberty*, in March 1967, but later recommissioned in 1982, the same year *Liberty* crewmembers reunited for the first time since the attack, and formed the USS *Liberty* Veterans Association (LVA), "to bring the true story of the attack on the USS *Liberty* and her heroic crew to the awareness of the American people."

NTC San Diego served as the site for several movies, like *Top Gun*, *Battle Cry*, *Here Comes the Navy*, and *In the Navy*, the Abbott and Costello film, as well as the television show *Pensacola: Wings of Gold* and the opening sequence for the television sitcom *C.P.O. Sharkey*.

Despite having had only limited schooling, they made me Educational Petty Officer in boot camp. Basically, I was a tutor for young men having trouble with their reading, writing and arithmetic. I was voted outstanding recruit by my peers and awarded a certificate of the same by my commanding officer (CO) at completion of boot.

PHILLIP F. TOURNEY
Outstanding Recruit

Phil Tourney receiving his "Outstanding Recruit" award in boot camp in 1964

My first assignment was aboard USS *Mauna Kea* (AE-22), an ammunition ship based out of Port Chicago, California. Our job was to pick up ammo and other munitions at Port Chicago and bring them by sea to a variety of U.S. ships off the coast of Vietnam. It was like a flea market of sorts, because after we unloaded our munitions, the other side would give us their cargo—the bodies of Americans killed in the war.

We would then take these bodies to U.S. Naval Base Subic Bay, Philippines, and from there they would be flown back to the U.S. We stacked the bodies like cordwood in green body bags, while trying as best we could to handle them with the dignity they deserved, and put them in the reefers (refrigerators) where the food was kept.

USS *Mauna Kea* (AE-22)

While carrying the bodies, I couldn't help thinking to myself, "This is someone's son . . . this could be me." While aboard the *Mauna Kea* this was the first time I experienced death in an up-close and personal way, and unfortunately it would not be the last.

The *Mauna Kea* was "laid down"—the formal commencement of construction—in 1955, launched almost exactly a year later, commissioned the next year, and decommissioned in 1995, with more than 38 years of active service. *Mauna Kea*, the oldest active ship in the Navy prior to decommissioning, was used as target practice and sunk in 2006 during the world's largest international maritime warfare exercise.

After finishing my tour with the *Mauna Kea*, she went into the yards and I was transferred clear across the country to the USS *Liberty* (AGTR-5). AGTR stood for Auxiliary General Technical Research.

2

Liberty

I had never heard of her before. She was stationed in Norfolk, Virginia, a long way from California. Upon arrival and seeing her for the first time, I was amazed at her appearance.

At 456-feet-long and 62-feet-wide, antennae were bristling all over the place, and she was a clean, sharp looking ship. I hadn't been in the Navy that long, but you didn't have to be to notice she was also an odd-looking bird.

A pristine USS *Liberty* (AGTR-5) in port at Norfolk Naval Shipyard (October 1966)

In fact, a "Chief of Naval Operations once called the *Liberty* 'the ugliest ship in the Navy,'" wrote James Bamford in *Body of Secrets: Anatomy of the Ultra-Secret National Security Agency.*

The Chief of Naval Operations (CNO), a position held by a four-star admiral, is the most senior naval officer assigned to serve in the Department of the Navy. The CNO is based in the Pentagon, and since the position was created in 1915, there have been 31 CNOs. I had the great honor of becoming close to one, Admiral Thomas Hinman Moorer, who served as CNO from August 1, 1967 to July 1, 1970.

Naval Station Norfolk had its beginnings during the Great War.

Right after the U.S. entered World War I, the federal government purchased 474 acres that would become the base. Construction began less than three months later, and by Armistice Day 1918, over 30,000 enlisted men were stationed there.

Naval Station Norfolk in Norfolk, Virginia

Spanning about four miles on the waterfront and seven miles of pier and wharf space, it is the largest naval station in the world, hosting five aircraft carriers, six guided missile cruisers, 22 guided missile destroyers, seven amphibious assault ships, seven submarines, 14 fleet ocean tugs, as well as 134 aircraft, supported by 14 piers and 11 aircraft hangars. Today, over 100,000 flight operations are conducted each year—275 flights per day. Norfolk Naval Base houses the largest concentration of USN forces anywhere in the world.

Admiral John Sidney
"Jack" McCain, Jr.

Officially, *Liberty* was under the control of Commander-in-Chief, U.S. Naval Forces, Europe (CINCUSNAVEUR), Admiral John Sidney "Jack" McCain, Jr., son of USN Admiral John S. McCain Sr., and father of U.S. senator John Sidney McCain III. McCain, Sr.—a pioneer of aircraft carrier operations—served in the Pacific theater in World War II (WW2), commanding all land-based air operations for the Guadalcanal campaign. "His operations off the Philippines and Okinawa and air strikes against Formosa and the Japanese home islands caused tremendous destruction of Japanese naval and air forces in the closing period of the war." He and McCain, Jr. were the first father-and-son pair to achieve a four-star admiral rank in the USN.

McCain, Jr. had been promoted to admiral just a few weeks earlier, and became CINCUSNAVEUR at the same time.

We learned years later, that several days before the attack, the command was taken away from McCain and transferred directly to the Joint Chiefs of Staff (JCS), encompassing a relatively small number of people. With just a few involved, it would be easier to keep secrets, as opposed to it being part of U.S. Naval Forces, Europe, where literally, thousands of people would know.

Liberty's captain at the time was D.T. Wieland, Jr., who held the rank of commander. I found out years later that Commander Wieland went into a deep depression when he found out what had happened to us, feeling he should have been there instead of his successor. After all, he was a "plankowner," a member of the crew of a USN vessel when commissioned. This means they "own" part of the ship and receive an official certificate stating this fact.

Liberty—originally named SS *Simmons Victory*—was a converted merchant marine cargo ship, known as a Victory ship, "a class of cargo ship produced in large numbers by North American shipyards during WW2 to replace losses caused by German submarines."

According to James Scott's *The Attack on the Liberty: The Untold Story of Israel's Deadly 1967 Assault on a U.S. Spy Ship*, which is referenced several times in this book, "The USS *Liberty*—named in honor of 10 cities and towns with the same name—officially was born." James's father, John, served aboard *Liberty* with me.

Besides having such a close connection to the *Liberty*, James, a 2016 Pulitzer Prize finalist, went above and beyond to write his book.

In the "Note on Sources" section in *The Attack on the Liberty*, James revealed what went into the creation of the book.

> Many of the reports I used to piece together the story of the USS *Liberty* came from two dozen archives and libraries scattered across the United States and Israel. The Freedom of Information Act pried loose other files from the Navy, State Department, Central Intelligence Agency, and the National Security Agency.

> Litigation proved the only means to obtain some records from the Navy. My diligent research assistant, Gideon Klaiman, scoured Israel's archives for *Liberty* records, which I had professionally translated from Hebrew to English in Israel.

> I relied heavily on hundreds of interviews I conducted with *Liberty* survivors, Navy personnel, Israeli military and intelligence officers, State Department officials, White House advisers, and CIA and NSA operatives, some of whom have never spoken publicly until now.

> The best material came from the personal files and records of the sailors who survived that awful day. Many of the officers and crewmembers still have razor-sharp bullets, bits of twisted shrapnel, and edges of blast holes that were excised off the ship's hull and superstructure by welders in Malta more than four decades ago.

> *Liberty* veterans shared with me scores of never-before-seen personal letters, telegrams, postcards, journals, reel-

to-reel tapes, and notes, which opened wide a window on the past.

In the 1960s, two WW2 Victory ships—SS *Iran Victory* and SS *Simmons Victory*—were reactivated and converted to technical research ships (TRSs): USS *Belmont* (AGTR-4) and USS *Liberty*.

The USN operated five ships of the AGTR type. The first three— USS *Oxford* (AGTR-1) [1961–1969], USS *Georgetown* (AGTR- 2) [1963–1969] and USS *Jamestown* (AGTR-3) [1963–1969]—were *Oxford*-class vessels converted from WW2 Liberty ships, which served the same purpose as the aforementioned Victory ships. The final two—USS *Belmont* [1964–1970] and USS *Liberty* [1964– 1968]—were *Belmont*-class vessels, converted from WW2 Victory ships.

Fred V. Fuller was a First Class Communications Technician (CT) aboard the *Belmont* who also worked for the National Security Agency (NSA) following his active duty time.

The USN established the Cryptographer rating in 1942, renamed it to Communications Technician in 1948, and changed the name again to Cryptologic Technician in 1976.

There are currently five CT sub ratings, or branches, an indication of the complexity of the rating. According to the Navy's website, "CTs perform a variety of duties worldwide at numerous overseas and stateside shore commands, aboard surface ships, aircraft and submarines and Naval Special Warfare. Duties include performing collection, analysis and reporting on communication signals using computers, specialized computer-assisted communications equipment, and video display terminals."

I served for 28 months aboard the *Belmont*, the sister ship of the *Liberty*, a carbon copy. The *Belmont* was commissioned two or three months before the *Liberty*. I recall vividly a few days after *Belmont* was commissioned, we got underway from Bremerton, Washington for our transit south along the west coast through the Panama Canal, then up to our home port in Norfolk. As we were steaming past San Diego, our CO was a good friend of the CO of the U.S. Naval Air Station, North Island—on the Coronado Peninsula—who was also a fighter pilot. It was a beautiful, clear, cloudless sunny day, apparently not unlike the day when *Liberty* was attacked.

The CO arranged to patch the fighter pilot CO into our intercom system. Booming over the ship's speakers throughout the ship, the pilot said, "I am going to do some practice strafing and bombing runs against you. I won't tell you which way I am attacking. See if you can spot me."

Well, we had the whole crew topside, except for a few snipes belowdecks that were needed to keep *Belmont* underway. He did several runs on us, over us, coming at us with full throttle, from all directions, just above the water. We never saw him until he was past us; we were sitting ducks.

All we heard was the "whoosh" and "boom" of the afterburners when he broke the sound barrier with each pass. There was nothing we could do in a real world situation, with our .45 pistols, shotguns and limited weapons. The fighter jet pilot was having a blast showing us what it would be like having our asses handed to us.

These ships were often referred to as "one-wayers," because if they were hit by a torpedo, they went down fast. I used to watch the old *Victory At Sea* television show reruns where I had seen so many of these ships similar to ours sink like a rock. *Victory at Sea* was a documentary series about naval warfare during WW2, and was broadcast by NBC from 1952–1953, and turned into a film in 1954.

The series won an Emmy award in 1954 and set the trend in establishing the historic television documentary genre. As a kid, I loved watching these old shows and always wondered what it would be like to be on a ship that got torpedoed.

New Hampshire native Lieutenant Commander David Edwin "Dave" Lewis was 19-years-old when he joined the Navy in 1950, attending the prestigious U.S. Naval Academy (USNA). Dave was in charge of the cryptologic detachment, or research spaces, of the ship.

> I was told I would have to go out on one of the AGTRs and have my "ticket punched" in order to get promoted.

One of those under Dave's command was Joseph C. Lentini, a 23-year-old Maryland native, who joined the Navy prior to his 18th birthday. Aboard *Liberty* he was a senior First Class Petty Officer CT serving as a supervisor in the Operations Branch, and oversaw all communications to and from the ship. Joe recounted a story about *Liberty*.

> When they brought the *Liberty* into Norfolk from Washington State, it made naval history, perhaps even world history. It was the only Navy ship that had a multiple car wreck on board at sea.
>
> The first captain—Wieland—got permission to bring the crew's cars aboard. The cars were all chained down on the upper deck, and broke loose in a storm, and they had a pileup on board.
>
> So right off the bat, the ship, looking backwards, made sure she was going to make some kind of a niche for herself in the annals of naval and world history.

The first thing I noticed when coming aboard *Liberty* was how easygoing everyone was, both officers and NCOs. My next thought was that I hit the jackpot and that this was going to be a dream job.

I was half right.

I made my first cruise aboard the *Liberty* as a Machinist's Mate (MM) in the engine room. I attained that rating through on-the-job training, and not through "A" School, a classroom setting where the Navy instructs sailors in their particular specialty. I was trained in all forms of standing watch, which meant checking the gauges of everything to make sure all was safe.

Given the fact the engine room was a place of extremes in terms of temperatures and pressures, it required regular monitoring if accidents were to be prevented.

An MM's job, according to the Navy, is to "operate, maintain, and repair ship propulsion machinery, auxiliary equipment, and outside machinery, such as: steering engine, hoisting machinery, food preparation equipment, refrigeration and air conditioning equipment, windlasses, elevators, and laundry equipment. Operate and maintain marine boilers, pumps, forced draft blowers, and heat exchangers; perform tests, transfers, and inventory of lubricating oils, fuels, and water. Maintain records and reports, and may perform duties in the generation and stowage of industrial gases."

I made one cruise with Commander Wieland before he was replaced by a new skipper, Commander William Loren McGonagle.

McGonagle, born November 19, 1925 in Wichita, Kansas, enlisted in the Navy in 1944, and in 1947 accepted a commission as an ensign. He served on the destroyer USS *Frank Knox* (DD-742), the minesweepers USS *Partridge* (AMS-31) and USS *Kite* (AMS-22), the fleet tug USS *Mataco* (AT-86) and the salvage ship USS *Reclaimer* (ARS-42).

The ceremony inaugurating his taking command of the ship took place with all the pomp and circumstance associated with the USN. As Commander Wieland departed the ship, a voice over the 1MC announced, "USS *LIBERTY* DEPARTING," and with that, McGonagle was now officially the captain of the *Liberty*.

The 1MC, or 1 Main Circuit, is the public address system for USN vessels. Used for transmitting information and orders throughout the vessel, it is loud enough so the entire crew can hear it. After spending a year in the engine room, a shipmate in my department and I

William Loren McGonagle aboard *Liberty* in 1967

requested a transfer to Repair Division in the shipfitter's shop, which was more to our liking, for two reasons. First, it was more "hand's on" type of work—welding and repairs, to be specific. Second, we would be out of the stifling heat of the engine room.

A shipmate, "my partner in crime" as I called him, was Americo "Rick" F. Aimetti, who was born in Brooklyn, New York in 1946. Rick attended boot camp in July 1964 and was stationed aboard *Liberty* in September 1965.

> I planned on making a career in the Navy. When I first got on board I was standing watch in the engine room, then they put me down in the boiler room because they were short boilermen.

In 1996, the Boilerman rating was merged into Machinist's Mate. Rick spent around one year in the boiler room, where the heat was sometimes tough to bear.

> I was supposed to be an Engineman but I never got to that point.

Enginemen operate, service, and repair internal combustion and diesel engines as well as other equipment.

> They needed help in R Division, Repair Division, so both Phil and I applied to transfer, because we were both down in the boiler room, and we both got approved. We did a lot together him and I. Whatever he did, I did, and whatever I did he did. Very few times were we apart. We were like a team.

It took a while for my request to go through the channels, so I had to stay in the engine room doing watches until someone else could take over my job. After a month my request was approved, and I switched from an MM to Shipfitter Pipefitter (SFP). The term "shipfitter" is derived from the words "ship" and "fit," essentially fitting parts of the ship together. The Shipfitter rating was established in 1921 then disestablished when the Shipfitter and Damage Controlman ratings were merged and replaced by the Hull Maintenance Technician.

Six months later I was promoted to E-4, Third Class Petty Officer.

Being part of ship's engineering, I was under the direct command of Lieutenant George Houston Golden, Chief Engineering Officer, who was also a *Liberty* plankowner. He was a Southern gent of the stereotypical persuasion and demeanor. Under his direction, I requested to learn every kind of damage control there was, especially fire-fighting.

Lieutenant Golden joined the USN at 17 and served his country for 30 years, through WW2, Korea and Vietnam, retiring as a lieutenant commander. George was admired throughout the ship, especially in the engineering department. Although stern when required, he was a very loving and caring officer and family man. His courageous actions during the attack contributed greatly to not only the crew's, but the ship's safety. If anybody deserved the Medal of Honor, George did.

Our duties always brought us to the west coast of Africa. When we were back at port I took classes on damage control, which I loved. Our instructors were vets who had seen action in WW2 and Korea. One instructor had been at Pearl Harbor when it was attacked and who impressed upon me the idea that the most dangerous thing encountered on a ship is fire. Putting out fires was like doing surgery— do it right and you save yours and everyone else's life; do it wrong and everyone dies.

In many respects, things aboard the *Liberty* were relaxed, and in other ways they weren't, especially when it came to drilling. We drilled and drilled and drilled, and at all hours—midnight, 2 A.M., 4 A.M., or whenever. When you heard the order, "GENERAL QUARTERS" (GQ), that meant you got your rear end moving and went to your battle station without wasting time.

Part of our drilling included manning the guntubs and the lookout towers. The guns were nothing as far as modern warfare at sea went. There were four .50 caliber machineguns—a mere 84 pounds and 65 inches—which were useful only in repelling boarders. As far as being effective against other vessels, that would be like shooting a grizzly bear with a BB gun.

Browning .50 Caliber Machinegun

Designed in 1918 by John Moses Browning and placed in service in 1933, the M2 Browning—M2 Machinegun or Browning .50 Caliber Machinegun—is a "heavy machinegun" used against lightly armored vehicles, boats, light fortifications, low-flying aircraft and infantry, and has been produced longer than any other machinegun in history.

I asked what it was the *Liberty* did and the response was always the same: We "mapped the ocean floor." Despite the fact I wasn't the smartest kid on the block, I figured out in short time that this was just the official answer and knew there must have been much more to it than that.

The fact that there were two different crews—the CTs, or "spooks" as we called them, and the ship's company—led me to figure out in due time we were a spy ship.

Joe explained what the CTs told anyone who asked what *Liberty* did.

> We were there to study radio wave propagation to help improve naval communications worldwide.

The CTs were a very secretive bunch. To the rest of us who were part of the ship's crew, they seemed arrogant. Naturally, when you get guys like them and guys like us on board the same ship, there are lots of confrontations. Their demeanor towards the ship's crew was very condescending, one of "Your job is to take care of us and make our lives comfortable, period." As an indicator of the kind of work they did, I never saw CTs dirty or dingy. There also was very little mingling between the regular crew and the CTs. The spaces where they worked were off limits to everyone, except the captain. What went on down there was secret and the rest of us dumb-asses were not privileged to know.

On four occasions I was sent to the CT spaces to do some welding and repairs, and in each case was escorted by an armed guard who never took his eyes off me for a second. While down there I was told, "Don't look at anything, don't talk to anyone. Do your job and get the hell out."

The first thing I noticed when going down there was that all the equipment was covered up with sheets. The few times I went down into those spaces I felt like I was in a foreign country and was always relieved to get out of there. I knew that as a mechanic, I was as welcome as a janitor with a mop and bucket would be in an operating room where they were doing brain surgery. We in the crew knew that they were probably spies, but we did not know who or what they were spying on.

Joe gave his take on why some tension existed between the two crews.

> We had two crews on board: the Naval Security Group, and they called us the spooks. We wore spit-shined shoes, starched and creased jeans and shirts, our fingernails were clean, our hair was cut and combed.

Naval Security Group (NAVSECGRU), active from March 1935 to September 2005, gathered intelligence for the U.S. and denied intelligence to America's adversaries, and according to *Blind Man's Bluff: The Untold Story of American Submarine Espionage*, was "the fabled cryptological service that had intercepted and decoded critical Japanese Navy communications during WW2." NAVSECGRU was also part of the NSA, the U.S. intelligence organization responsible for the worldwide monitoring, collection, and processing of information and data for foreign intelligence and counterintelligence purposes, known as signals intelligence, or SIGINT, communications intelligence, or COMINT, and electronic intelligence, or ELINT.

The other crew on board was the guys who took care of the ship. They had their sleeves rolled up and grease up to their elbows. They were the guys who were the real sailors, the ship's crew.

The very aft part of the ship—one level below main deck—was the CT berthing quarters. That was another reason that sometimes there was a little hate and discontent between the ship's crew and the CTs. The ship's crew slept in the bow, and in any rough weather, that is not the place that you wanna be. All the CTs were in the aft end, with thick mattresses and three-tier bunks. The bunks opened up to store stuff in them and there were storage lockers against the bulkheads for each one of us. There was a big head, or toilet, with showers. Our sleeping space was right next to the chow hall—also used for movies and bingo. We lived pretty well.

Another "spook," CT2 Robert J. Schnell, who we called "Buddha," was born in Montana in 1943 and enlisted in the Navy in 1963.

A buddy of mine that I met in boot camp, told me to tell them you wanna be a CT. And I said, "Why?" And he said, "Because the school's in Florida. We'll go to Florida for the winter." And I thought, "Oh boy, yeah, that's a great idea."

Minnesota native Glenn Roger Oliphant was a 22-year-old Third Class Electronics Technician, Radar, (ET) who joined the Navy in 1965, and was stationed aboard the *Liberty* less than a year before the attack.

Originally known as Radio Technician, the ET rating was created in 1948. ETs maintain all the electronic equipment aboard Navy ships, and then some.

On the *Liberty*, we just had the one radar, and so I guess my boss figured that I should know almost everything that we had responsibility for, so I worked on the transmitters and a couple of the receivers, and also I worked on the IFF [Identification Friend or Foe], so I got a well-rounded education as far as the electronics that we were responsible for.

Our spaces were above deck, for the most part. The transmitters were on the main deck. The radar was of course up in the pilot house. The ETs bunked with all of the CTs aft of the chow hall, so I knew a lot of those fellas very well.

One of the few CTs I befriended was Phillip Charles Tiedtke, who was born in 1944 in Santa Cruz, California and joined the Navy in 1964. We lifted weights together but he never talked about his job.

As I said, the job of the ship's company was to operate and maintain the ship, and make the CTs as comfortable as possible.

The west coast of Africa was where the *Liberty* was typically sent for routine monitoring.

On our missions there, we would cruise up and down the coast at five or six knots, day and night. One knot is equal to one nautical mile per hour (mph), approximately 1.151 mph.

In recent years I have at times asked some of the CTs why we always went to Africa and the common answer on their part has been that they couldn't talk about it.

My best guess was that the atmospheric conditions in that part of the world were such that it was optimum for listening in on radio traffic, no matter where it was coming from, similar to how at nighttime you can pick up radio stations that you can't during the day.

Every month or so, we would pull into some African port to resupply: we would buy food and fuel, and in the process help out the local farmers and merchants in those countries by buying the fruits of their labors. We would all get "liberty," meaning we were free to go on shore and do whatever we wanted, for as long as we wanted, since we were not on duty. It was up to us to report back in.

Joe explained why we spent so much time in West Africa and our typical route.

There were Russians and Chinese in Africa at the time.

The ship sailed the coast of West Africa from the north, Monrovia [the capital of Liberia], all the way down to the south to Cape Town [South Africa]. Eventually under Captain McGonagle, the ship stopped going to Cape Town because of apartheid. We went to Monrovia, Dakar [the capital of Senegal], Abidjan [the economic center of the Republic of Côte d'Ivoire, or Ivory Coast], Angola [officially the Republic of Angola]. That was our little niche in the world.

For us in the ship's crew, life was not the high-energy, high intensity drama usually associated with the spy business. Life was pretty boring, and in many ways, it was similar to the storyline of the movie *Groundhog Day* starring Bill Murray where every day was just like the one before it, with nothing new or exciting taking place.

After finishing my second cruise aboard *Liberty*, I was back in Virginia.

3

Orders

In April of 1967 we received orders to head back out on what would be the fourth cruise for the ship. As we were making preparations to leave, we noticed some trouble with the TRSSCOM, the 35-foot-tall communications dish that bounced radio signals off the Moon so as not to give away the ship's position. It was leaking hydraulic fluid, and Captain wanted it fixed right away because he was eager to get underway.

TRSSCOM was an acronym for **T**echnical **R**esearch **S**hip **S**pecial **COM**munications, and was utilized for Earth-Moon-Earth communications. A special gyroscope-stabilized 16-foot parabolic antenna transmitted radio signals toward the Moon, where they would bounce back to Earth and be received by an 84-foot parabolic antenna at a Naval Communications Station in Maryland or Hawaii. In order for the signals to be transmitted successfully, "both locations had to be able to see the Moon at the same time," as explained in *Body of Secrets*.

Naval Radio Station Cheltenham (Maryland) was established in 1938 on more than 500 acres of farmland, and in 1953 was re-designated as Naval Communications Station, Washington, D.C., although it was officially known as Naval Communications Detachment Cheltenham. In 1960, the USN showed off its Moon Relay Communications System by bouncing radio signals off the Moon, which took all of 2.5 seconds to communicate with Naval Communications Station Pearl Harbor (Hawaii) from the Moon's surface.

While Cheltenham—which at its peak accommodated more than 500 military and civilian personnel, as well as their families— played a critical role in monitoring the Japanese attack on Pearl

Harbor in 1941 and 1962's Cuban Missile Crisis, it was deactivated in 1998. Two years later the U.S. Congress "directed the Federal Law Enforcement Training Center (FLETC) to locate suitable properties within the metropolitan Washington, D.C. area to be used for firearms requalification and pursuit driver training programs for area law enforcement officers," and in 2001, the site that once housed Cheltenham was transferred to FLETC.

Pennsylvania native John Edward Gidusko, who served aboard *Liberty* on the cruise prior to this one as an Electronics Material Officer, gave further details about the TRSSCOM.

> The brand spanking new installation of the TRSSCOM antenna aboard *Liberty* was fraught with problems. The shipyard wanted a few more days before *Liberty* sailed, but McGonagle was impatient to get going.
>
> Captain McGonagle was known as a "steamer," meaning he would rather be at sea than in port. He gave the shipyard one more day to finish up, but they needed more time than the captain would give them.
>
> As a result, hydraulic oil leaks were prevalent throughout the system and prevented maximum use of the antenna.

Ultimately, the antenna was repaired by the *Liberty*'s shipfitter crew, of which I was a part.

John Edward Gidusko in the *Erasing the Liberty*
donation trailer (February 2016)

John passed on November 26, 2016, and for not being part of the crew during the attack, few have done more for the USS *Liberty* than him. As his obituary stated, "[H]is greatest driving force was maintaining and protecting a website promoting information on the attack on the USS *Liberty*, a ship he served aboard." His passing is a great loss to all those driven to get the truth out. May you rest in peace, John.

4

Abidjan

We departed on May 2, and it was rough seas from Norfolk to Abidjan—the economic capital of Ivory Coast and the most populous French-speaking city in West Africa—where we were to be for a four-day port call. In hindsight, this was obviously a bad omen for what was to come. The seas were high and water was coming over the bow, and whatever it was I was doing at any particular time was interrupted periodically by me heading for the side of the ship so I could throw up into the Atlantic.

One of my shipmates, New York State native Stephen Blair Tracy, clearly remembered the trip.

> I was one of the fortunate ones who didn't get sea sick. There were few of us. This was the only time I ever witnessed people actually turning "green." I don't remember the percentages, but there were a lot more sick than weren't.
>
> One particular evening during the roughest seas, four of us were playing cards—Hearts, I think—in our sleeping quarters in the forecastle [the forward part of a ship, abbreviated fo'c'sle or fo'c's'le and pronounced "foaxul"]. This part of the ship is the most forward and therefore felt the worst of the seas.
>
> With guys moaning and groaning and puking, some of us still had fun. Our card table was secured to the deck, the deck was waxed and the chairs were loose. In high seas, the bow would rise on a swell and then drop like a

stone. If that weren't enough, this place on the ship was adjacent to where the anchors hung off the bow. When the ship dropped from a high swell, the anchors would fly out and then slam back against the hull, making the loudest noise I ever heard. To put it in perspective, these were one-ton steel anchors slamming our sides. What was real funny though was when the ship went up the swell, the guy in the "south" seat would slide all the way back to the bulkhead, and when the ship dipped down, he would slide back to his position and play his card. Ditto for the guy in the "north position." I remember doing this for hours while looking at some of my shipmates lying in their bunks miserable.

Bob recalled rough seas on the previous cruise.

The second day we were out we ran into a storm off Cape Hatteras. I went out for breakfast on the mess deck, and here's this pretty large room in the aft end of the ship, rocking and rolling, and the coffee from my cup spilled out into the grease in the eggs and bacon, and I covered my mouth and went straight topside and threw up, and continued to do so for the next three days.

Steve described his easy days at sea.

The trip across the Atlantic was uneventful as I recall. My duties as a deckhand were pretty mundane—swab, peel paint, paint, peel paint, swab, repeat. We spent evenings playing cards and writing letters home.

I found out while writing this book with Dave Gahary that Steve came from a distinguished American and USN family—with one of his relatives known as the "Father of the Modern American Fighting Navy"—although you never would know that from his modest, down-to-Earth, demeanor.

My family was not a typical military family; no one in my immediate family had served any serious time with the armed services for several generations. That would soon change in the 1960s.

In the middle '60s, the Vietnam buildup and the draft had my father very concerned, as four of his children were draft-eligible young men. He had not served on active duty in the armed services, but not for the lack of trying. My father won an appointment to Annapolis in the 1920s to the great pride and admiration from his friends and family, particularly his mother. In his first semester at the Naval Academy, it was discovered that he was colorblind. In those days, that was a total disqualification. He was sent home. My grandmother cried for days.

My father, however, coped very well. He enrolled in prestigious Cornell University, earned his bachelor's degree, and a master's in mechanical engineering.

His grandfather—my great-grandfather—was Benjamin Franklin Tracy, a farmer, landowner, lawyer, politician, and military man of great distinction, the quintessential American statesman and gentleman. He ran a 2,000-plus-acre farm in the southern tier of upstate New York, raising crops like wheat, tobacco and soy beans and raising standard bred horses. He was a loyal American and devoted to duty.

During the Civil War, he served directly under General Ulysses S. Grant in the field and eventually became the Commandant of the Elmira Prison, the "Andersonville of the North."

He was decorated and recognized for his heroism and dedication to prison reform. He rose to the rank of general in the U.S. Army, and received the Medal of Honor in the Battle of the Wilderness (May 5–7, 1864) during the Civil War.

One of Elmira's barracks was converted into a military prison in the summer of 1864, and due to the horrendous conditions there it was referred to as "Hellmira" by some inmates. In the year of its existence, "2,970 of the 12,100 prisoners would die from a combination of malnutrition, continued exposure to harsh winter weather, and disease from the poor sanitary conditions . . . combined with a lack of medical care." At war's end, prisoners were "required to take a loyalty oath and given a train ticket home." The camp was shuttered, razed and converted to farmland, where work is underway to reconstruct the camp.

He entered politics after the war and eventually became the Secretary of the Navy under President Benjamin Harrison, a cabinet position at the time. He was the President's closest advisor.

As Secretary of the Navy, he oversaw the creation of the first steel ships in the Navy, including the infamous USS Maine. He was later dubbed the "Father of the Modern American Fighting Navy."

USS *Tracy* (DD-214)—a *Clemson*-class destroyer present for the Japanese attack on Pearl Harbor—was named after him, as well as the town of Tracyton, Washington, and a fjord in Alaska, Tracy Arm.

USS *Tracy* (DD-214) refueling alongside USS *California* (BB-44)

His political ambitions were for real, as he considered a run for the White House. However, in 1889 his Washington house caught fire—from a gas lantern—destroying it and killing his beloved wife and daughter. His home was right down the street from the White House and the first person to his aid was none other than the President himself! Life was different then.

Needless to say, the Navy was always a part of our family's life, even if we weren't directly involved.

My older brother, Benjamin Franklin Tracy III, joined the Navy Reserve prior to the Vietnam buildup and got out before the draft buildup. My brother James joined the Air Force and served admirably in Thailand. My younger brother John and I both joined the Navy Reserve at our father's urgency. He always said, in the Navy you know you have a bed to sleep in, not a foxhole. John later ironically served aboard the USS *Saratoga*.

"The *Liberty* had arrived in Abidjan [on May 22], its first port of call in a planned four-month cruise along the west coast of Africa," wrote James Scott in *The Attack on the Liberty*.

Once we hit Abidjan—the economic capital of Ivory Coast and the most populous French-speaking city in West Africa—some of us got liberty and headed for the Hôtel Ivoire. We were in port for two days and everything was situation normal.

Steve remembered the West African port city.

Other than Canada, this was my first experience in a foreign land. I was shocked at how poor the people were, particularly in the neighborhoods we traveled, including the local bar district. I remember the dirt streets blended in with the dirt floors; nothing paved, no floors laid. The beer was cheap, though not very cold.

Bob has vivid memories of the port-of-call.

We got to Africa and we pulled into Abidjan, and we were planning I think it was a five-day stay in Abidjan. We had overnight liberty; we didn't have Cinderella liberty, which means you had to be back to the ship by midnight.

Bob was at a local bar with some shipmates.

We ran out of money, and it was two or three o'clock in the morning, and the bar was gonna be open on all night anyway, so we thought we'd go pick up some money and go back out and have a couple more drinks since we were having such a good time.

Early one morning, as I sat in a bar with a few of my shipmates, the doors swung open and two Shore Patrolmen— military police—from the *Liberty*, came in. They shouted out loud that all *Liberty* crewmen were to report to the ship immediately. Their demeanor was stern and urgent, something I had not seen before.

Being called back to ship in such a hurry was unusual in itself, because when we got shore leave, we were basically on our own recognizance. I didn't know what was going on, but considering the fact that we were a spy ship, I knew it had to be related to this in some way.

Steve's liberty was interrupted as well.

Our stay in Abidjan was cut short. Very suddenly we were all called back to the ship and told to get ready to sail. I recall that one of our shipmates at that time was messing around with the wrong girl and the locals were chasing him down the pier as we were getting ready to toss the lines. It was quite funny.

After Bob returned for more money to continue his partying, he wasn't prepared for what he saw.

> So we get back to the ship and the skipper is in his
> bathrobe on the quarterdeck, barking orders and trying
> to get ready to pull out. It really made me nervous the
> fact that we'd almost missed ship's movement and that
> woulda been a court-martial offense.

Military justice is meted out through the Uniform Code of Military
Justice (UCMJ), which has its foundations in the U.S. Constitution,
which states that "Congress shall have Power . . . To make Rules for
the Government and Regulation of the land and naval forces." The
UCMJ was passed by Congress in 1950, "and signed into law by
President Harry S. Truman the next day."

UCMJ Article 87 states that, "Any person subject to this chapter
who through neglect or design misses the movement of a ship, aircraft,
or unit with which he is required in the course of duty to move shall
be punished as a court-martial may direct," where "Movement" is
defines as "a move, transfer, or shift of a ship."

The maximum punishment for "design" is a dishonorable
discharge, forfeiture of all pay and allowances, and confinement for
2 years, and for "neglect," a bad-conduct discharge, forfeiture of all
pay and allowances, and confinement for 1 year.

Once on board, we were all tasked with getting the ship ready for
sea. A somber mood crept over everyone as we made preparations.
Not only had our shore leave been cut short, but also, given the fact
our missions were generally uneventful, this new development and
urgency spooked us all. Lieutenant Golden told us we were headed
out to sea. We had heard on the radio there was something going on at
that time in the Middle East between Israel—America's "ally"—and
the Arabs.

Although most people might believe Israel is an ally of the U.S.,
the fact is this is not true.

Raymond L. McGovern is a former U.S. Army infantry/intelligence
officer and 27-year Central Intelligence Agency (CIA) analyst. Ray
served this country from the administrations of John F. Kennedy
through George H. W. Bush, where his "duties included chairing
National Intelligence Estimates and preparing the President's Daily

Brief. He even briefed one-on-one to President Ronald Reagan's most senior national security advisers from 1981 to 1985."

Ray explained why Israel is not an ally of the U.S.

> Israel is not our ally. To be an ally, you need to have a mutual defense treaty. There is no mutual defense treaty between the Unites States of America and Israel.

Ray explained why there is no treaty.

> After 1973, when the Arabs did launch an attack on Israeli occupied territory, the U.S. went to the Israelis, in a very, very discreet, diplomatic way, and said, "Look, we don't like this happening to you. We think that a good solution would be a mutual defense treaty." And the Israelis said, "You know, thanks very much, but no thanks."

Ray finished up by explaining why Israel declined.

> Number one, a mutual defense treaty requires internationally recognized borders. There was no way the Israelis wanted to raise the issue of the occupied territories in their current borders as opposed to the legal ones that they had before 1967. Number two, if you have a mutual defense treaty with another government, it's sort of expected that if you're going to attack or invade a third country, as Israel has done with respect to Lebanon for example, you're supposed to tip off the other country that this is what you're going to do, so they know what to expect. The Israelis didn't want any part of that either.

5

Soviets

B eing a lowly sailor way down on the chain of command, I had no idea, nor did any of my shipmates, that a secret deal was being devised while we steamed from Africa.

In the book *The Liberty Cipher: Cold Warfare Series IV* by Patrick J. Pacalo, evidence is provided that sheds light on how the world's two superpowers, the U.S. and the Union of Soviet Socialist Republics (USSR), used their militaries—and even entire countries—as pawns in their struggle for dominance, and what Top Secret NSA documents reveal about the attack on my ship.

The book "is a work of nonfiction based upon material found in the National Archives, the Johnson Library, various open sources, and the National Security Archive; also records from the U.S. Navy were used in putting this work together. Interviews with survivors of the attack on the USS *Liberty* were also used."

Pacalo was assisted heavily by Captain Robert Flynn Kamansky, M.D.

Captain Kamansky, a former U.S. Army surgeon and dentist, says he's been researching the massacre since 2009—seven-days-a-week—with a *Liberty* shipmate of mine, Don Pageler.

The Liberty Cipher points out that on May 26, while we were headed to Rota, Spain, North Atlantic Treaty Organization (NATO) forces were put on alert, and the next day, the great powers were swinging a deal.

It was the height of the Vietnam War, and the U.S.-backed South Vietnamese forces were locked in a deadly battle with the Soviet-backed North. A deal, however, was in the making. The Soviets would restrain their communist clients if the U.S. applied pressure to Israel to put the brakes on its illegal land grab.

"By May 27, American and Soviet messages to Israel counseling restraint had been received," states *The Liberty Cipher*.

In fact, there was a lull in the fighting, "with the Soviets backing off in Vietnam as a payback for U.S. pressure on Israel," states the book, but no one in the mainstream media seemed to pick up on the deal.

"[W]hile some in the press might have seen a possible link to the war in Vietnam and the attack on the *Liberty*," states the book, "no members of the press drew out a direct connection between the two series of events, at least not for the public eye to examine."

Much greater insight into the U.S./USSR relationship is provided by English-born Dr. Anthony R. Wells, chairman of the board of the USS *Liberty* Alliance, primarily composed of former high-ranking U.S. military men and diplomats, whose mission spread the true story of the *Liberty* massacre far and wide.

All have passed on, and Tony is all who's left. Significantly, Tony is the only living person to have worked for British intelligence and served in the Royal Navy as a British citizen and also to have worked for U.S. intelligence and the USN as a citizen of the U.S.

> I was humbly invited onto the board as a very young man by Admiral Tom Moorer because I was part of a group, and I was detailed to review the whole June war in the mid-'70s. I saw all the British and American intelligence, I interviewed Secretary of State Dean Rusk twice, personally.

> I had wonderful conversations with him, with the man who was running the thing for President Johnson directly, was talking with the Russians during the whole war, working with the British Prime Minister Harold Wilson, so, I had access.

> And by default I became the third chairman because these other wonderful gentlemen who were on the board

for decades passed away, and I've been to multiple, unfortunately, funerals at Arlington National Cemetery, honoring these wonderful people.

So, here I am now, able to, if you like, defend their birthright, which I'm proud to do, naturally. [The *Liberty* crew] needs to be honored, they need to be respected. They need to be formally honored, in Washington, by the president of the United States, before they all pass away.

Tony explained how Israel's illegal and reckless land grab almost brought the U.S. and USSR into direct conflict, and how close we all were to World War 3.

[Israel] nearly brought the United States and the Soviet Union into confrontation—as Dean Rusk explained it to me—greater than even during the situation of the Cuban Missile Crisis in 1962. It looked like [the Israel Defense Forces (IDF)] was gonna march on Damascus, which was a huge, huge Soviet ally and surrogate. So that, from Moscow's point of view, could not happen without major Russian military intervention. And that was the fear in Washington with Dean Rusk and President Johnson, and with Harold Wilson in London.

And so the *Liberty* was in the middle of all this, listening to all the communications. And remember, Liberty wasn't just about Israel, it was about all the main players, which were Jordan, Egypt, Syria, and of course, the Soviet Union.

[The USSR] had plans to move into Syria. They actually got all the overflight rights for their airborne divisions from President Tito in Yugoslavia, to overfly Yugoslavia from their bases in Hungary to go into Syria.

As Tony explains in his fine book, *A Tale of Two Navies: Geopolitics, Technology, and Strategy in the United States Navy and the Royal Navy, 1960-2015*, Israel's complete disregard for its only friend, the U.S., put the entire world on edge.

> Damascus was the line that the Soviets could not allow Israel to cross, and Washington was well aware of it. Pressure from the U.S. on Israel to accept a cease-fire was exerted very much with this in mind, as well as concern about Israel's true intentions.

Although "the United States had always stressed that it would intervene only to save Israel from invasion," they were prepared for the worst.

> The Sixth Fleet remained passive. The whole striking force of the Sixth Fleet, except for the 2,000-strong Marine battalion, cruising the Sea of Crete, was in a good position for a quick move toward the 200-mile zone off the eastern Mediterranean coast. This was about 20 minutes' flying time for a U.S. Navy F-4 Phantom to main Arab targets.
>
> There was a U.S. naval force east of Suez patrolling the Gulf, Arabian Sea, and Red Sea area. A destroyer was sent south from the Sixth Fleet at the end of May. Normally a ship from this detachment would have gone north, but as a precaution this was not done, leaving three destroyers in the area and a command ship. This happened on June 2, at the same time that U.S. ASW [Anti-Submarine Warfare] forces were moving from the North Atlantic into the Mediterranean.

What complicated matters was the USSR's view of the influence the U.S. wielded over Israel.

> [Premier of the Soviet Union Alexei Nikolayevich] Kosygin had certainly miscalculated in his assessment of the ability of the U.S. to influence Israel.

Tony explained the matter in further detail in his book.

> What had motivated Israel to perpetrate what appeared to have been an egregious act against the USS *Liberty?* What were the total circumstances, strategic and operational, that had led the Israeli leadership to make the fateful decision to attack and destroy a U.S. eavesdropping ship operating in international waters at the end of the Six-Day War? I concluded in 1976-77 and still believe today that the strategic backdrop and U.S.-Soviet relations hold the answers to these questions. Your author concluded that Israel's actions during the Six-Day War brought U.S.-Soviet relations to a stressful peak not seen since the Cuban Missile Crisis.

> Why would Israel attack the *Liberty* on June 8? The Soviet Union was a key player, not a mere presence in the shadows, but a demonstrative protagonist. The Soviets were supporting the new Syrian regime with economic and military aid, while Palestinian guerillas were intensifying their operations against Israel from Syrian bases. At the same time, the Soviets increased their support for Nasser. In mid-May 1967 the Syrians warned the Soviets that the Israelis were going to invade Syria, occupy Damascus, and topple the Baathist regime. The Soviets were obstructionist, derailing international peace efforts.

> It was at this point that USS *Liberty* and its brave crew was forward deployed. It was at the "pointy end of the spear;" in one sense, as an eavesdropping ship, she was the point itself. What did Washington want? The administration wanted to be inside the minds and see the intentions of all the main players, including Israel. The *Liberty* was on station to help unravel the plans, goals, and operations of the key players. The U.S. president and secretary of state realized that Israel's war plan could spell disaster for U.S.-Soviet relations should it produce an attack upon

Syria, Moscow's client. Their advance into Syria brought superpower confrontation dangerously close.

Did the Soviets plan to intervene, and why?

The first answer is "yes;" the why is that Israel intended to invade Syria and take Damascus. This single fact is the key. In response the Soviets planned to do two things: provide military resupply Syria and intervene directly. The Soviets began operations on June 8, 1967, the day that the *Liberty* was attacked. Their plan was to drop paratroopers in Syria and place them between an advancing Israeli army and Damascus.

How did the Soviet Union plan to execute retaliation?

An-12 Cub aircraft [Antonov An-12, NATO reporting name Cub], the standard Soviet paratrooper and cargo transports, flew from fields in Hungary across Yugoslavia and then over the Adriatic and Mediterranean to Syria.

Antonov An-12 "Cub"

The Soviet operational plans and actions were not spontaneous reactions to the Israeli advance. They were well planned in advance; Yugoslavia had granted overflight rights. The Soviets were poised to take on the

Israelis. The threat to intervene was made emphatically when the Syrian forces collapsed as Israelis stormed the Golan Heights on June 9, a collapse that left the road to Damascus virtually undefended.

The Cold War balance was now becoming dangerously out of kilter. The hotline quickly became an extraordinary successful means of preventing a major conflict. By that channel Moscow made it clear: if the Israelis did not desist, the Soviet Army would execute a massive airborne drop into Syria and confront the Israelis.

The "hot line" was not actually a red phone, but a teletype machine, an "Electronic Teleprinter Cryptographic Regenerative Repeater Mixer II (ETCRRM). Four—a spare on each side in case of malfunctioning—ETCRRM IIs were used for the Washington-Moscow Hotline, two in Washington, two in Moscow.

Rusk told me that he and President Johnson "had never assumed any other" than the Soviets would use their airborne forces.

USS *Liberty* was in the middle and was finding out more than the Israelis would tolerate. Secretary [of State] Rusk concluded that the Israelis wanted *Liberty* sunk without trace or survivors, no one to tell what had been done or by whom. The attack was conducted by intense airborne and torpedo boat strikes to minimize communications from *Liberty*. *Liberty's* destruction would ensure that she could no longer collect vital intelligence, while potentially garnering U.S. support for Israel through a false belief that an Arab country had been responsible. [See Peter Hounam's *Operation Cyanide: How the Bombing of the USS Liberty Nearly Caused World War Three* for more on the false flag aspects of the *Liberty* massacre] Perhaps it might even push the United States over the edge and support Israel's invasion of Syria and possible entry into the outskirts of Damascus, or at least leave Washington publicly neutral, while privately supporting Israel.

However, a retaliatory strike by the United States against, for example, Egyptian airfields, would have precipitated the very crisis that Dean Rusk sought to avert. If the Israelis had continued into Syria and the United States attacked Egyptian airfields, one can only speculate on the Soviet reaction.

The Israelis were dragging the United States into a war without the Americans really knowing why. Secretary Rusk believed that Israel had no concern for the consequences of its actions for U.S.-Soviet relations as long as Israel security objectives were achieved. *Liberty's* survival denied Israel any ability to exploit its loss and thus compel President Johnson to urge constraint on Israel, which was also under intense pressure from Moscow.

The brave crew of the *Liberty* ensured that their ship survived. They fought for their ship with all means at their disposal. Their courage and survival constitute the enduring hallmark and legacy of USS *Liberty*. These brave men, by fighting for their ship and not giving up, saved the United States from a potentially disastrous embroilment with the Soviet Union over Israel.

Secretary Rusk was vehemently stating, against strong opposition from the U.S.-based Israeli lobby, that the *Liberty* attack had been deliberate. Why would he do this? Dean Rusk was privy to all the intelligence, some key parts of which have not been disclosed to this day.

The USS *Liberty* was spying on Israel, directly and indirectly (via surrogate communications intercepts), and on all the other protagonists in the region. It was listening to the Soviet Union's communications with its clients, Egypt and particularly Syria (and indeed, the Soviet Union was listening to the Israelis).

In 1967 and thereafter the United States, for self-evident reasons, did not wish the world to know that it possessed this seagoing intelligence-collection capability, than anything within the Soviet Ocean Surveillance System or anywhere else.

So how important was *Liberty?* Very—it represented the ability to milk all the local Soviet communications and to translate and transmit them in very short time frames and decision-makers.

Secretary Rusk and President Johnson and Prime Minister Harold Wilson in London wanted to know from every source possible not only whether Israel was about to do something so rash that the Soviets would launch forces into Syria, but if so when and how the Soviets might intervene.

The extra personnel embarked on board *Liberty* while en route to the eastern Mediterranean were critical augmenters to extend the ship's capabilities for these purposes. She could do things that no other collection system, organization, or human being could in 1967.

To his undying credit, Secretary Rusk was a man of such integrity that he would follow only his conscience, what he knew it to be true from all and every source of very special intelligence available. The attack on the USS *Liberty* was deliberate.

USS *Liberty* in happier times

6

Valdez

I learned later there was already another spy ship in the area, the USNS *Private Jose F. Valdez* (T-AG-169). USNS stands for United States Naval Ship, and is used for non-commissioned ships belonging to the U.S. Navy. Like *Liberty, Valdez* was tasked with intercepting, or collecting SIGINT and reporting information back to the NSA.

Fred has intimate knowledge not just about TRSs, but about the *Valdez*.

> The civilians on board *Valdez* were merchant seaman, who served like the crew of *Liberty* who ran the ship: the deck force, firemen, machinist mates, shipfitters, signalmen, cooks, storekeepers, CO, XO. The guys working in the security spaces on *Valdez*—like *Liberty*— were USN CTs. After *Liberty* relieved *Valdez* off the Gaza coast, *Valdez* was sent to Hoboken, N.J. for some refitting and upgrades.
>
> I understand *Valdez* had no air conditioning, so they requested that it be fitted with central air conditioning. Apparently there was no money for this poor man's technical research ship, so the Navy painted *Valdez* white to reflect the sun.

Although some believed *Valdez* was capable of doing *Liberty's* job, Fred explained why that was not the case.

> On 1 September 1967, as a civilian working for the NSA, I received orders to proceed from Fort G.G. Meade to Hoboken.

Located in Maryland, Fort George G. Meade—named for a Civil War general who served as commander of the Army of the Potomac—is a U.S. Army installation that houses the NSA, U.S. Cyber Command, and several other Department of Defense units.

Valdez was not mentioned on my paper orders, however my unwritten verbal orders were to board *Valdez* and report to the NAVSECGRU to provide training to the NAVSECGRU CT contingent on how to modify their ELINT configuration to enable the demultiplexing, identification, collection, acquisition and reporting of tactical and strategic VHF/UHF multichannel communications systems. This is a capability *Valdez* never had before. Other AGTRs were fully capable of performing these functions; *Valdez* was not. I spent four extremely busy and long days aboard *Valdez* at sea, and when they pulled into Norfolk, I felt that I had accomplished my mission, but it was a total jury rigged operation. I disembarked and made my way back to Fort Meade.

According to a document declassified and approved for release by the NSA on November 8, 2006, *Liberty* was selected "because she had superior speed (18 knots vs. 8 knots for *Valdez*), because her VHF/UHF multichannel collection capability was better, and because she was, unlike *Valdez*, at the beginning of a deployment."

Body of Secrets explained the backstory of the *Valdez* and the *Liberty*, why my ship was sent to the Med, and the clear proof that Israel was the aggressor in the war, not its Arab neighbors as it claimed.

The *Valdez*, one small ship monitoring an enormous continent, was later [replaced] by the USS *Liberty*, a large floating listening post. A veteran of WW2 like the *Valdez*, *Liberty* [while the SS *Simmons Victory*] had also served honorably during the Korean War, making the lonely transit across the Pacific 18 times to bring supplies to American forces fighting there. Worn, its hull streaked with rust, the ship was finally retired to a naval boneyard in 1958, but five years later it was recalled to active duty for service in the Cold War and fitted with four .50 caliber machineguns.

Half the Earth away, behind cipher-locked doors at NSA, the talk was not of possible African coups but of potential Middle East wars. The indications had been growing for weeks, like swells before a storm. On the Israeli-Syrian border, what started out as potshots at tractors had quickly escalated to cannon fire between tanks. On May 17, Egypt (then known as the United Arab Republic [UAR]) evicted UN peacekeepers and then moved troops to its Sinai border with Israel.

A few days later, Israeli tanks were reported on the Sinai frontier, and the following day Egypt ordered mobilization of 100,000 armed reserves.

On May 23, Gamal Abdel Nasser blockaded the Straits of Tiran, thereby closing the Gulf of Aqaba to Israeli shipping and prohibiting unescorted tankers under any flag from reaching the Israeli port of Elat. The Israelis declared the action "an act of aggression against Israel" and began a full-scale mobilization.

As NSA's ears strained for information, Israeli officials began arriving in Washington. Nasser, they said, was about to launch a lopsided war against them and they needed American support. It was a lie. In fact, as Menachem Begin admitted years later, it was Israel that was planning a first strike attack on Egypt. "We . . . had a choice," Begin said in 1982, when he was Israel's prime minister. "The Egyptian army concentrations in the Sinai approaches do not prove that Nasser was really about to attack us. We must be honest with ourselves. We decided to attack him."

With the growing possibility of U.S. involvement in a Middle East war, the Joint Chiefs of Staff needed rapid intelligence on the ground situation in Egypt. Above all, they wanted to know how many Soviet troops, if any, were currently in Egypt and what kinds of weapons they had. Also, if U.S. fighter planes were to enter the conflict, it was essential to pinpoint the locations of surface-to-air missile batteries. If troops went in, it would be vital to know the locations and strength of opposing forces.

Under the gun to provide answers, officials at NSA considered their options. Land-based stations, like the one in Cyprus, were too far away to collect the narrow line-of-sight signals used by air defense radar, fire control radar, microwave communications, and other targets.

Airborne SIGINT platforms—Air Force C-130s and the Navy EC-121s—could collect some of this. But after allowing for time to and from the "orbit areas," the aircrews would only have about five hours on station— too short a time for the sustained collection that was required. Adding aircraft was also an option but finding extra signals intelligence planes would be very difficult. Also, downtime and maintenance on those aircraft was greater than for any other kind of platform.

Finally there were the ships, which was the best option. Because they could sail relatively close, they could pick up the most important signals. Also, unlike the aircraft, they could remain on station for weeks at a time, eavesdropping, locating transmitters, and analyzing the intelligence.

At the time, the USS *Oxford* and *Jamestown* were in Southeast Asia; the USS *Georgetown* and *Belmont* were eavesdropping off South America; and the USNS *Muller* was monitoring signals off Cuba. That left the USNS *Valdez* and the USS *Liberty*. The *Valdez* had just completed a long mission and was near Gibraltar on its way back to the United States. On the other hand, the *Liberty*, which was larger and faster, had just begun a new mission and was relatively close, in port in Abidjan.

On May 23, NSA decided to send *Liberty* to the Middle East, and at 8:20 P.M. a FLASH message was sent to my ship:

> MAKE IMMEDIATE PREPARATIONS TO GET UNDERWAY. WHEN READY FOR SEA ASAP DEPART PORT ABIDJAN AND PROCEED BEST POSSIBLE SPEED TO ROTA SPAIN TO LOAD TECHNICAL SUPPORT MATERIAL AND SUPPLIES. WHEN READY FOR SEA PROCEED TO OPERATING AREA OFF PORT SAID. SPECIFIC AREAS WILL FOLLOW.

A FLASH message is the highest level message—out of five—issued by the Combined Communications Electronics Board, composed of the U.S., UK, Australia, New Zealand and Canada. FLASH messages—where brevity is mandatory—"are to be handled as fast as humanly possible, ahead of all other messages, with in-station handling time not to exceed 10 minutes." The other four message levels "are interrupted on all circuits involved until the handling of FLASH messages is completed."

Bamford continued.

> For eight days, at top speed, the bow cut a silvery path through 3,000 miles of choppy Atlantic Ocean. The need for linguists was especially critical on the *Liberty*, which, because of her West African targets, carried only French and Portuguese language experts.

> Therefore, five Arabic linguists—two enlisted Marines and three NSA civilians—were ordered to Rota to rendezvous with the *Liberty*. Although the ship already had numerous Russian linguists, it was also decided to add one more, a senior analytical specialist. NSA had originally

wanted to also put Hebrew linguists on the ship, but the agency just didn't have enough.

As head of the research spaces, Dave explained why there were no Hebrew linguists on *Liberty*.

We had no Hebrew linguists onboard, and we were ordered never to copy anything Israeli or British Commonwealth. Those were always the two caveats, anywhere in the world where I was stationed, I always had those same two caveats. So we didn't copy Israeli circuits to start with. We weren't permitted to. I know the Brits do. I know the [U.S.] Air Force got some intercept, but Navy was never allowed to. We always had that caveat.

Dave believed the Israelis used—and use—their power in the U.S. political infrastructure to make sure that America can't spy on them, although the Israelis have made a cottage industry of spying on the U.S.

Bamford continued.

On June 5, 1967, at 7:45 A.M. Sinai time (1:45 A.M. in Washington, D.C.), Israel launched virtually its entire air force against Egyptian airfields, destroying, within 80 minutes, the majority of Egypt's air power. On the ground, tanks pushed out in three directions across the Sinai toward the Suez Canal. Fighting was also initiated along the Jordanian and Syrian borders. Simultaneously, Israeli officials put out false reports to the press saying that Egypt had launched a major attack against them and that they were defending themselves.

About the same time in Tel Aviv, Foreign Minister Abba Eban summoned U.S. Ambassador Walworth Barbour to a meeting in his office. Building an even larger curtain of lies around Israel's true activities and intentions, Eban accused Egypt of starting the war. Barbour quickly sent a secret FLASH message back to Washington. "Early this morning," he quoted Eban, "Israelis observed Egyptian units moving in large numbers toward Israel and in fact considerable force penetrated Israeli territory and clashed with Israeli ground forces. Consequently, GOI [Government of Israel] gave order to attack." Eban told Barbour that his government intended to protest Egypt's action to the UN Security Council. "Israel is [the] victim of Nasser's aggression," he said.

Eban then went on to lie about Israel's goals, which all along had been to capture as much territory as possible. "GOI has no rpt [repeat] no intention taking advantage of situation to enlarge its territory. That hopes peace can be restored within present boundaries." Finally, after half an hour of deception, Eban brazenly asked the United States to go up against the USSR on Israel's behalf. Israel, Barbour reported, "asks our help in restraining any Soviet initiative."

7

Rota

Despite the fact the seas were calm, the trip towards Rota, Spain was rough because of the hurry we were in to get there. We ran at full speed ahead—maximum speed—around 18 knots, for eight days, until June 1.

We arrived at Naval Station Rota, picked up supplies, and more importantly, four newcomers—three U.S. Marine linguists and one civilian, 23-year-old Washington native Alan Merle Blue, who worked for the NSA.

Naval Station Rota, or NAVSTA Rota, covering more than 6,000 acres, is the largest American military community in Spain and is entirely U.S.-funded. NAVSTA Rota had its beginnings in 1953, when Spain's dictator, Francisco Franco, strengthened relations with the U.S. as a way to boost the local economy.

Naval Station Rota

According to *Body of Secrets*, Rota "was the Navy's major launching site for airborne eavesdropping missions over the Mediterranean area."

Our crew now stood at 294 brave souls: 272 enlisted, including nine CPOs, 16 officers, three Marines and three civilians.

USS *Vulcan* (AR-5)

"[T]he majority of the *Liberty*'s 16 officers," writes James Scott in *The Attack on the Liberty*, "were under [the age of] 30."

Joe had intimate knowledge of why we stopped in Rota.

> We dropped off all our linguists that were for the west coast of Africa and brought on new people who spoke the Arabic languages. We did not have anyone brought on board that specifically spoke Hebrew or could communicate in Israel, I guess because they were our friends. We did have a couple of CTs on board who were Jewish and spoke what Hebrew they had learned in synagogue. We weren't there to monitor Israel.

Maine native William Michael "Billy" LeMay, Sr., a 22-year-old Second Class Electrician's Mate (EM) in charge of the Electrical Department, recalled the heightened tension on board.

The EM rating, established in 1883, disestablished in 1884, and reestablished in 1898, took its current name in 1921. EMs "are responsible for the operation of a ship's electrical power generation systems, lighting systems, electrical equipment and electrical appliances."

> My duty station was the main generator room, just outside where the CTs were. And for the first time, because we picked up Marines when we hit Rota, there was a guard

outside the door. On all the other cruises there was never guards, but for this cruise, we did have a Marine as a guard outside the door with a gun.

Billy's USN career began with an eerie connection to the *Liberty*.

I was first assigned to the USS *Vulcan* [(AR-5)], a repair ship out of Norfolk, Virginia, which was almost welded to the pier. We only went out two times in two years, and one of them was during the skirmish down in the Dominican Republic.

The Dominican Civil War began April 24, 1965, and ended September 3, 1965, in the Dominican capital, Santo Domingo, brought on by a coup.

The Communists were trying to take over an island down there, and they emptied the Norfolk, Virginia base and all the ships went down there. We were down there for a month and repaired minesweepers, engines, and stuff like that.

Fred was there as well.

Belmont's first operational deployment, after getting underway from Norfolk, they, like *Liberty*, received emergency orders to cancel their scheduled deployment to Africa and proceed at flank speed to conduct operations to provide support in the Dominican Republic. *Belmont* was the first U.S. Navy ship to arrive, and I believe the last to leave. It proved to be an extremely productive mission.

Incredibly, *Liberty* was repaired by *Vulcan* from March 24 to April 21, just a month before we headed from Rota to the Med.

53

8

Mediterranean

As an indicator that our collective sixth sense was working overtime and telling us that something bad was approaching, tensions amongst the ship's crew were high. Everyone was agitated—snapping and barking at each other for relatively small things. Sometime around noon the next day, after our stop at Rota, we were on our way, passing the Rock of Gibraltar and then, as Lieutenant Golden had promised, out to sea.

In making the approximately 2,300-mile trip across the Mediterranean, we did full speed. There was a headwind against us of about 30 or 40 knots, almost as if some higher power was trying to keep us away from our destination.

Along the way, we saw three Soviet destroyers that kept about 6,000 yards distance between us and them. The Mediterranean was calm, but we made it rough by putting the pedal to the metal. The water sprayed us constantly as we heaved up and down on our hasty trip.

We knew we were headed into a war zone, so Captain McGonagle requested an armed escort, a destroyer of all things—a warship designed to defend against attacks—but was denied.

The official explanation from Washington was that there was nothing to fear—the *Liberty* was a U.S.-flagged ship and the flag we proudly flew was our protective shield. After all, we were America, and the last country that picked a fight with us on December 7, 1941 paid for it dearly.

As we approached our destination, *Liberty* crewmembers were rooting for Israel, hoping she would wallop her Arab enemies. Obviously not knowing what was to come, we showed our support for the Jewish state by making Israeli flags of different sizes and placing them all over the ship.

How could we have known any better? It was, after all, only about 20 years since WW2 was over, and growing up in America, we had all gotten a heavy dose of how badly Jews had been treated. How could we not root for poor, seemingly defenseless Israel?

Despite being assured we were safe, the unease amongst the crew remained. It was not just the rough-and-rowdy enlisted men who had a bad feeling in their guts about the mission, but the officers as well. They were harder, sharper, more direct, less patient, and just plain antsy. They had always drilled us a lot anyway, but now they drilled us a hell of a lot more and paid attention to every detail. No mistakes were tolerated.

Basically, all the drills we in damage control did on a regular basis in dealing with an attack were stepped up considerably. We drilled in plugging holes in the ship's skin that might be created because of rocket and cannon fire.

We drilled in shoring up bulkheads in case we were hit by a torpedo. We drilled in putting out fires of any sort. It was almost as if Captain McGonagle knew we were to be attacked.

On June 4 we heard on the radio that Israel launched her sneak attack on the Arabs. The fast pace of the war and what appeared would be an easy victory for Israel led us to believe it would all be over soon.

Joe explained why *Liberty* raced to the Med.

> We were in port when the Israeli military launched a preemptive strike against the Arab states. We knew they were gonna do it, but they did it way ahead of when they said they were gonna do it. We would never have been in the Med had they not had a Six-Day War.

One of the things we noticed right away as we neared our destination was that ships of all sorts—tankers, cargo ships and just about every other thing you could imagine—were all headed in the opposite direction, as if they were fleeing the area. Despite this bad omen, our jittery, antsy mood had changed to one of excited invincibility, because our American flag—our force field—was waving high where it could not possibly go unnoticed, and no one was going to get on the bad side of the red, white and blue. When June 7 came around, the weather turned in our favor. Mother Nature's wet, windy, temperamental mood suddenly changed and was replaced with beautiful, clear skies and calm seas. Although we did not know it at that time, it was to be the calm before the storm.

On that evening, we wrapped up our 6,000 mile trip as we approached the Egyptian-controlled Gaza Strip. For all intents and purposes the war between the Jewish state and the Arabs was a done deal, although we could still hear and see some mopping up taking place on the horizon.

"Obtaining the earliest intelligence that the Russians were taking part in the fighting was one of the principal reasons for sending the *Liberty* so far into the war zone," writes Bamford in *Body of Secrets*.

Joe explained what *Liberty*'s mission was—and how she did it—after we arrived in the Med.

> We were off an area where there was active combat going on. That was why we were there: to see how in real combat the Arab states guide their missiles, do their commands, what codes they use, so we could get as much free information as we could in a real wartime situation.
>
> We started slowly doing a circle, a long oval-type circle, around five to eight knots, up and down the coast around the Sinai Peninsula, Egyptian territory. But we were 13 miles offshore, clearly in international waters by anyone's standards, and we were painted like a U.S. ship, numbered and lettered like a U.S. ship, flew the American flag like the U.S. ship that we were, and of course all our sailors were wearing Navy uniforms.

The Six-Day War, from June 5 to 10, 1967, was precipitated by Israel, who had launched preemptive strikes against the United Arab Republic—now Egypt—Syria and Jordan.

We were later told that a warning had been sent out by the JCS that we were to remain at least 100 miles away from the conflict, although we never received it. Considering the fact we were basically a giant floating radio station, there was little chance that we "missed" it if it had actually been sent.

Joe explained why the "warning" message could not have happened, let alone the way the JCS claimed.

> It makes no sense at all that it would be rerouted to the Philippines. A message sent by the JCS to a ship in the Sixth Fleet in the Mediterranean would go to a communications center that sent messages only to the Sixth Fleet via the "fleet broadcast system." And all the messages to all the ships would be transmitted in order of importance and it was up to each ship in the Sixth Fleet to go through all the messages and pick theirs out.

> It's almost impossible for a message sent to a ship in one fleet to end up in another, let alone end up in a land-based station. Once someone understands how the naval communications system works, this story makes no sense at all.

The Fleet Broadcasting System (FBS) was used to transmit all U.S. Navy operational orders to ships at sea. The FBS was also the system that allowed U.S. Navy Chief Warrant Officer and communications specialist John Anthony Walker, Jr. to lead one of the most devastating spy rings ever uncovered in this country, lasting from 1967 to 1985. While spying for the Soviets, he helped them decipher more than one million encrypted naval messages, considered "the most damaging Soviet spy ring in history."

9

Noratlas

While steaming towards our destination, we weren't the only ones taking in the sights. We were being observed for several days by aircraft.

Once daybreak arrived, we received visitors in the form of overflights of our ship. I didn't see the initial flights because I was belowdecks doing my job, but others told me about them. The planes were unquestionably Israeli, as the Star of David was easy to see, and knowing that our "friends" were checking on us caused the general mood to improve dramatically.

Rick has vivid memories of that day.

> It was a clear, beautiful day, and every morning at quarters, on the main deck, I would look up at the mast and watch the flag flying, which is something I like to do. I'm a flag lover, and I love our flag, and I love seeing it flying on a ship. And I knew that morning that the flag was flying; I saw it with my own eyes. You can't tell me there was no flag flying; sorry, my eyes don't lie. I watched it the whole day. Every time I'd go out, I'd always look up there. So I saw it numerous times, and I knew the flag was flying.

> I saw the planes flying over in the morning and remember seeing billows of smoke on land.

The way my shipmates described them, these surveillance planes were low and slow, the overflights lasting approximately six hours. Around noon, the flights stopped altogether.

Larry B. Thorn, a 24-year-old Minnesota native and Second Class Machine Repairman on board the *Liberty*, witnessed the flyovers.

> I was standing on the main deck looking at this plane flying over and around us. I saw the silhouette of the pilot.

Kenneth R. Gauthier, a 20-year-old Third Class CT from Lafayette, Louisiana, was assigned to the *Liberty* on October 31, 1966 and remembered the fly-bys.

> I was outside and saw some of the airplanes flying by and doing surveillance.

Steve remembered the overflights.

> On the morning of June 8, the sky was bright and cloudless. I was on deck with my fellow deck crew. Fred Kerner and I watched as a box-car-like plane flew low over us. I recall seeing the Star of David on the side and was relieved that it was our friends, the Israelis. We even saw the pilot's face and waved to him. I don't recall that he waved back.

As it was not possible for them to mistake the fact we were Americans, the general belief amongst the crew was that Washington and Tel Aviv were working together to make sure we were safe.

Body of Secrets detailed the reconnaissance of our ship by a Nord Noratlas.

> The reconnaissance was repeated at approximately 30-minute intervals throughout the morning. At one point, a boxy Israeli Air Force Noratlas 2501 circled the ship around the starboard side, proceeded forward of the ship, and headed back toward the Sinai.

"It had a big Star of David on it and it was flying just a little bit above our mast on the ship," recalled crewmember Larry Weaver. "We really thought his wing was actually going to clip one of our masts. . . . And I was actually able to wave to the co-pilot, a fellow on the right-hand side of the plane. He waved back, and actually smiled at me. I could see him that well. I didn't think anything of that because they were our allies. There's no question about it. They had seen the ship's markings and the American flag. They could damn near see my rank. The underway flag was definitely flying. Especially when you're that close to a war zone."

The Nord Noratlas was a French military aircraft—used by the Israelis for cargo and paratroop transport, as bombers on long-range strikes into Egypt, and for maritime reconnaissance—with 425 produced from 1949-1961. At the outbreak of the Six-Day War, the Israeli Air Force (IAF) had 23, 16 of them former West German planes, used for maritime patrol missions, dropping supplies and ammunition, and evacuating the wounded. One Noratlas was destroyed on the first day of the war during a Royal Jordanian Air Force strike. As France was one of only a handful of countries willing to sell Israel modern armaments, the IAF purchased six of the planes beginning in 1956 and phased them out in 1978.

Nord 2501 Noratlas

The Attack on the Liberty added more details to the overflights.

> High above the *Liberty* in the cockpit of the Nord 2501 Noratlas reconnaissance plane, an Israeli observer stared down at the spy ship.
>
> The plane had been airborne since 4:10 A.M., patrolling Israel's coastline to detect ships beyond radar range. Other than the *Liberty*, the sea was largely empty. The recon plane dropped as low as 3,000 feet and circled a half mile away to better study the foreign vessel.
>
> The observer radioed that he had found what looked like a destroyer 70 miles west of Gaza. The observer soon corrected his earlier report. He had spotted an American supply ship.
>
> From the cockpit, the observer noted the *Liberty*'s unique hull markings, GTR-5, which identified it as a general technical research ship. The flight engineer later recalled that the ship lacked cannons. "It was a gray color," he said. "Not too big, not too small, like a cargo ship."

Belowdecks, Joe and the other CTs were well aware of what was happening topside.

> On the 7th and the 6th of June, we sent as many as a half-a-dozen what they call SITREPs—situation reports—to Washington, for overflights. We had been overflown several times by low-flying, slow-moving, propeller-driven, Star of David, reconnaissance aircraft, so low in fact, that our men on deck waved to the pilots and the pilots waved back.
>
> These SITREPs provided clear documentation of the overflights; date, time, aircraft type and any pertinent comments.

Israel knew we were there, and they knew who we were, and what we were doing, a day or two before the 8th of June.

Perhaps more significantly, the U.S. government had clear documentation that Israel knew we were there.

One of my close shipmates in my division was Third Class Shipfitter, Metal, Dulio Demori. Born in Italy, 24-year-old Dulio came to the U.S. in 1956 and enlisted in the Navy in 1964, and attended boot camp with Rick. He was topside when we were being surveilled.

It was prior to lunchtime or about midday, when I first saw black smoke in the faraway distance. And I had no clue that there was a war going on between Israel and her enemies. Shortly thereafter a plane came about and circled our ship. It flew low and slow. You could actually see the head of the pilot. I think they should have had the ability to properly identify the ship. I didn't pay much attention and I went to lunch.

James Clayton "Smitty" Smith was a 20-year-old Third Class Damage Controlman, born in Tampa, Florida but raised in western New York. Smitty, as he was called by the rest of us, served 13 years as an enlisted sailor, making Senior Chief Petty Officer, E-8, and retiring after 25 years as an O-4, Lieutenant Commander.

Around four months after he entered the Navy, in October 1966, he was stationed aboard *Liberty*, his first ship.

Smitty was tending to the "repair lockers" when he witnessed the surveillance plane.

They have in there firehoses, oxygen breathing apparatuses for firefighters, and various equipment for fighting fires. It's called a "repair" locker but it's a "damage control" locker in reality. And they had shoring in there that we had to use to shore up the bulkheads after the torpedo hit. It's just four-by-fours and metal shoring that you put against the bulkhead to make it stable where it won't cave in.

That's what a damage control man did; he just took care of all that equipment.

Repair Locker 2 was forward on the main deck and Repair Locker 3 was aft on the second deck, so you had to transit the whole main deck and then go down one more, to the mess decks.

I had checked out one of the two lockers and then gone aft or forward, whichever it was, to the other one, and was checking out the equipment there, and as I walked across the main deck, you could see the reconnaissance plane flying over us, making several passes. I can't tell you how many.

10

EC-121

L ittle did I know, but more eyes were in the sky. A Lockheed EC-121 Warning Star was listening in on war chatter miles above the fighting.

The Warning Star, one of 232 built for the Navy and the Air Force, was a military version of the Lockheed L-1049 Super Constellation, an airborne early warning system and intelligence gathering aircraft. The EC-121 also played a role in the Distant Early Warning Line, or DEW Line, operational from 1957 to 1985, a system of radar stations in the Arctic, the Aleutian Islands, the Faroe Islands, Greenland, and Iceland, to detect Soviet bombers during the Cold War, and to provide evidence of an invasion by land or sea.

Introduced in 1954 and re-tired in 1978, Warning Stars had a maximum speed of 299 mph and a cruising speed of 255 mph, a range of 4,250 miles, a service ceiling of 25,000 feet and could house a six-man flight crew. They were also the forerunner to the much more well-known Boeing E-3 Sentry, or AWACS (Airborne Warning And Control System).

Lockheed EC-121 Warning Star

Bamford uncovered the EC-121 information for *Body of Secrets*, and clear evidence that Israel was 100% sure they were attacking an American ship, my ship.

As the Israelis continued their slaughter, neither they nor the *Liberty* crew had any idea that witnesses were present high above. Until now. According to information, interviews, and documents obtained for *Body of Secrets*, for nearly 35 years NSA has hidden the facts that one of its planes was overhead at the time of the incident, eavesdropping on what was going on below. The intercepts from that plane, which answer some of the key questions about the attack, are among NSA's deepest secrets.

In the "Acknowledgments" section of *Body of Secrets*, Bamford thanks USN CPO Marvin E. Nowicki, who served aboard the EC-121 at the time, and "had the unusual qualification of being a Hebrew and Russian linguist," accumulating "over 2,000 hours in such spy planes over his career."

Two hours before the attack, the Navy EC-121 . . . had taken off from Athens and returned to the eastern Mediterranean for its regular patrol. Now it was flying a diagonal track from Crete to Cyprus to El Arish and back.

[A]bout the time the air attack was getting under way, Nowicki heard one of the other Hebrew linguists excitedly trying to get his attention on the secure intercom. "Hey, Chief," the linguist shouted, "I've got really odd activity on UHF. They mentioned an American flag."

Nowicki asked the linguist for the frequency and "rolled up to it." "Sure as the devil," said Nowicki, "Israeli aircraft were completing an attack on some object. I alerted the evaluator, giving him sparse details, adding that we had no idea what was taking place." For a while the activity subsided.

[T]he Hebrew linguist called Nowicki again. "He told me about new activity and that the American flag is being mentioned again. I had the frequency but for some strange reason, despite seeing it on my spectrum analyzer, couldn't hear it on my receiver, so I left my position to join him to listen at his position. I heard a couple of references to the flag during an apparent attack. The attackers weren't aircraft; they had to be surface units (we later found out at USA-512J it was the Israeli motor torpedo boats attacking the *Liberty*). Neither [the other Hebrew linguist] nor I had ever heard MTB attacks in voice before, so we had no idea what was occurring below us. I advised the evaluator; he was as mystified as we were."

[T]he intercept operators in the EC-121 . . . continued to eavesdrop on voices from the war below, but they heard no more mention of the American flag. "Finally," said Chief Nowicki, "it was time to return to Athens. We recorded voice activity en route home until the intercepts finally faded. On the way home the evaluator and I got together to try to figure out what we copied. Despite replaying portions of the tapes, we still did not have a complete understanding of what transpired except for the likelihood that a ship flying the American flag was being attacked by the Israeli air and surface forces."

After landing on the Greek air force side of the Athens airport, Nowicki and the intercept crew were brought directly to the processing center. "By the time we arrived at the USA-512J compound," he said, "collateral reports were coming in to the station about the attack on the USS *Liberty*.

The first question we were asked was, did we get any of the activity? Yes, we dared to say we did. The NSA civilians took our tapes and began transcribing. It was pretty clear that Israeli aircraft and motor torpedo boats attacked a ship in the east Med. Although the attackers never gave a name or a hull number, the ship was iden- tified as flying an American flag. We logically concluded that the ship was the USS *Liberty*, although we had no idea she was even in the area and could become the object of such an attack."

"As I recall, we recorded most, if not all, of the attack," Chief Nowicki said. "I heard a couple of references to the flag during an apparent attack."

Chief Nowicki, who is Jewish, had hoped Israel had made a mistake when it attacked my ship, according to *Body of Secrets*.

Nowicki, who later received a Ph.D. in political science and taught public administration at the college level, is an enthusiastic supporter of Israel, who originally assumed his information would help clear Israel. Instead, it convicts the government.

If the Israelis did see the flag, then the attack was coldblooded murder—like the hundreds of earlier murders committed by Israelis that day at El Arish.

On September 20, 1995, Egypt "discovered two mass graves in the Sinai containing the remains of Egyptian prisoners of war and unarmed civilians shot by Israeli soldiers during the 1967 war."

The New York Times reported on the issue the following day.

The charges first came to prominence when a retired Israeli brigadier general, Arieh Biroh, said in interviews that in October 1956, he and another officer killed 49 Egyptian prisoners of war in the Sinai Desert.

At the same time, an Israeli historian said that as many as 300 unarmed Egyptians were killed in both the 1967 war and in the war of 1956. Those reports led to other allegations and revelations. The discovery of the two graves, one near a former Egyptian air base about three miles from El Arish and the other about 18 miles from town, was described today in the government-owned newspaper *Al Ahram*. The paper said the two shallow graves held the remains of at least 30 and possibly 60 people. It quoted several Bedouins in the region as saying they had witnessed the killing of Egyptian soldiers after their surrender on June 6 and June 7, 1967, and had helped to bury them.

The paper said an expedition organized by reporters had uncovered the two graves with the help of an Egyptian guide who had served as a sergeant during the 1967 war. The former sergeant, Abdelsalam Moussa, said he had helped to bury some victims in one grave. The newspaper showed pictures of one grave that it said contained the remains of 30 people.

Mr. Moussa, now 55, said he had been ordered to bury some of his comrades by Israeli soldiers who took him prisoner. "I saw a line of prisoners, civilians and military, and they opened fire at them all at once," Mr. Moussa was quoted as saying. "When they were dead, they told us to bury them."

Al Ahram also quoted a Bedouin, Suleman Moghnem Salameh, who said he saw Israelis kill about 30 Egyptians soldiers and officers after they surrendered, leaving them for the Bedouins to bury. Israel responded by sending Elli Dayan, a Deputy Foreign Minister, to discuss the matter. During his visit here, he offered compensation to the families of victims but noted Israel's 20-year statute of limitations.

The Attack on the Liberty added more to what Bamford had uncovered.

Miles above the *Liberty* in the back of a Navy spy plane, Petty Officer Second Class Michael Prostinak tuned the dials on his receiver in search of Israeli communications. The Hebrew linguist had lifted off from the Athens airbase in an EC-121 that morning for an eight-hour mission over the Middle East to eavesdrop on the fourth day of the war.

Though his Hebrew lagged behind his Spanish skills, Prostinak had learned to pick up on key words, such as "tanks," "artillery," and "mortar fire." He eavesdropped on a frequency long enough to get a basic understanding. If it had potential intelligence value, he recorded it. If not, he turned the dials. More than the language, Prostinak listened for the excitement in a voice that almost always indicated action.

That's what grabbed his attention this afternoon as the Willy Victor [Navy nickname for the EC- 121] roared along the Egyptian coast. The flurry of Hebrew made it impossible for Prostinak to discern whether he heard aircraft or ground forces. He could sense from the excitement that something was going on far below. He strained to listen and translate.

He then heard something that shocked him. He flipped on the secure intercom to his supervisor. "Hey, Chief, I've got really odd activity," Prostinak called out as he hit the record button. "They mentioned an American flag."

Why our own intelligence agency, the NSA, kept this hidden from us—and the American people—for all this time, is not just disturbing, it's heartbreaking.

11

Drill

I awoke at 3:30 on the morning of June 8 because I had Sounding and Security watch duty. Sounding and Security watch, basically a damage control watch, was the most important watch on the ship. I had to follow a regular route and conduct a continuous security inspection of all spaces, inspecting all watertight hatches and scuttles. I also had to check for fire, fire hazards, theft, sabotage, or any other irregularities that would affect the physical security of the ship. I was also required to take soundings at regular intervals and compare them to the previous day.

Soundings measured the amount of liquid in certain compartments, tanks, and voids using sounding tubes, taken on a regular schedule or when considered necessary for the safety of the ship. My job also included making sure all tanks of potable water were drinkable. I would report to the bridge every hour on the hour with the news that all was OK.

I went to lunch around noon, and soon afterwards a GQ drill was announced over the 1MC. Captain wanted a chemical drill done, which meant me crawling into what was called an "impregnated" suit. I grabbed my firehose and nozzle and made my way to the main deck, pretending to wash down any chemicals on the ship. The heat inside that suit was enough to make me woozy to the point where I thought I would pass out. Somewhere around 1:45 P.M.—just a few minutes before I would no doubt have keeled over—the drill was done. I crawled out of the suit and put it away.

Damage Control Central hailed me and informed me that one of the phones in the starboard—the right-hand side of the ship, facing forward—gun mount on the forecastle—the forward part of a ship, abbreviated fo'c'sle or fo'c's'le and pronounced "foaxul"— was not working. Indiana native David Skolak, an E-3 Interior

70

Communications electrician (IC), another engineer like myself, accompanied me to the gun mount where the broken phone was located. I told him what needed to be done and his response was, "No problem, Tourney, I'll get her working." This was about five minutes before 2 P.M.

According to the USN's website, ICs "install, maintain and repair the equipment needed for interior communications within ships and shore facilities," like "public address systems, interior telephone systems, alarm systems, engine telegraphs to communicate orders for changes in engine speed from the bridge to the engine room, the ship's gyrocompass, the rudder position indicator," as well as ship-to-shore or ship-to-ship communications.

We stood there for a few minutes near the gun mount, shooting the bull. One of the things we both remarked on was that of all the places we would not want to be during an attack, this was it; the guntub. We knew that in any attack, the guntub, as well as the guy manning it, would get taken out as a first priority. We fought back the shivers associated with this discussion by reminding ourselves and each other that everything was OK. We were Americans and Israel was our ally, we thought. Therefore, anyone becoming aggressive with us would immediately be crushed by our good friends, the Israelis, just as your buddy would step in and start throwing punches if you were jumped by someone.

I had to get back to my workstation, so I said goodbye to Skolak and the gunner and made my way down the starboard ladder to the main deck, and then on to my workstation in the shipfitter's shop on the starboard side. As soon as I opened the hatch, stepped in and closed it, I heard an order announced over the 1MC to test the motor whaleboat.

A few moments after the order had been given I heard a huge explosion right next to the hatch I had just closed. The only logical explanation in my mind was that whoever was carrying out the order to test the motor whaleboat had done something wrong and the boat had blown up as a consequence.

The idea we were under attack was the farthest thing from my mind.

Joe recalled what he remembered of the drill.

The captain came on the 1MC and gave us a "well done." From Captain McGonagle, that was appreciated by the crew. But I remember clearly that his comments were, "But, we're gonna keep having these drills. We have to be vigilant because we are near a war zone. We are close enough that you can see some smoke from the battle. You men were outstanding. Try to improve. Well done and secured from general quarters."

When the captain mentioned seeing "smoke," a lot of the guys grabbed their cameras and went topside. I was still in the Comm [Communications] Center and I stayed there because I had some work to do.

The next thing I remember was an announcement over the 1MC from the Officer of the Deck [OOD], the guy who runs the ship when the captain's not there, to stand clear of the O1 level aft while testing the motor whaleboat.

Another CT, E-3 Donald W. Pageler, a Kansas native, was brand new to the Navy and the *Liberty* when he came aboard.

I turned 21 on February 1st, I got assigned to the *Liberty* in late March, we went to sea May the 2nd, and we were attacked on June the 8th.

The first thing I remember is McGonagle was running a GQ drill at 1 o'clock. We secured from the GQ drill at 1:35, 1:40. I was off duty, so I went up on the fantail to smoke a couple of cigarettes. I was just on my way down onto the ladder to my sleeping compartment, which was at the aft end of the ship and was right aft of the mess deck. I was halfway down the ladder when I heard all the metal hitting and the GQ alarm sounded again. So I just went on down the ladder, through my sleeping compartment and on to the mess deck where my GQ area was. My GQ station was Repair Party 3 on the mess deck. I was supposed to be in charge of a submersible pump. I was so green, that's probably why they didn't assign me to the intelligence spaces where I worked, because I was so [new to] my job that they wanted more senior guys up there.

Not realizing that a rocket had just exploded directly outside the hatch, I grabbed the handle and opened it once more to go out and investigate the trouble. I had just barely put one foot outside, when I felt myself grabbed by the shirt collar and violently jerked back inside. I turned and saw it was First Class Petty Officer Dale Neese.

"Get back!" he barked, "We're under attack!"

12

Jets

B illy was the first of my shipmates to see the jets.

The day of the attack was beautiful. The ocean was calm as could be, just like a mirror. I referred to the water like glass.

Just before the attack, I was up on the deck, and I saw an explosion or something on the beach, and we got a GQ drill. I think they told me it was chemical warfare that day.

We did the GQ and it ended. After GQ I went back up on the main deck because we had to check the carbon arc searchlight up on the O4 level, the highest place you could be on the deck, and not climb a mast.

Carbon arc searchlights were built by General Electric and first appeared in 1893 in Chicago at the World's Columbian Exposition. Around 10,000 were made, with most ending up in Europe during WW2.

So as I'm walking up there to check out the carbon arc searchlight, just as I got there a jet fighter, and I believe it was black with no markings on it, was flying very low, the same direction the ship was going. There was a lieutenant up there and I believe his job was to identify any planes that flew over or anything like that. So as I got up there

I turned around to him and I said, "Sir, did you see that fighter?"

And he goes, "Where?" Well, I turned around and I pointed at the fighter, and as I pointed at the fighter, the first strafing came. And he went from the bow to the stern, diagonally across the ship, not right down the center of it. I turned and I looked at the officer, and he was bloody like I was, just all kinds of little bloody holes coming out of him."

What Billy saw was a French-made Dassault Mirage IIIC.

The Mirage, a single-seat, all-weather interceptor-fighter aircraft, was armed with two 30 mm cannon, one air-to-air missile and two AIM-9 Sidewinder missiles. It's hard to fathom—even today—that the Sidewinder was developed by my own USN in the 1950s.

Mirage IIICJ – "Shahak 41"— du Squadron 119 en juin 1967

Billy, who still carries 52 pieces of shrapnel in him, said his next thought was to get out of where he was.

Now I didn't grab him, I didn't do any of that, but I ran to the ladder, slid down it—never hit a rung, just like you see in the movies—slid down, went into the ship;

I could finally get inside because there was no entrance into the ship on the deck that I was on. As I got in there,

there was glass all over the place, and that's when my body realized that my left knee had been shattered and I fell to the deck.

Ken was topside when the jets began their assault.

All of a sudden there was a huge explosion behind me. I turned around and I saw a jet going straight up.

Joe remembered the initial assault.

It was a beautiful, clear day. We were looking forward to going up and sunbathing at the noon hour, which was normal for us.

The photographer was called to the bridge because on radar they had tracked, initially, surface craft, coming, from what we believed—which turned out to be true—an Israeli port, on a direct line with our ship. And shortly after they noted the surface craft, they noted high-speed aircraft passing over those vessels on the same track. And they wanted the photographer to see if he could get a picture of the jets as they flew over.

The photographer was another CT, and he was focusing on that lead jet, and he said he saw orange-like flame coming from the jet. And the next thing that happened was he was picking himself up off the deck. That jet had come from the aft end of the ship, circled wide, and come straight down the centerline, and when the fellow was trying to take a picture, the pilot opened fire.

The guy lived to tell the tale, in fact they even gave him the telephoto lens he was using, because the slug that would've killed him went down the barrel of the telephoto lens, backstopped on the camera, and knocked his butt on the ground.

Rockets tore right through the guntubs, and my shipmates

Bob recalled the air attack.

I had a midwatch [the middle watch, from 0000-0400 (midnight-4 A.M.)] the night before, so I slept in till about noon, and I got some lunch and we had a GQ practice.

After the GQ practice we were sitting back in our spaces; there were some tables back in our quarters where you could play cards and things like that, so we were all sitting around talking about the fact that the Arabs really don't have the *cojones* [Spanish for "a man's testicles," meaning boldness or courage needed to do something, nerve] to attack us because we're protected by the Israelis.

About that time, it sounded like somebody threw a handful of ball bearings on a piece of glass and they stuck. And it was right above our heads. No one spoke, we didn't wait, everybody was headed for their GQ station before we actually heard [the general quarters announcement] on the 1MC.

I went directly to my GQ station where I worked, like
two levels below the main deck, below the waterline.
We immediately cranked up our equipment and started
listening for anything we could find. We could hear the
explosions and somebody brought one of the wounded
guys down toward our spaces and they were told to take
him to the mess decks, but he was shot up, very bloody,
blood all over the place, and I knew we were in big
trouble.

We had to turn off our equipment because it started
smoking, which we did, and someone came in and said,
"Stay low because the shells are starting to penetrate the
side."

Buddha remembered the jet attack.

Pretty soon after [GQ] I heard what sounded like
somebody was dragging big chains over the deck, and
came to find out that was the planes strafing us. The hatch
opened up and a guy kinda tumbled down the ladder; he'd
been hit. Seemed like we were under attack for maybe
half-an-hour or so.

Steve remembered the attack.

The [ship's] store was several decks below and toward
the aft of the ship. While standing in line, passing time
with other sailors, we heard a muffled explosion. We kind
of shrugged, thinking it might just be a boiler "issue."
Then the GQ alert sounded. We all took off as fast as we
could.

I raced forward toward the forecastle and then up to the
main deck. I ran out through the hatch below the forward
starboard gun mount, running several yards as I took in
the sight: the bridge was engulfed in smoke, fires raged,

rocket holes everywhere. I slammed on the brakes, looked at the vent for which I was responsible, saw it was still secure from earlier and turned to run back to the hatch. I looked up and saw a jet heading at us very low. I dove forward against the bulkhead as he fired more rounds on us. I held my hat in my hand as I dove and later noticed that it had several holes from shrapnel.

No match against Israeli jets

There was an injured petty officer leaning against the bulkhead with what looked like a puncture wound in his chest. With strength I didn't know I had, I lifted him and carried him inside where I and others got him on a mattress for the "ride" to the mess decks, our new hospital.

I was stunned at that sight: dozens of wounded men, loud moans, the smell of death. There was little I could do to help, so I darted to my assigned repair party as quick as I could. Before I left the mess decks, I spotted R.J. Reilly who was sitting vigil with his brother Tom, who was badly injured. I was supposed to be working alongside Tom on deck when we were attacked.

The blood-drenched *Liberty* after the massacre

Some of the thousands of rounds that pierced *Liberty's* skin

The air attack seemed to go on forever. Our repair party was located inside the forecastle and rocket fire kept hitting the deck above us. We alternated our loud prayers with foul-mouthed pleas for our planes.

And then, it was over, so we thought. Some of us peeked out on the deck, looking to the sky hoping to see our jets, but saw nothing but the smoke from our ship.

We were contacted by the bridge, which requested two relief crew members to come up immediately. I was one of them.

We ran quickly, not certain if the air attack was over. We went up the ladder on the port side to the bridge. I was stunned again by what I saw: the Captain, looking and acting like John Wayne, a tourniquet wrapped on his leg, barking out orders; officers and sailors slumped against the bulkhead, blood and guts everywhere, so much smoke; and the stench.

I remember being somewhat surprised that the Captain had a camera and was shooting pictures of everything.

Larry, who was belowdecks, recalled the jet attack.

I'm standing there during the attack in Repair Party 3 and you could hear the bullets going through the skin of the ship.

Dulio was also belowdecks when the jets launched their vicious attack.

Normally after lunch I would go up to the forecastle, and on top of an ammunition box, I would lay down a towel and get a suntan. By the grace of God I did not do that on that particular day, and that saved my life.

81

After lunch I went back to the metal working shop where I was assigned. Shortly thereafter we heard a very loud noise, not having a clue what it was all about. The GQ alarm was sounded and you were supposed to proceed to your battle station.

I stepped outside on the main deck and ran for the first hatch. As I entered, I glanced to my left and I saw the corpsman with a medic alongside him. It was our mailman, Spicher, lying in a pool of blood. Later on I found out he was one of the fatalities.

I proceeded to go down belowdecks to the forward part of the ship where I was assigned to a repair party. By the time I reached my destination, I looked overhead, and there was a good-sized hole that was made by an Israeli rocket, and the blue sky was clearly visible. For the first time in my life I was really scared and I never prayed so hard to come out of this alive.

Dazed and shocked sailors survey the damage

As fate would have it, when the jets arrived, Smitty was teamed with Postal Clerk Second Class John Clarence Spicher, a 30-year-old married father of a two-year-old son, who was also a *Liberty* plankowner.

After lunch we went to GQ station for a drill, and we got finished with the drill, I don't know, I guess an hour later or so, and then we were gonna go back to normal ship's routine, and that's when the first jets came in.

When they sounded GQ, I immediately went down to the mess decks, which was where my repair locker was, and got on my headset and my phones.

Then all of a sudden word spread through the channels that there was a fire on the O1 level port side, which was where my gasoline was stored for my pumps, so I figured that must've exploded or somehow caught fire.

Other people were supposed to go fight that but they were having problems activating their oxygen breathing apparatus—OBAs—so I went up there, and somehow, me and the PC [Postal Clerk], John Spicher, we ended up going out on the main deck and fighting that fire. He had the nozzle and I had the hose behind him.

And I could see the jets then, as they circled the ship and strafed us. John and I stayed out there until we got that fire put out, and then we headed indoors, inside the superstructure, and I was the first one in and he was the last one in, and unfortunately he got shot up. He died there inside that superstructure.

After that fire was put out, I went forward because they said there was another fire, which was in fact the motor whaleboat burning. And I grabbed another hose, which was of no use because it was full of bullet and shrapnel holes, so I went inside the superstructure and grabbed another hose, and put that fire out on the motor whaleboat, which was on the O1 level starboard side.

Pennsylvania native Ernest A. "Ernie" Gallo, a 24-year-old CT, was one of the last of my shipmates to see Spicher alive.

> John Spicher, our postal clerk, was badly wounded, and one of our corpsmen was working on him. He turned to us and said, "This man needs mouth-to-mouth resuscitation."
>
> I guess he gave him a shot of morphine, and he instructed us to keep his Mae West [a nickname for a life jacket] tightly around his chest because he had a lot of shrapnel in his chest, and that was the problem.
>
> So one of us worked on keeping his jacket as tight as possible, and we took turns giving him mouth-to-mouth resuscitation. We continued to do this until the corpsman came back and said he had passed. And with that, I said some prayers over him. I'm Catholic, and I whispered a prayer in his ear. That's all we could do.

Glenn recounted what happened right after the GQ ended.

> We had had a GQ drill, and there were several of us who went down to the mess decks, and we were gonna have a cup of coffee.
>
> And so I remember sitting there, and we were talking, and then all of a sudden there were two relatively close explosions, and they were so loud. And as soon as you heard the noise, there was a vibration. It was almost like the ship was shaking.
>
> From what I learned, a rocket had hit the deck above the transmitter room and it exploded but it didn't explode through the deck; it kind of glanced off then exploded. I had suffered acoustic trauma, they called it. My ears were ringing, and I've had ringing in my ears virtually from that point on. I suffered a hearing loss from that attack.

Israel targeted all the watertight hatches

The GQ alarm sounded, so everybody quick just left the mess decks and ran to where their GQ station was. Well, fortunately for me, mine was very close. I just had to go up a couple of ladders, and I was on the main deck, and I could go on the inside of the ship, into the Radio Transmitter Room.

As I was going up the ladders and going to the Radio Transmitter Room, there were a number of other explosions, and the same feeling of the ship just shaking.

As soon as I got to the Radio Transmitter Room, the Radiomen were saying on the 1MC to me, "We need a transmitter, we need a transmitter." And so I looked over to the transmitter that they normally use, and it was being used, and I told them it was being used.

I didn't hear anything for about a minute or two, and then they were screaming, "We need a transmitter, we need a transmitter!" I told them that they had to use another transmitter. And they had the ability to activate different transmitters from their station, and so they did that.

We also had a receiver in the room, and normally that receiver would pick up what was being transmitted. I was hearing this buzzing sound. It sounded like a buzz saw, that's how I described it. It was almost constant, but there would be a gap, like 15 seconds where there was no buzz sound.

Don remembered the air attack.

Somebody grabbed me and another guy and said, "Go to the bridge and bring down wounded."

During the air attack all I really remember is going up to the bridge one time and somebody opening the hatch at the aft end of the bridge with somebody on a stretcher saying, "Here, take this guy below."

I remember we grabbed the stretcher and hauled the guy three or four sets of ladders down to the mess decks where we had a hospital set up. I'm sure I made multiple runs up there but I really don't remember that much.

Billy struggled with his wounds.

So I crawled around through a hatch into the officers' quarters and this sailor comes up to me and says, "Hey, you hurt?" And I looked up at him, and I said, "No, I love crawling on the deck." Of course there was blood everywhere; he knew I was hurt. We laughed even a little bit, if I remember right. He saw my leg bleeding quite badly, so he put a tourniquet on it, and he says, "I can't carry you myself to sick bay, I've gotta go get help." So he left. And I don't know how long it was. It seemed like a long time, but I think I might've even blacked out a couple of times while he was gone. But he came back and he had that Stokes stretcher, whatever it is, that wire mesh where they can twist you around, and put you any direction to get you to where they wanna put you.

They put me in it, and as we're coming around the corner to go down another ladder into the mess decks, which had already been assigned as sick bay, I believe, the corpsman came by and said, "Take the tourniquet off his leg, we don't want him to lose his leg."

So they put me down, he started to take the tourniquet off, and all of a sudden there was this tremendous explosion. A lot of heat, and I could see blue sky through the hole. Evidently a rocket must've hit, or something hit the side of the ship where we were, and came through.

This guy that was helping me, they claim, had a hole through his wrist, and it might even be that part of him is inside one of my wounds. Then they took me down to sick bay and they put me on the table.

The GQ alarm was sounded and I made my way to my duty station. After going down the ladder, I slipped and fell and found myself under the trampling feet of sailors as they made their way to their stations. I rolled over to my right side to get out of their way, got on my feet and joined the stampede to get to my station as well. I got into battle-dress and got my gear ready.

CPO Harold J. "Hal" Thompson was the on-scene leader. As soon as I arrived, he said he'd been hit and was leaving to get medical care. Since I was assistant on-scene leader, that meant I was in charge.

"It's all yours now, Tourney," Thompson said as he made his way down the passage, and I, not in the least bit thrilled with my new promotion, yelled back "Hey, thanks a lot chief."

I began my duties by making sure all persons in the damage control party were accounted for and ready to do business. Several were missing, which was not surprising, considering the torrent of explosions I could hear taking place just one deck above me. Suddenly—just like the "thousand points of light" George H.W. Bush described in his presidential acceptance speech—holes began appearing everywhere around us from the rocket and cannon fire as they struck the side and deck of the ship, allowing in sunlight where before there was none. I caught a piece of shrapnel four inches long, just above the elbow on my right arm. I pulled it out, threw it on the deck and moved everyone in my department to the main deck.

I didn't know it, but some new jets had joined the slaughter, eight minutes after the first had begun to blow our ship to hell

Super Mystere B.2 из 105-й АЭ ВВС Израиля, июнь 1967 г.
Super Mystere B.2 of the 105th Air Squadron of Israeli AF, June 1967.

Dassault Super Mystère B.2 — 105th Air Squadron, IAF, June 1967

Two French-made Dassault Super Mystère fighter-bombers, armed with two 30 mm cannons with 150 rounds per gun, two Matra rocket pods with 18, 68 mm rockets each, and four missiles, made multiple runs, unloading all of their armaments into our defenseless vessel. The Super Mystère "was the first Western European supersonic aircraft to enter mass production." Fortunately for the *Liberty* and her crew—and their families—the Mystères were not armed with their 5,000 pounds of payload, perhaps thinking they wouldn't need such ordnance to sink a virtually unarmed WW2-era cargo ship.

Once on the main deck, Rick and I were not prepared for what we were about to see. The first place I went was to the same guntub I had visited earlier. I saw nothing but a pile of human remains—blood, hunks of flesh and fragments of bone. We knew there was no life to be saved at the guntub, so we moved on. All the while, cannon and rocket fire were raining down on us.

Israel targeted the guntubs first

Dead and wounded bodies were everywhere on the main deck. In between volleys of machinegun fire and rockets we darted out from what we thought was safe cover, grabbed them one at a time, dragged them across the deck and threw them through the hatch. Others down below picked them up and took them someplace where they could be treated. It took us about 15 minutes to clear the decks of those who were alive and could be saved.

All told, there were about 25 guys up there who had been hurt and needed help. I think the worst case I saw was Seaman Apprentice Thomas R. Reilly, Jr., who was on his back, alert, and covered head-to-toe with gray paint. Considering the number of wounds he had sustained, the paint—as thick as cold molasses—probably saved his life, as it served as a giant bandage.

Once Rick and I assessed that there was no one else alive on the main deck, I was ordered to go to the log room, the location of Damage Control Central. When I got there, Ensign John Scott, my superior, was burning documents. This is standard procedure in the U.S. military, as all documents—no matter how seemingly insignificant they are—must be destroyed in the event of an attack. You do not allow your enemy to get any information on anything, and who else but an enemy would be attacking us? After speaking for a few minutes, he ordered me back on deck to assess the damage and to put out any fires.

On my way back, the passageways were littered with wounded men, all bloody and moaning. My shipmates called out to me asking for help. Some of them would ask, as if I were a doctor, "Hey, man, can you do something about this?"

I got to the bridge and saw that Captain McGonagle was badly wounded in the leg but still in command. Rocket and cannon holes were everywhere, and burning napalm was dripping through the holes and into the bridge compartment. I tried hitting the napalm with the CO_2 canisters I had, but the fire was so intense that CO_2 was basically useless, so I requested a fire team with water hoses. In hindsight, I realize this was just a waste of time, since the hoses had been shot up like a snake hit with birdshot from a shotgun.

I threw the two empty CO_2 canisters overboard and told the captain I would be back with some better equipment to put out the fires, and he said, "Do what you can, sailor." Despite the fact we were under attack and he was badly wounded, he was calm and professional, in a surreal way.

Before I left, I looked at my good friend, Francis Brown—a Third Class Quartermaster, who was steering the ship. We drank beer together, played cards and shot pool, and he had just hit the ripe old age of 20 a month before. We stood there for a moment, not saying a word but simply locking eyes.

I went to find more CO_2 canisters, and as soon as I got hold of one—in less than five minutes—I flew back up the port—the left-hand side of the ship, facing forward—ladder to get to the bridge. When I got to the top, I stepped in something wet, causing me to slip and fall on my back violently. The CO_2 canister flew out of my hands and came crashing down with a bang that caused everyone, including McGonagle, to look in my direction.

As soon as I got up, I saw what it was that had caused me to slip and fall. My good friend, Francis Brown, had caught a machinegun bullet or a piece of shrapnel to the back of the head and his blood was everywhere. His eyes were closed and his face was swelled up like a balloon. It was something that no human being should ever see, especially when it is your good friend.

My first thought when seeing this was, "Those Arab bastards, they just blew my friend to pieces!"

Down below, Joe clearly remembered what happened when the attack began.

I was already at my GQ station when I heard the announcement.

GENERAL QUARTERS, GENERAL QUARTERS, THIS IS NO DRILL. MAN YOUR BATTLE STATIONS. THE SHIP IS UNDER ATTACK. GENERAL QUARTERS. THIS IS NO DRILL.

Down in the Comm Center, we were doing what we were supposed to be doing: trying to get comms [communications] up. We didn't know what was going on topside; we could hear it, but we weren't living it. Every time a rocket hit, down inside, it was like somebody hit a trashcan with a baseball bat.

We were two decks below the main deck. Bullets were not flying around our space. The explosions didn't impact our space other than the noise and the confusion.

So we're trying to get communications with some of our stations, and initially were rather calm about it. As the noise went on, it became obvious that we needed to get communications. It sounded so critical that the two maintenance men had started emergency destruction on some of our code gear.

It was the first time I'd seen them happy, really happy; they were enjoying what they were doing. They were cutting up equipment and smashing up equipment. We had not been ordered to do it, but it sounded so bad down there, that we fully expected to have the ship taken by somebody. We weren't thinking "sunk and dead," we were thinking "captured and you better get rid of this stuff."

The jets were targeting the wheelhouse, the four machinegun mounts, and all the antennas. And they knew where they were; they put at least two rockets through each machinegun mount. They hit every watertight hatch topside; every one of them had rocket holes through them. They hit every antenna on board. They hit all the life raft stations. They hit the captain's gig [taxi].

Dave, speaking on film, added more insight into the attack by the jets.

If you look at the photographs of the *Liberty* after the attack, on the first strafing run they used heat-seeking missiles that took out the tuning section of every transmitting antenna on the ship. In less than two seconds they had taken out all our communication capability.

Joe recalled where he was when he was hit.

I was in the Comm Center when a rocket hit topside, and I felt the concussion. It felt like somebody had blown on my leg. That is, if you've ever been at fireworks and a rocket has gone off, at Fourth of July, and you felt the explosion, it's like a little puff, a little push, that's what I felt.

But when I looked down at my leg, my dungarees, on my left leg, had like a razor cut, about six inches along my upper thigh. And the first area of skin was severed in my leg. It looked gross. It didn't hurt particularly. Fred Walton, one of the other supervisors was standing next to me and said, "It must've been shrapnel." I looked up at the overhead and there were no holes, so I said, "Fred, it couldn't be shrapnel, there's no holes."

What Dave and Joe explained is proof that Israel not only knew they were attacking a USN ship, but that they were attacking the USS *Liberty*.

Anyone with any knowledge of air-to-ship-attacks knows that it would be impossible to hit 44 antennae in less than five seconds without knowing exactly where they were. On top of this, the Israelis were jamming all our frequencies, both USN tactical and international maritime distress.

Naturally, they would've had to know our frequencies in order to jam them. Obviously, someone had provided the Israelis with this information. To claim that the attack was a mistake is not only ludicrous, but a slap in the face to *Liberty* crewmembers, the USN, and the entire country. In fact, Richard Belfield was told by an NSA insider that Israel knew the exact identity of my ship and had the codes.

Belfield, an award-winning television producer, director, author and playwright, has made programs "for every British terrestrial channel as well as the National Geographic TV Channel, Discovery, the A&E Network and WGBH in the USA." His work that has drawn the most attention, however, is his film *The Day Israel Attacked America*, where he "acquired a copy of the audiotape of the attack as it had unfolded, the real time conversations between Israeli Air Force pilots and their controllers back at base."

In 1980, a former analyst from the NSA told me that the frequencies the *Liberty* was transmitting on were given to the Israelis two days before, so they could never be in any doubt this was an American ship. He said when the attack started, and the reason why the NSA knew it was an Israeli attack, was because those specific frequencies were jammed.

Dave elaborated.

> They had to know what those frequencies were before
> they could jam them.

This NSA insider has no doubt that Israel knew it was the *Liberty*
they were attempting to sink with all hands on board, an act of mass
murder incomprehensible to most over these past 50 years.

> My source was in the NSA listening post in Brindisi, and
> is absolutely adamant that that's what happened.

Brindisi is a city in southern Italy on the coast of the Adriatic Sea,
halfway down the outside of the "heel" on Italy's "boot." The NSA
listening post was located on San Vito dei Normanni Air Station, a
U.S. Air Force facility.

This information coupled with the below, turns it from a slap in the
face to a kick in the crotch.

The Attack on the Liberty explains in vivid and painful detail
that the Israeli pilots knew they were attacking a U.S. ship, the USS
Liberty.

> The transcript of radio communication between the pilots
> and air controllers . . . also revealed that moments before
> the attack began, Israeli forces questioned whether the
> ship might be American.
>
> Approximately two minutes before the pilots first strafed
> the *Liberty*, a weapons system officer in general head-
> quarters blurted out: "What is it? Americans?"
>
> "Where are Americans?" one of the air controllers asked.
>
> The officer didn't answer. Lieutenant Colonel Shmuel
> Kislev, the chief air controller at general headquarters in
> Tel Aviv, queried his counterpart at Air Control Central.

"What are you saying?"

"I didn't say," the other replied, his tone implying that he didn't want to know.

Despite the doubts about the ship's identification, Kislev—seated just a few feet away from the commander of the Israeli Air Force—neither halted the impending assault nor ordered his fighters to inspect the ship for identifying markings or a flag as the planes zeroed in on the *Liberty*. His only concern seemed to be whether any antiaircraft fire targeted his fighters.

"Does he have authorization to attack?" one of the controllers asked.

"He does," Kislev snapped.

The pilots blasted the *Liberty*'s bridge, machineguns, and antennae, killing and injuring dozens of stunned sailors, firefighters, and stretcher bearers. Fires erupted on deck and blood soaked the bridge. Kislev ordered a pair of Super Mystère fighters to join the attack with napalm, which he deemed "more efficient."

Napalm, developed in 1942 in a secret laboratory at Harvard University, is a contraction of the ingredients of the incendiary: **na**phthenic and **palm**itic acids. First used—in WW2 in Europe and Japan, then the Korean War and Vietnam War as well—against buildings and later humans, since it sticks to skin—with no way to remove it—and causes severe burns when ignited. Napalm can impact humans in several ways: burning, asphyxiation, unconsciousness, and death.

Napalm fires create an atmosphere of greater than 20% carbon monoxide—leading to asphyxiation, or suffocation—and firestorms with self-perpetuating winds of up to 70 mph. One napalm bomb dropped from a low-flying plane can impact an area of over a half acre.

Scorched by napalm

One of the pilots then instructed another. "We'll come in from the rear. Watch out for the masts," the pilot warned. "I'll come in from her left, you come behind me."

"Authorized to sink her?" asked one of the controllers.

"You can sink her," Kislev ordered, asking a minute later for a report on the pilot's progress in the attack. "Is he screwing her?"

The Israelis were using sexual innuendoes in their transmissions as American sailors were being massacred.

"He's going down on her with napalm all the time," replied another controller.

Besides the sexual references, they also made light of the unimaginable suffering they were inflicting.

A pilot joked during the strafing runs that hitting the defenseless ship was easier than shooting down MiGs, a reference to Soviet jet-fighters often used by Arab militaries. Another quipped that to sink the *Liberty* before the torpedo boats arrived would be a "mitzvah."

A mitzvah is a Jewish rite of passage, used in the terms *bar* and *bat* mitzvah.

"Oil is spilling out into the water," one pilot exclaimed. "Great! Wonderful! She's burning! She's burning!"

One of the air controllers parroted the pilot. "She's burning!" the controller cried out. "The warship is burning!"

Shortly before planes exhausted all their ammunition, Kislev finally asked the pilots to look for a flag. He then ordered a third pair of fighters to join the attack. One of the pilots buzzed the ship moments later and spotted the *Liberty*'s hull number. He radioed it to ground control, albeit one letter off. The air controller ordered him to disengage.

"What country?" asked one of the air controllers.

"Probably American," replied Kislev.

"What?"

"Probably American."

More than 20 minutes before the fatal torpedo strike that killed 25 [men], Israel's chief air controller conclusively identified the *Liberty* as an American ship.

Years later Kislev confessed that when the pilot radioed in the *Liberty*'s hull number, any doubt about the ship's identity vanished. "At that point in time, in my mind, it was an American ship," he admitted in a British television documentary. "I was sure it was an American ship."

Pilots and air controllers were not the only Israelis aware of the *Liberty*'s identity. [T]wo naval officers—one in the Navy war room in Haifa, the other a senior liaison in the air force command center in Tel Aviv—testified that before the torpedo attack, both suspected the target was the *Liberty*. Neither officer intervened to halt the attack.

13

SOS

The Israelis, using their unmarked jet aircraft to knock out our means of communication, must've believed they completed their mission. And they would've been right, if not for one, lone 24-foot whip antenna that escaped targeting, and one brave *Liberty* sailor who risked life and limb to do his job. In fact, if not for the actions of this young man, I would not be writing this, and the fate of my ship and its history, as well as world history, would be much different today.[1]

Incredibly, for over 40 years this story of heroism in the face of fire was not known to most of the *Liberty* crewmen.

Dave explained why that was.

> Both Jim Ennes and myself were medevaced off the ship the following day. It was only a few years back that Jim found out that his sailor, Terry Halbardier, was a hero, and he called me and asked if I would endorse a recommendation for the Silver Star, and I thought it was great. We would all be dead if it weren't for him.

Texas native James Terry Halbardier, a 21-year-old Third Class ET, explained in various interviews what happened that day.

> On the first pass the jets knocked out our ability to call for help. The one remaining antenna, which I had shut down because it had some problems in the tuner—which is

---

[1] There is disagreement among some members of the crew as to whether some information in this chapter is accurate due to the delay in reporting of Terry's actions and other anomalies.

probably why it didn't get hit—I had to jury rig a coaxial cable directly from the transmitter to the antenna.

Since the antenna was shut down, it wasn't generating any heat.

A coax, or coaxial cable, is a type of cable that has an inner conductor surrounded by an insulating layer, like the cable lines that most of us have in our homes.

With the jets still strafing the *Liberty*, Terry ran onto the deck and attached new wire to the antenna so the radiomen could send out an SOS to anyone out there.

Dave summed up Terry's actions nicely.

> He hooked the one antenna that was operational to the one transmitter that was operational. He got hit with shrapnel three times while he was carrying the coax. To me that's a hero.

Almost 42 years passed before Terry got his Silver Star, presented by U.S. Representative Devin Gerald Nunes (R-Calif), at his district office, the text of which appears below.

> The President of the United States of America takes pleasure in presenting the Silver Star to Electronics Technician Third Class James Terry Halbardier, United States Navy, for conspicuous gallantry and intrepidity in action while serving on board the USS *Liberty* (AGTR-5), on 8 June 1967. The USS *Liberty* was attacked by Israeli aircraft and motor torpedo boats in the Eastern Mediterranean Sea on the fourth day of the Six-Day War. Petty Officer Halbardier, without hesitation and with complete disregard for his own personal safety, fearlessly and repeatedly exposed himself to overwhelming rocket and machinegun fire to repair a damaged antenna in an open deck area during heavy aerial attacks. Aware that all of the ship's transmitting antennas had been destroyed and that communication with higher authority depended

upon antenna repair, Petty Officer Halbardier risked his life to run connecting coaxial cable across open decks from the antenna to the main transmitter room. His efforts allowed the ship to establish communications with distant elements of the Sixth Fleet and call for assistance. Despite being wounded, Petty Officer Halbardier ignored his injuries until the antenna had been repaired and the call for help had been received and acknowledged. His courageous actions were critical in alerting distant Navy commanders to the ship's need for assistance and were instrumental in saving the ship and hundreds of lives. Petty Officer Halbardier's outstanding display of decisive leadership, unrelenting perseverance, and loyal devotion to duty reflected great credit upon him and were in keeping with the highest traditions of the United States Naval Service.

The wording on Terry's award reads differently than all the others: it identifies Israel as the attacker.[2]

Many *Liberty* crewmembers believe the SOS that was made possible due to Terry's brave actions caused a quick chain of events

[2] One Medal of Honor (the Navy's highest and most prestigious decoration awarded for acts of valor), two Navy Crosses (the Navy's second-highest decoration awarded for valor in combat), 13 Silver Star Medals (the U.S. military's third-highest decoration for valor in combat, awarded for gallantry in action against an enemy of the United States), 20 Bronze Star Medals (a decoration awarded for either heroic achievement, heroic service, meritorious achievement, or meritorious service in a combat zone), nine Navy Commendation Medals (decoration awarded for sustained acts of heroism or meritorious service), 208 Purple Hearts (the oldest U.S. military decoration, established by George Washington, awarded in the name of the President to those wounded or killed while serving with the U.S. military), 294 Combat Action Ribbons (a U.S. Navy and U.S. Coast Guard decoration awarded when a military member engaged the enemy, was under hostile fire, or attacked by the enemy, and "actively participated in ground or surface combat"), the Presidential Unit Citation (awarded to a unit for extraordinary heroism in action against an armed enemy, which must display such gallantry, determination, and esprit de corps in accomplishing its mission under extremely difficult and hazardous conditions so as to set it apart from and above other units participating in the same campaign) and the National Security Agency Exceptional Service Civilian Award.

to occur that "forced Israel to back off," when the attackers heard that "help was on the way."

Don drove up to the ceremony. Ray McGovern was there as well. He flew from Virginia to see Halbardier receive the Silver Star Medal. They were the only two present from out-of-town, and Ray was asked for comment from local media.

> We have a Silver Star, the third highest award in the Navy, given to a person without whom there'd be no tale to tell. *Liberty* would be at the bottom of the Mediterranean.

Terry lived with me in Colorado for about a year in the mid-1990s after he wanted out of Texas following his divorce. We did various maintenance jobs together in Aspen and Telluride, and that whole time he was fixing up his van so he could hit the road and sleep in it.

Terry died August 11, 2015. May you rest in peace, Terry.

14
Torpedoes

The jets realized they couldn't sink us—plus they were out of ammo—so they called off their attack and left. Before we could breathe a sigh of relief however, the voice of Captain McGonagle came over the 1MC, ordering the ship's crew to prepare for torpedo hit, starboard side.

I looked out to see motor torpedo boats (MTBs) coming at us at a high rate of speed. Unlike the jets, one of the boats was proudly flying a Star of David flag. When I saw the flag and how fast they were coming at us, I foolishly assumed our beloved "ally" had scared off the jets and were coming to our rescue. That delusion lasted for only a minute.

I found out later they were three *Daya*-class MTBs named after birds of prey—*Aya* (T-203), *Daya* (T-204), and *Tahmas* (T-206)— coming from Ashdod, Israel's largest port.

The three *Daya*-class motor torpedo boats that attacked *Liberty*: *Aya* (T-203), *Daya* (T-204), and *Tahmas* (T-206)

Redesigned from French-built Meulan—wood-hulled—boats, they were diesel-powered with a top speed of 42 knots, and armed with heavy machineguns, 20 and 40 mm cannons and capable of carrying two torpedoes.

At 2:40 P.M., from around a half mile away, T-203 opened fire with their .50 caliber machinegun.

Two minutes later, T-206 launched their two torpedoes from the same distance. Somehow, both missed.

An MTB closing in for the kill

USS *Liberty* taking evasive maneuvers

Another two minutes passed by and the other MTBs fired their torpedoes, around the same time.

T-204 launched one torpedo from around a mile, and it veered away from the ship.

T-203 launched both their torpedoes from a little over a mile away, and one veered off track, but the other was coming right for us.

In our heads, the countdown began as that fifth torpedo approached. I was on the starboard side, only one deck above the waterline.

As we had been trained to do, we hunkered down in "torpedo attack mode." This meant bending your knees and elbows, putting your hands against the bulkhead and relaxing your neck. This last action is nearly impossible knowing that death is approaching.

As I crouched there, waiting for the explosion, I remembered the *Victory at Sea* documentaries I watched as a kid. I was sure we would blow up and sink to the bottom like a rock.

My talk with God was short but sweet—"Lord, if this is the way it's gotta be, then it's gotta be. I'm sorry if I ever disappointed you."

The seconds peeled away like minutes, as I waited for the blast.

When the explosion came, it was literally deafening. Being directly above it by a mere eight feet, my eardrums were blown out, something I live with to this day.

Although my feet remained on the deck, at the same time I was airborne.

We all were, because the ship was picked up completely out of the water by the explosion. When it came back down it bounced like a ball that had been tossed onto the pavement.

Now, with what I had left of my hearing, I could hear new sounds. There was moaning and groaning and wailing; not of wounded men but rather of a wounded ship as metal gave way to the rush of seawater within the compartment directly below.

That the ship had not blown up meant the torpedo had not hit the engine room. If it had and all that cold seawater had hit the boiler, we would have been blown to smithereens.

The ship settled and then started to list. It seemed impossible that she would not go down, but miraculously—and I do mean miraculously—she steadied herself.

A view of the massive hole in dry dock

Dave had been aboard *Liberty* about 10 months when Israel launched their vicious, unprovoked attack and recounted what happened when the torpedo struck our ship.

I was covered with a 30-year supply of burnt Navy paint.

Like me, Dave lost both his eardrums, confirmed by a medical exam afterwards.

They told me one eardrum was burnt 98% and the other one was 85% blown out, so I didn't have much to hear with. I was in the hospital four different times. They gave me two new ear drums. I was among the very, very fortunate people. I was blessed with paint instead of being killed instantly. Virtually everybody within 20 feet of me was killed instantly.

I am also blessed with total amnesia from the time the skipper said, "Stand by for torpedo attack starboard side," until I came to on the mess decks. I'm fortunate in that respect. I didn't see all the gore.

One sailor who wasn't killed from the torpedo was Joe, who explained what happened right before it hit.

> Lieutenant Commander Dave Lewis, who was in charge of the research spaces, he was the lead officer down there, was coming my way. It's the last thing I remember, because that is exactly when the boats got there and the Israelis launched torpedoes at us, and one hit the room I had just stepped out of. I got bounced around. I don't remember it.

Buddha shed a lot more light on what happened with Dave and Joe.

> And then they said "PREPARE FOR TORPEDO ATTACK, STARBOARD SIDE." So we had everybody lay flat on the deck, with their battle helmets toward the starboard side, and the last thing I remember was my desk flying across part of the compartment and smacking me.
>
> I think it was the water that woke me up when the water came in the compartment. And everything was dark and we were going across the ceiling and the pipes in the water that stunk of fuel.
>
> We went towards the ladder and they kept telling people to get that big hatch open because of the watertight seal in the compartment.
>
> Just a single hatch was taking way too long to get people out of there. I finally got out and I knew where there was a sledgehammer that was stuck in the corner in the coffee mess, and I grabbed it and started pounding the dogs on that watertight hatch off. I finally got it loose and got the big compartment open, and everybody started coming out a lot faster. And once they exited you could hear people hollerin' for help and what not.

Buddha didn't just get the hatch open to let his shipmates out, he went back in to look for more.

So I went back down in the compartment and I think the first person that I got hold of was [Dave] Lewis. I didn't know this for years until at one of the reunions it came out that Mr. Lewis was the one who was asking for help. He said he was blind and couldn't see and would somebody help him.

So I went and got him and put his hands on my shoulder and told him I would lead him out of there. I led him up the ladder and got him out and told him them to take him to the mess decks, that he needed help.

I went back down and I don't know if I pulled anybody else out, but I found Joe Lentini, and his leg was wrapped in a door jamb. I bent it outta the way and pulled him outta there and put him on my shoulder. I guess his leg was broke and he couldn't walk, so I carried him up the ladder and put him down on the deck and told them to get him to the mess decks and he needed help.

I went down I think for the third time and I couldn't find anybody else, so I came up and Joe was still laying there, so I picked him up to the next level, up a flight of stairs on my shoulder, and he was a pretty heavy guy, I remember that. I about passed out from the smoke and the weight of him. I got him up there and they finally got him to the mess deck. When I got there, I finally recovered from the smoke.

Buddha wasn't done helping out.

There were fires up in the captain's gig, so I grabbed a firehose and went up there. Then I lost all my water pressure and turned around and looked, and here come a torpedo boat, and he was shooting a machine gun at us and it blew holes in the firehose till I had no water pressure. I remembered a firehose clear on the fantail, so I went up around the forecastle and back down the other side, on the port side, and got a firehose and came out there. The whaleboat had already burned all up, so it wasn't of any use.

Bob will never forget that day.

I heard 'STAND BY FOR TORPEDO ATTACK, STARBOARD SIDE!" and I immediately said to myself, "Holy shit!"

I was down on the deck, hard hat on, and I heard a loud thump and just a couple of seconds after that, the explosion was so tremendous, unbelievable.

I remember flying up in the air and landing back on the deck, and I could still feel the wind and the heat from the explosion and the stuff bouncing off my arms, my head, and my face. And apparently I guess I lost the hard hat somewhere, but I hit the deck hard, and I could feel the ship was rolling, and then it started rolling back. And I couldn't hear anything either, but then I started to feel water come up around me. And I didn't even realize the bulkhead in front of where I was laying was totally gone. I remember seeing little fires out in front of me; it didn't even dawn on me the bulkhead was gone.

So I went away from that bulkhead and down to where the entrance to the passageway was. Got down there and already water was up to my knees, and there's a guy that was in [an] office who was trying to get out; his foot was cut by the door.

He said, "Give me a hand." So I pushed back on the door and he was able to get his foot out. And then he and I went down the passageway and by the time we got down

> there we were swimming, and by the time we got around to where the ladder was we were hanging onto pipes in the overhead.
>
> Finally the hatch was opened, I started going out, somebody pushed me toward the hatch from behind me—I have no idea who that was—and I hit the stairs and went up and they handed me a life jacket.

Glenn remembered clearly what he was doing when the torpedo was on its way.

> I was trying to figure out if I could get another transmitter to work in case something happened to the one they were using, and then they said, "STAND BY FOR TORPEDO ATTACK."
>
> All of a sudden the torpedo hit, and the next thing I know I was knocked backwards from the transmitter room to a wall, probably 10 or 12 feet. I had hit the wall standing up and then I slid down. I looked down and I had urinated in my pants; you don't even know this happens to you, it's a body reaction.
>
> The ship started tilting, going back down, and then the announcement came over the 1MC, "PREPARE TO ABANDON SHIP." I remember somebody say over the 1MC, "Save us, God." There was another person in the transmitter room with me, and I went over to the hatch to go outside, and it had been dogged down very, very hard. This was my first reaction because I knew where my life raft was, but it had completely burned up; there was nothing left.
>
> One of the other fellas came around the corner and said, "It looks like we're gonna sink." So I went over to my locker for my life jacket.

Don has vivid memories of the torpedo strike.

I remember about the time McGonagle came on, which would've been around 2:35 P.M., and said, "PREPARE FOR TORPEDO ATTACK," and we had some old salt on the mess deck who had enough savvy to say, "Throw yourself across the wounded." So, I remember doing that, and it was a good thing because it was like a giant was on one side of the ship, picked up the ship and then we slowly sank back down. And if we hadn't done that, all those guys would've rolled off onto the deck.

I remember one of my shipmates was on his knees on the mess decks with his rosary beads saying goodbye to life.

Then after we took the torpedo hit, somebody said, "Take the submersible pump forward." I got there just about the time one of the officers was making the decision to order the hatch to be closed to make the ship watertight, and all I remember is thinking to myself "Damn, I'm glad I'm not him and have to live with it the rest of my life wondering if there's anybody down there alive or not." I don't think there was, but who would ever know for sure?

Billy continued to struggle on the mess decks.

I would black out, come back to, black out, come back to, and I can remember just lying there and hearing "PREPARE FOR TORPEDO ATTACK." I don't remember the torpedo hitting, so I must've blacked out again. But I did come to, and I can remember they said, "PREPARE TO ABANDON SHIP." And I can honestly tell you, this is not because I'm a hero or anything like that, my first thought was, "Please leave me here, because it wouldn't do any good, I'd only attract sharks."

They cancelled the "ABANDON SHIP." I can remember lying on the table, saying, "What would John Wayne do?

He'd go to his duty station." So I tried to go to my duty station and fell on the deck. They picked me up and put me back on the table.

Then later on they came by and gave me morphine. I don't remember ever feeling pain for some reason. I'm sure I had it and I might've expressed it, but in my opinion they never had to give it to me because I never felt it. And I don't know why.

For the rest of the day I kept blacking out and waking up, blacking out and waking up.

Smitty recalled the torpedo strike.

And then they said, "STAND BY FOR TORPEDO AT-TACK." And, don't ask me why, but I went down below to my GQ station on the mess decks, which if the torpe-do's gonna hit you don't wanna be belowdecks, but I went down there, I'm guessin', because I didn't wanna die alone out on the main deck.

When that torpedo hit it rocked the ship considerably, and when the ship settled back down, they were getting ready to prepare to abandon ship. Apparently all of the life rafts on the main deck, or the O1 level, were all shot up during the attack.

The torpedo boats took care of those if the planes didn't get 'em on the first run. We started taking the wounded up to the main deck from the mess decks, and then decided that's not a good idea. They rescinded the "ABANDON SHIP" order because there were no life rafts to use and we couldn't get anybody off of there anyway.

I was a 20-year-old kid in charge of Damage Control Forward, on a ship that had just suffered over 70% casualties. I had no communications, so my only way of getting my orders was to speak personally with Ensign Scott in Damage Control Central. After locating him and asking what I was to do, he instructed me to go find out where the torpedo had hit. So I, along with Rick, went down into the bowels of the ship to the CT spaces where the spooks worked.

When we arrived, I banged on the steel door with my fire ax. The lock on the door was electronic and required a code to open it, which I obviously didn't have. On the other side of the door, a voice said, "You're not authorized to enter this area."

"Oh yes I am!" I answered. "I'm here to assess the damage. You better open the door now or I'll break it down with my fire ax!"

Buddha was behind the door, as I just found out, thanks to Dave Gahary, almost 50 years later. He finally agreed to open the door.

> I made him promise, when I opened that door, that he'd never ever speak about what he saw in there. And he said he wouldn't. He kept his word.

Sadly, a short time after Dave Gahary interviewed him for this book, Buddha passed away on September 15, 2017 from an extended illness.

Robert J. Schnell aboard USS *Liberty*

The door opened.

I went straight to the main hatch, and since I had been down in the spaces before doing grunt work for the spooks, I knew the lay of the land. The main hatch was sealed, along with the scuttle hatch, which is the smaller hatch within the larger one. I turned the scuttle hatch counterclockwise, very slowly, since the compartment just had a hole blown in the side of it and might already be filled with water. As I slowly turned it, I heard air escaping in our direction, meaning the compartment was not filled yet, but was filling.

I continued opening the hatch slowly, when to my surprise, I heard frantic banging on the other side. Knowing life was there, I turned the wheel as fast as I could and threw the hatch open. As soon as it opened, Marine Sergeant Bryce Lockwood and another shipmate came scrambling out. Rick and I grabbed the two and yanked them out of the hole.

Lockwood, thinking we had locked him in there and left him to die, turned on both of us with fury, calling us a couple of dirty, no-good SOBs.

Neither I nor Rick said anything; we just continued to look for more life.

Just then Ensign Scott entered carrying a battle lantern. He ordered me to give him my belt, which I did, and he tied my belt around the handle and lowered the lantern into the water to check for any signs of life. After a few silent moments, we looked at each other.

"What do you think, Tourney?" he asked.

My response was as short as my prayer had been earlier when I thought I was a dead man for sure.

"Sir," I said, "I think we'd better seal her up."

And we did.

Rick still lives with that decision.

To this day I don't know if we locked anybody down there. Were they unconscious because of the blast and then drowned, who knows? So that's something you gotta keep in your head and live with.

Joe explained what he experienced after the blast.

> I never heard the torpedo blast because it knocked me out; that's how close I was to it. I have no recollection. I came to, and I was in the dark on my face in water. I tried to stand up, and as fate would have it, I tried to get up on my left leg. Since it was dark I couldn't see, but both bones of my left leg below the knee were broke, and right through the skin. I fell back down and called out for help. "My leg's broken, I can't see. Somebody get me outta here."

> And then I passed out again, either fully or partially, because the next thing I remember was being carried up the ladder that I was laying at the bottom of and being shoved through the hatch and moved up to the next deck.

Nebraska native Ronald G. Kukal, a 27-year-old First Class Petty Officer CT has vivid memories of the torpedo blast, and how it has come to affect his life.

> I was within 30 feet of the explosion, by myself in the corner of the compartment where my supervisor's desk was. Seconds from the torpedo's impact, I heard a voice from somewhere say, "Get down, and get down now." My movement was delayed, and somehow I ended up on the deck, nose to the steel plate. I still don't know how I got down there. I heard the explosion and the shrapnel overhead, hitting the bulkheads, the equipment. Men died all around me, as they weren't low enough to escape the shrapnel. Looking back there has never been a doubt in my mind as to why I am still here, not one doubt at all.

Ken barely made it out alive.

> While I was down at my GQ location in the research center there was activity going on, some kind of destruction of

information. You could hear the explosions happening on the top of the ship; nothing was reaching inside the compartment that I was in.

There was a point in time when they said "STAND BY FOR TORPEDO ATTACK—GET ON THE FLOOR." So everybody lay down on the floor, but evidently that torpedo that was coming missed the ship, because they gave a brief notice that everything was OK. So we stood up.

After that, there was another "STAND BY FOR TORPEDO ATTACK—IMMINENT," or something like that. I got back down on the floor, and turned around and looked behind me and there was a huge safe. I thought, if that safe falls over, it's gonna crush me right there. So I moved over far enough away from the safe so if it fell, it wouldn't crush me.

Then all of a sudden there was a huge explosion; fire came in, smoke came in, and water immediately came in. I knew everybody was trying to get out, and I knew they would try to get to that ladder as fast as they could. I don't know if the hatch was opened or closed at that point in time, but I decided to try to get around the back side and come to the hallway. So instead of going straight to the ladder, which was the closest way, I went around to the back door of the room I was in and tried to go through the hall that was between the two rooms downstairs. When I got halfway through the hallway, the walls were crushed in; I could no longer go any further.

Now while I'm trying to do this, the water must've been maybe 12 to 18 inches from the top of the overhead [ceiling]. And that's the level the water stayed at. So I'm trying to avoid going near all the wires and things running on the top of the room, trying to get some air in that little 12-to-18-inch space, with the smoke and oil and all that stuff up there. I could not get around the room to the ladder because the hallway was crushed. So I turned around and went all the way back the other way and went back to the ladder. I can't remember hearing anybody else there; I just don't, it's blocked out of my mind.

When I got back to the ladder, the hatch was closed. I tried to get up the ladder and somebody pulled me down from the ladder. I don't have any idea who it was. I got pushed back down into the water. At some point in time, and I don't know how long it was, somebody opened the scuttle hatch. Whoever was down there with me went up the ladder first.

When I got to the top of it there were two guys standing on the first floor of the research center, and I think they grabbed me and pulled me the rest of the way. I'm told one of them was Phil Tourney. I went through the mess area, and I remember seeing a guy laying on one of the tables, and on his socks the word was ARMSTRONG. I don't know if he was dead or alive.

Bob remembered when he exited the superstructure.

We went out of the CT spaces into a hallway and then up topside. My head was pounding, and there was so much shrapnel on the deck. I remember there was quite a list on and the starboard side; it was very close to the water on the starboard side. There was so much shrapnel on the deck that it stuck in the bottom of my leather shoes and I kept sliding down toward the water, and I'd grab a railing to where I could pull myself up to where I could sit on a hatch.

I remember the captain said he needed people to go up and fight the fires, and every time I tried to stand up I would just slide and fall. I started picking out pieces of shrapnel from the bottom of my shoes. Joe Lentini came up, blood pouring out of his shoe and he had a big gash in his eyebrow, so myself and another guy took him up to head him down to the mess decks where they were taking all the wounded.

Somebody else took him on down, and I was grabbed to do some damage control, so I went with a party to go down and start filling holes in the skin of the ship. So we started pounding spherical cones into those holes. And then somebody said that they thought the [MTBs] were gonna come back, they were still firing at us, so somehow we ended up in the forecastle lying on the deck with a bunch of other guys.

After that I went back out with the damage control team. My buddy Larry Goins, he thought I was dead, I thought he was dead, and I ran into him, we hugged each other. I remember trying to offer assistance, whatever I could do, and some said, "Well stay out of the way unless somebody needs something." There were a lot of us standing around. We just kind of leaned up against the bulkheads to try and stay out of the way, and if anybody [needed] us for something we'd get up and do it. That's the way I spent the night of June the 8th.

I could make no sense of it. Why would a friend do this to us? We had all been pulling for Israel the whole time. We wanted them to win, and their payback for our loyalty to them was to try to murder us—all of us. There was no warning—nothing to indicate that such a thing was coming our way. It was much like Judas, who betrayed his friend with a kiss—a kiss of death.

I can't speak for the rest of the crew, but for me, the knowledge this had been done by a friend filled me with seething rage. I was determined to do whatever was necessary and at whatever cost to save the ship in whatever way I could. For some reason, knowing we had been betrayed by a "friend" made me stronger.

As angry as I was at that time however, it would be nothing compared to the anger I would experience later when I learned the terrible truth that we were betrayed not only by Israel, but also by others even closer to home.

I found out much later that two of these MTBs were involved in another attack on ships in international waters, a month after they tried to sink us, known as the Battle of Rumani Coast.

After Israel's successful land grab, its coastline was significantly enlarged and now included the coast of the Sinai Peninsula. Seeking to enforce Israeli sovereignty over this new stolen area, the Israeli navy began patrolling the Sinai coastline up to the approaches of Port Said in the UAR—Egypt.

A month and a day after their vicious attack against us, an Israeli destroyer, *Eilat*, sailed toward the Sinai coast and rendezvoused with the *Aya* and *Daya*.

On the evening of July 11, the MTBs picked up on radar two Egyptian MTBs about 15 miles away from them and about 12 miles from *Eilat*. They moved to intercept, with *Eilat* closing from the north and *Aya* and *Daya* from the east. After a 20-minute battle, both Egyptian MTBs were ablaze, which caused their torpedoes to explode. There were no Israelis lost and no Egyptians survived.

15

Machineguns

Rick and I left the main deck, and little did we know a new phase of the war against our lives had just begun. We climbed back up to the main deck, just to make sure there were no more survivors waiting to be rescued. To our shock, it turned out there were men alive on the deck. As before, we grabbed them and threw them into any hatch, corner, or anything that appeared to offer some form of protection for them as they fought to stay alive.

Now, instead of the jets firing at us with machineguns, it was the gunners aboard the MTBs. They shot at anything that moved, including firefighters and stretcher bearers. It seemed to last forever. One of the guys I was pulling to safety got hit right above the knee with a .50 caliber, resulting in an explosion of blood and bone. I took off my shirt and tied the sleeves around the top of his leg as tight as I could get it to stop the bleeding. We got him down to the mess decks and untied the tourniquet for just a few seconds so that they wouldn't be forced to amputate his leg later. Then we retied it and left the area.

Rick and I went back up on the main deck, still under fire from the gunners on the MTBs. Now, not only were they shooting at the firefighters and stretcher bearers, but at the waterline as well, right in the direction of the boilers and from no further than 100 feet away. It was obvious to me what they were trying to do: blow up the ship by hitting the boilers.

Throughout the entire time they were firing at anything that moved, they circled the ship like vultures. There was no way, from such a close distance, that they could have missed the identification markings: an eight-foot-high "5" and a four-foot-high "GTR" along both bows, and 18-inch-high black letters spelling "LIBERTY" across the stern.

They were English words written in the Latin alphabet, not Arabic—as they would later claim, making up the excuse that they thought we were the rickety Egyptian horse freighter, *El Quesir*, which had been tied up in port during the time of the attack, which Israel certainly knew.

This view of *Liberty* makes a mockery of Israel's "mistaken identity" claim

The sound of machineguns and all the rest of the hell taking place at that moment were interrupted by a new order from McGonagle, "ALL CREW PREPARE TO ABANDON SHIP." Obviously he thought we were going under, as the ship was still listing badly to the starboard side where the torpedo hit.

When we started our voyage from Norfolk we had enough life rafts for 294 crewmembers. Now, however, most of the life rafts had been destroyed by rockets, gunfire or napalm, with only three left, large enough to hold as many as a dozen men each. I personally jettisoned one of them into the water and watched as all of them inflated. Just a few minutes later, though, I saw them being machine-gunned by the MTBs. In something that causes my blood to boil to this very day, I watched in horror as one of our destroyed rafts was taken aboard an MTB as a trophy, while the other two were sunk. Perversely, the captured life raft was put on display in Israel several years later.

Glenn was an eyewitness to this war crime.

> They were bringing up the wounded from the mess decks, over a dozen guys there, and all of a sudden there were shell fragments flying around the air. I remember Lloyd Painter saying, "Everybody, get back to the mess decks." Fragments were flying everywhere.

> I didn't see the MTB, but they were shooting their .50 caliber machineguns on the side of the ship, and some of the shell fragments were flying in our area. A couple of times I actually saw pieces of the metal flying overhead when I was crawling on the deck.

> I crawled back over to the port side of the ship and I was standing there and saw two life rafts float behind the ship, possibly 100 yards behind the ship, and then I saw some puffs in the water by the life rafts. I could see the life rafts deflated, and then within a few seconds there came an MTB, and they stopped right next to the life rafts. And they picked up one of the life rafts with a hook and took it on board.

> Then that MTB started speeding up and he turned, because he was going perpendicular to the ship, now he was going parallel with the ship, but he was very close to the ship. I looked over and the guy manning the machinegun on the bow of that torpedo boat slammed it over toward me, so I quickly lay down on the deck.

> I looked to see that machine-gunner was pointing right at me. So I backed off and then I could hear the MTB moving along the port side of the ship going toward the bow of the ship. When it got to the front part of the ship, I stood up and saw it going past. It had quit shooting at the ship then.

These life rafts were put over the side to evacuate our most seriously wounded, and the gunning of them was a war crime. When I saw them being shot to pieces, I knew there was no hope for the *Liberty* crew. Israel clearly understood the meaning of the phrase "Dead men tell no tales," and they were not about to allow even one of us to live to tell our story.

The gunfire from the MTBs stopped, and the only explanation I can offer for this is that the rotten bastards ran out of ammo.

The nightmare of the MTBs left, only to be replaced by another one.

Torpedo hole in the USS *Liberty*

16
Helicopters

First it was the jet aircraft and then the MTBs. Now came something else. I heard it at first from far away, despite the fact that my eardrums had been blown out by the torpedo blast.

Far off in the distance came the unmistakable "whomp, whomp, whomp" sound of a troop-carrying helicopter. It was approaching the ship from the starboard side, the same side where the torpedo hit.

Soon, I saw what I heard, as the helicopter appeared just above the horizon and approached us like birds of prey.

Two Aérospatiale SA 321 Super Frelon helicopters were coming in for the kill.

The Super Frelon—or Super Hornet—is a French-made, three-engined, heavy transport helicopter armed with one window-mounted 20 mm cannon, four homing torpedoes and two Exocet missiles. Israel had just ordered 12 Hornets in 1965, with the first arriving in 1966, and four more at the start of the Six-Day War.

Aérospatiale SA 321 Super Frelon

As it neared, a call came over the intercom: "ALL SHIP'S PERSONNEL PREPARE TO REPEL BOARDERS." This meant there was going to be a firefight.

Although it was not part of my duty to hand out the few small arms we had on the ship, Rick and I made our way to the gun locker as fast as we could. Both of us—having seen our friend Francis Brown with his head blown open—were filled with such a rage that we could envision nothing better than delivering a little payback to those who killed him.

I could do nothing to stop the jets, with their rockets, 30 mm cannons, and napalm. I could do nothing in fighting back against the MTBs.

But by God, if it was going to be a man-to-man fight with whoever was on board those helicopters, then I was going to try and make up for lost time. We ran down to the gun locker only to find it locked up tighter than Fort Knox. The master-at-arms, the only one with a key to the locker, was nowhere to be found. Considering the high number of dead and wounded, we figured he was among them.

The locker was not that big, nor were our war machines that impressive—some old WW2-era M1 Garands, some .45 pistols and a few 12-gauge shotguns. Nevertheless, we were desperate for something to fight back with, even if it were only a BB gun. Someone—I can't remember who; it may even have been me—grabbed an ax and started beating the lock on the locker. It yielded nothing; it was beaten to death but would not give.

We left the area, unarmed and just as defenseless as we had been earlier when the jets and MTBs attacked.

As the helicopter hovered about 50 feet above the deck, I could see that my worst suspicions had been proven correct: this was not a rescue helicopter. Instead, like a hornet-swollen hive, there were commandos on board—special forces—armed with submachineguns used for close-quarter combat. They were here to finish what their fellow assassins had been unable to: they were going to murder the entire crew of the *Liberty*. Then, once we were all dead and they were free to move about as they pleased, they would place explosives in strategic areas of the ship, detonate them and sink us all: the perfect crime, leaving no witnesses.

As the helicopter hovered for a moment, I saw that the troops inside were preparing to board the ship. From no more than 75 feet away, I stood like a dumb-ass in an open doorway where they had a clear shot at me, and locked eyes with one of my would-be assassins who was sitting on the floor of the chopper. His legs were hanging out and he had one foot on the skid below, waiting for the order to rappel down to the ship's deck and finish us all off.

I stepped out of the hatch and stood on the deck of my battered and bloody ship. I thought about everything that happened over the course of the last hour or so. My good friend, Francis Brown, his brains splattered all over the bridge . . . David Skolak, who was left in chunks of flesh, bone and internal organs . . . and all the other men, whom I had never gotten to meet or know, and who were now gone forever.

And so, the only thing I could do in that moment in letting my killers know what I thought about what they did to my ship, friends and country, was to give them the finger. The one Israeli with whom I had locked eyes merely chuckled at the sight of something as impotent and harmless as my middle finger, and in the midst of all his machinegun-toting buddies, he simply smiled and gave me the finger back.

Glenn Oliphant has vivid memories of the helicopters.

There was an announcement on the 1MC, "PREPARE TO REPEL BOARDERS." I remember that specifically.

About 20 minutes later, we were milling around on the deck, because we were scared the ship was still gonna sink, and off in the distance—about a half-a-mile away—I could see these two helicopters coming. They were very close to each other, about 50 yards apart, parallel to each other.

And as they got closer, I could tell they were like troop-carrying helicopters, and then when they got pretty close, say 100 yards away, I could see they had a door-gunner, and behind the door-gunner, I could see armed troops back in there. They were coming up very close to the ship, and

127

I was standing there and the door-gunner pointed his gun at me. So I quick ducked down again. But I could hear that they were going along the port side of the ship, fairly slow, and I don't know if they ever went on the starboard side of the ship.

Suddenly, without any apparent reason or warning, the helicopter hauled ass out of there like a vampire being exposed to sunlight. The sight of them scurrying off sent a wave of euphoria through the crew.

I continued my search for the living, and being in charge of damage control, I was free to go anywhere I wanted on the ship. For whatever reason, I wanted to check on Captain McGonagle and see if they had taken care of my friend Francis Brown properly.

When I got there, Francis was gone and McGonagle was standing upright with a tourniquet on his leg.

No sooner had I arrived—three-and-a-half hours after the helicopters left—I heard someone shout, "HELICOPTER APPROACHING FROM STARBOARD SIDE, SIR!"

Sure enough, another damned helicopter—another Hornet—with Israeli markings, loaded again, I thought, with SOBs wanting us all dead, was heading towards us, and began hovering above us.

A sack was dropped from the helicopter that landed on the main deck next to Rick, who recounted what happened.

They came real close to the forecastle and this guy came out like he was gonna toss me something, so I looked up at him. So he tosses a brown paper bag—about six inches high—over to me and I caught it.

I looked inside the bag, and there were a couple of oranges weighing it down.

Inside with the oranges was the business card of 41-year-old USN Commander Ernest C. Castle, the American naval attaché for the U.S. Ambassador to Israel, who had scrawled something on the back of his card.

I took out the card and looked at it, and it said, 'HAVE YOU CASUALTIES?' I looked up at him and thought to myself, "What are you freaking nuts?! Look at the freaking deck, there's people lying all over the place!" There were bodies all over the place, and parts all over the place, and blood all over the place. What kind of a note is that?!

Somebody told me to bring it up to the bridge, so I went down from the forecastle and around and up the ladder to the bridge. When I was about three quarters of the way up there somebody came down to meet me and took the bag and took it the rest of the way up to the captain.

Upon reading this, McGonagle became furious. He limped out of the enclosed part of the bridge to the wing and yelled, "GET OUT OF HERE! WE DON'T WANT ANY HELP FROM YOU!"

The helicopter left, marking the end of Israel's military assault on our ship. We had defeated the aggressors without firing a single shot, merely by staying alive and remaining afloat.

More than 30 years later, with the release of the EC-121 tapes, more evidence was provided that proved the Israelis knew they were attacking a U.S. ship.

According to communications intercepted by the EC-121 circling miles above the attack, at 3:12 P.M., one of the helicopters reported seeing an American flag flying from *Liberty*'s mast.

17

LBJ

To understand how the president of the U.S. could so callously abandon our ship in its most desperate hour, it would be necessary to look at the man more closely.

Lyndon Baines Johnson was born on August 27, 1908, in a small farmhouse in Stonewall, Texas, the oldest of five children born to Samuel Ealy Johnson, Jr. and Rebekah Baines.

Unbelievably, he was a Lieutenant Commander in the U.S. Naval Reserve, and served from 1940 to 1964, and received the Silver Star Medal, the American Campaign Medal, the Asiatic-Pacific Campaign Medal, and the World War II Victory Medal.

His Silver Star citation reads in part:

> For gallantry in action in the vicinity of Port Moresby and Salamaula, New Guinea, on June 9, 1942. While on a mission of obtaining information in the Southwest Pacific area, Lieutenant Commander Johnson, in order to obtain personal knowledge of combat conditions, volunteered as an observer on a hazardous aerial combat mission over hostile positions in New Guinea. As our planes neared the target area they were intercepted by eight hostile fighters. When, at this time, the plane in which Lieutenant Commander Johnson was an observer, developed mechanical trouble and was forced to turn back alone, presenting a favorable target to the enemy fighters, he evidenced marked coolness in spite of the hazards involved. His gallant actions enabled him to obtain and return with valuable information.

The Attack on the Liberty pointed out LBJ's fondness for Israel, and Jews.

Israel enjoyed its strongest relationship with the U.S. under Johnson.

LBJ wasn't the first U.S. president to warm to Israel, however.

President John Kennedy, one of the first presidents to grasp Israel's influence on domestic politics, strengthened relations and sold sophisticated surface-to-air missile batteries to Israel.

LBJ was also a Christian Zionist, one who believes that the creation of the state of Israel and the return of the Jews to the Holy Land is in accord with Biblical prophecy.

The president's support stemmed from his religious upbringing in the dusty hill country of Texas. Family elders had preached that the destruction of Israel would trigger the apocalypse. "Take care of the Jews, God's chosen people," Johnson's grandfather scrawled in a family album. "Consider them your friends and help them any way you can." The president never forgot those teachings, as illustrated by a speech he gave to members of B'nai B'rith, a national Jewish organization. "Most, if not all of you, have very deep ties with the land and with the people of Israel, as I do, for my Christian faith sprang from yours," Johnson said. "The Bible stories are woven into my childhood memories as the gallant struggle of modern Jews to be free of persecution is also woven into our souls."

The president's fondness for Israel had as much to do with politics as biblical stories. The nation's six million Jews in 1967 accounted for only a fraction of the 200 million Americans, but Jews commanded a larger role in political life than the population figures might otherwise have indicated. Many American Jews monitored the issues, voted, and involved themselves in business organizations, labor unions, and civic groups. Others occupied important leadership roles in newspapers and in the television and motion picture industry. Jews donated and raised millions for political candidates, mostly Democrats. Many also lived in major cities in crucial political states, including New York, Newark, Boston, Philadelphia, Los Angeles, and Chicago. Candidates recognized that these large populations could determine the outcome of states that accounted for 169 of the 270 electoral votes required to win the White House.

Support for the Jewish state has a long history, as *The Attack on the Liberty* made clear.

The U.S. under Johnson increased aid to the Jewish state. "No one who has an insider's view," noted Robert Komer of the National Security Council, "could contest the proposition that the U.S. is 100% behind the security and wellbeing of Israel. We are Israel's chief supporters, bankers, direct and indirect arms purveyors, and ultimate guarantors."

Very significantly, LBJ's worldview was decidedly "Jewish."

Johnson surrounded himself in office with Jewish and pro-Israel advisers. The shrewd politician picked brothers Walt and Eugene Rostow to serve as his national security adviser and undersecretary of state for political affairs, respectively.

The president chose Supreme Court justice Arthur Goldberg as ambassador to the United Nations, replacing him on the bench with Abe Fortas, another Israel supporter. John Roche, a former dean at Brandeis University, wrote many of Johnson's speeches. The president also relied on close Jewish friends for advice, including high-profile lawyers Ed Weisl and David Ginsburg, who often represented the Israeli Embassy. Johnson never missed a call from Democratic fundraiser Abe Feinberg, because, as one senior aide noted, "it might mean another million dollars." United Artists Chairman Arthur Krim and his wife, Mathilde, a former gunrunner for early Zionist guerrillas, spent so many nights in the White House that Room 303 became the couple's regular quarters.

There is evidence as well that LBJ may have been Jewish.

LBJ: *"There is little doubt that he was Jewish."*

An April 11, 2013 article in *5 Towns Jewish Times,* an independent weekly newspaper serving the five towns of Nassau County, New York, entitled "Our First Jewish President Lyndon Johnson?," may provide some important insights into why LBJ abandoned Americans and allowed Israel to get away with premeditated, cold-blooded murder on the high seas.

A few months ago, the Associated Press reported that newly released tapes from U.S. president Lyndon

Johnson's White House office showed LBJ's "personal and often emotional connection to Israel." The news agency pointed out that during the Johnson presidency (1963-1969), "the United States became Israel's chief diplomatic ally and primary arms supplier."

But the news report does little to reveal the full historical extent of Johnson's actions on behalf of the Jewish people and the State of Israel. Most students of the Arab-Israeli conflict can identify Johnson as the president during the 1967 war. But few know about LBJ's actions to rescue hundreds of endangered Jews during the Holocaust—actions that could have thrown him out of Congress and into jail. Indeed, the title of "Righteous Gentile" is certainly appropriate in the case of the Texan, whose centennial year is being commemorated this year. Appropriately enough, the annual Jerusalem Conference announced this week that it will honor Johnson.

Historians have revealed that Johnson, while serving as a young congressman in 1938 and 1939, arranged for visas to be supplied to Jews in Warsaw, and oversaw the apparently illegal immigration of hundreds of Jews through the port of Galveston, Texas.

A key resource for uncovering LBJ's pro-Jewish activity is the unpublished 1989 doctoral thesis by University of Texas student Louis Gomolak, "Prologue: LBJ's Foreign Affairs Background, 1908-1948." Johnson's activities were confirmed by other historians in interviews with his wife, family members and political associates.

Research into Johnson's personal history indicates that he inherited his concern for the Jewish people from his family. His aunt Jessie Johnson Hatcher, a major influence on LBJ, was a member of the Zionist Organization of America. According to Gomolak, Aunt Jessie had nurtured LBJ's commitment to befriending Jews for 50 years. As a young boy, Lyndon watched his politically active grandfather

"Big Sam" and father "Little Sam" seek clemency for Leo Frank, the Jewish victim of a blood libel in Atlanta. Frank was lynched by a mob in 1915, and the Ku Klux Klan in Texas threatened to kill the Johnsons. The Johnsons later told friends that Lyndon's family hid in their cellar while his father and uncles stood guard with shotguns on their porch in case of KKK attacks. Johnson's speechwriter later stated, "Johnson often cited Leo Frank's lynching as the source of his opposition to both anti-Semitism and isolationism."

Already in 1934—four years before Chamberlain's Munich sellout to Hitler—Johnson was keenly alert to the dangers of Nazism and presented a book of essays, *Nazism: An Assault on Civilization*, to the 21-year-old woman he was courting, Claudia Taylor—later known as "Lady Bird" Johnson. It was an incredible engagement present.

Five days after taking office in 1937, LBJ broke with the "Dixiecrats" and supported an immigration bill that would naturalize illegal aliens, mostly Jews from Lithuania and Poland. In 1938, Johnson was told of a young Austrian Jewish musician who was about to be deported from the United States. With an element of subterfuge, LBJ sent him to the U.S. Consulate in Havana to obtain a residency permit. Erich Leinsdorf, the world famous musician and conductor, credited LBJ for saving his live.

That same year, LBJ warned Jewish friend, Jim Novy, that European Jews faced annihilation. "Get as many Jewish people as possible out of Germany and Poland," were Johnson's instructions. Somehow, Johnson provided him with a pile of signed immigration papers that were used to get 42 Jews out of Warsaw. But that wasn't enough. According to historian James M. Smallwood, Congressman Johnson used legal and sometimes illegal methods to smuggle "hundreds of Jews into Texas, using Galveston as the entry port. Enough money could buy false passports and fake visas in Cuba, Mexico and other Latin American countries. Johnson smuggled boatloads and planeloads of Jews into Texas. He hid them in the Texas National Youth Administration. Johnson saved at least 400 or 500 Jews, possibly more."

During World War II Johnson joined Novy at a small Austin gathering to sell $65,000 in war bonds. According to Gomolak, Novy and Johnson then raised a very "substantial sum for arms for Jewish underground fighters in Palestine." One source cited by the historian reports that "Novy and Johnson had been secretly shipping heavy crates labeled 'Texas Grapefruit'—but containing arms— to Jewish underground 'freedom fighters' in Palestine."

On June 4, 1945, Johnson visited Dachau. According to Smallwood, Lady Bird later recalled that when her husband returned home, "he was still shaken, stunned, terrorized, and bursting with an overpowering revulsion and incredulous horror at what he had seen."

A decade later while serving in the Senate, Johnson blocked the Eisenhower administration's attempts to apply sanctions against Israel following the 1956 Sinai Campaign. "The indefatigable Johnson had never ceased pressure on the administration," wrote I.L. "Si" Kenen, the head of AIPAC [American Israel Public Affairs Committee] at the time. As Senate majority leader, Johnson consistently blocked the anti-Israel initiatives of his fellow Democrat, William Fulbright, the chairman of the Senate Foreign Relations Committee. Among Johnson's closest advisers during this period were several strong pro-Israel advocates, including Benjamin Cohen— who 30 years earlier was the liaison between Supreme Court justice Louis Brandeis and Chaim Weizmann) and Abe Fortas—the legendary Washington "insider."

Johnson's concern for the Jewish people continued through his presidency. Soon after taking office in the aftermath of John F. Kennedy's assassination in 1963, Johnson told an Israeli diplomat, "You have lost a very great friend, but you have found a better one." Just one month after succeeding Kennedy, LBJ attended the December 1963 dedication of the Agudas Achim Synagogue in Austin. Novy opened the ceremony by saying to Johnson, "We can't thank him enough for all those Jews he got out of Germany during the days of Hitler." Lady Bird would later describe the day, according to Gomolak: "Person after person plucked at my sleeve and said, 'I wouldn't be here today if it wasn't for him. He helped me get out.'" Lady Bird elaborated, "Jews had been woven into the warp and woof of all [Lyndon's] years."

The prelude to the 1967 war was a terrifying period for Israel, with the U.S. State Department led by the historically unfriendly Dean Rusk urging an evenhanded policy despite Arab threats and acts of aggression. Johnson held no such illusions. After the war he placed the blame firmly on Egypt: "If a single act of folly was more responsible for this explosion than any other, it was the arbitrary and dangerous announced decision [by Egypt that the Straits of Tiran would be closed to Israeli ships and Israeli-bound cargo]."

Kennedy was the first president to approve the sale of defensive U.S. weapons to Israel, specifically Hawk anti-aircraft missiles. But Johnson approved tanks and fighter jets, all vital after the 1967 war when France imposed a freeze on sales to Israel. Yehuda Avner recently described on these pages Prime Minister Levi Eshkol's successful appeal for these weapons on a visit to the LBJ ranch. Israel won the 1967 war, and Johnson worked to make sure it also won the peace. "I sure as hell want to be careful and not run out on little Israel," Johnson said in a March 1968 conversation with his ambassador to the United Nations, Arthur Goldberg, according to White House tapes recently released.

Soon after the 1967 war, Soviet premier Alexei Kosygin asked Johnson at the Glassboro Summit why the U.S. supported Israel when there were 80 million Arabs and only 3 million Israelis. "Because it is a right thing to do," responded the straight-shooting Texan.

The crafting of UN Resolution 242 in November 1967 was done under Johnson's scrutiny. The call for "secure and recognized boundaries" was critical. The American and British drafters of the resolution opposed Israel returning all the territories captured in the war. In September 1968, Johnson explained, "We are not the ones to say where other nations should draw lines between them that will assure each the greatest security. It is clear, however, that a return to the situation of 4 June 1967 will not bring peace. There must be secure and there must be recognized borders. Some such lines must be agreed to by the neighbors involved." Goldberg later noted, "Resolution 242 in no way refers to Jerusalem, and this omission was deliberate." This historic diplomacy was conducted under Johnson's stewardship, as Goldberg related in oral history to the Johnson Library. "I must say for Johnson," Goldberg stated. "He gave me great personal support."

Robert David Johnson, a professor of history at Brooklyn College, recently wrote in *The New York Sun*, Johnson's policies stemmed more from personal concerns—his friendship with leading Zionists, his belief that America had a moral obligation to bolster Israeli security and his conception of Israel as a frontier land much like his home state of Texas. His personal concerns led him to intervene when he felt that the State or Defense departments had insufficiently appreciated Israel's diplomatic or military needs."

President Johnson firmly pointed American policy in a pro-Israel direction. In a historical context, the American emergency airlift to Israel in 1973, the constant diplomatic support, the economic and military assistance and the strategic bonds between the two countries can all be credited to the seeds planted by LBJ.

Additional Note:

Lyndon Johnson's maternal ancestors, the Huffmans, apparently migrated to Frederick, Maryland from Germany sometime in the mid-18th century. Later they moved to Bourbon, Kentucky and eventually settled in Texas in the mid-to-late 19th century.

According to Jewish law, if a person's mother is Jewish, then that person is automatically Jewish, regardless of the father's ethnicity or religion. The facts indicate that both of Lyndon Johnson's great-grandparents, on the maternal side, were Jewish.

These were the grandparents of Lyndon's mother, Rebecca Baines. Their names were John S. Huffman and Mary Elizabeth Perrin. John Huffman's mother was Suzanne Ament, a common Jewish name.

Perrin is also a common Jewish name. Huffman and Perrin had a daughter, Ruth Ament Huffman, who married Joseph Baines and together they had a daughter, Rebekah Baines, Lyndon Johnson's mother. The line of Jewish mothers can be traced back three generations in Lyndon Johnson's family tree. There is little doubt that he was Jewish.

The aforementioned Captain Kamansky, who is an ardent American-Jewish Zionist (Zionism supports the creation of a Jewish homeland in modern-day Palestine) and claims to have spent the last seven years and around $150,000 of his own money investigating the attack on my ship, uncovered some startling information on Israeli spy Mathilde Krim, as well as another Israeli spy embedded in the U.S. government—Helmut Sonnenfeldt, a National Security Council (NSC) adviser—her connections to LBJ, and to the *Liberty*.

The Jewish Sonnenfeldt was born in Berlin, Germany in 1926 and was a U.S. foreign policy expert and a veteran staff member of the NSC, also holding several advisory posts in the U.S. government and the private sector, and later occupying positions in academia and in think tanks.

Dr. Kamansky explained Sonnenfeldt's connection.

> Sonnenfeldt was caught by the [Federal Bureau of Investigation] FBI—three days before the *Liberty* was attacked—giving classified information to the Israeli Embassy in Washington, D.C. When he was caught, he said, "It was only a little bit of spying."

On August 24, 2005, *The Washington Post* reported on Sonnenfeldt and another longtime American-Jewish spy-for-Israel, Richard Norman Perle, one of the neoconservative architects of the 2003 invasion of Iraq.

> The leaker (and author of the report) was CIA analyst David Sullivan, and the leakee was Richard Perle. CIA Director Stansfield Turner was incensed at the unauthorized disclosure, but before he could fire Sullivan, the latter quit. Turner urged Senator Jackson to fire Perle, but he was let off with a reprimand. Jackson then added insult to injury by immediately hiring Sullivan to his staff. Sullivan and Perle became close friends and co-conspirators, and together established an informal right-wing network which they called "the Madison Group," after their usual meeting place in—you might have guessed—the Madison Hotel Coffee Shop.

> Perle's second brush with the law occurred a year later in 1970. An FBI wiretap authorized for the Israeli Embassy picked up Perle discussing with an Embassy official classified information which he said had been supplied to him by a staff member on the National Security Council. An NSC/FBI investigation was launched to

identify the staff member, and quickly focused upon Helmut Sonnenfeldt. The latter had been previously investigated in 1967 while a staff member of the State Department's Bureau of Intelligence and Research, for suspected unauthorized transmission to an Israeli Government official of a classified document concerning the commencement of the 1967 war in the Middle East.

Captain Kamansky addressed a problem that even exists today with American Jews who are Israeli spies and their influence to avoid prosecution.

And because of Sonnenfeldt's political connections, they didn't do anything about it.

He was also caught in 1949, when he was in the Army, spying on classified data, and his CO said he didn't trust him. He got off on that. And he was also caught in 1953 giving information to the Israeli Embassy.

The FBI had all this and stonewalled it; didn't tell anybody, until a congressional investigative committee uncovered it.

What kind of information was he giving the Israeli Embassy three days before the massacre on the USS *Liberty*?

The FBI has declassified 500 pages for us, but there are 200 of the 500 that we cannot see at all. In those 200 pages is what they caught Sonnenfeldt doing three days before the *Liberty* attack.

He was giving ship codes to the Israeli Embassy. That could've been legal to do, because Johnson as president could've given them the codes, but he didn't wanna be caught doing it, so he gave it to Sonnenfeldt to give to the Israeli Embassy.

Why would LBJ want to give codes to a U.S. Navy ship to Israel?

Because the Krims were responsible for 80% of his money from Hollywood for his reelection. He was having an affair with [Mathilde Krim], and he was hoping to get reelected and use the Krims again for money.

Why would the Krims want to give the codes to a U.S. Navy ship to a foreign power?

Because they were spies; they were Irgun. They were spies for Israel.

The Irgun was a Zionist paramilitary organization operating from 1931 to 1948. It was classified as a terrorist group by many individuals and entities and was responsible for bombing the King David Hotel, in which 91 were killed and 46 injured, as well as 59 other targets across Europe and the Middle East. Perhaps the most famous member of this terror group was Menachem Begin, the sixth prime minister of Israel and the founder of the hardline Likud party. He also headed Irgun, and is the man credited with the creation of the truck bomb.

Guilt by Association: How Deception and Self-Deceit Took America to War by Jeff Gates, is a fascinating read. Jeff, an attorney and investment banker, who has advised the governments of 35 countries on financial matters, served as a convoy commander in Vietnam, and spent seven years as U.S. Senate Committee on Finance counsel. In that position he impacted federal pension law and employee stock ownership plans, present in around 10,000 U.S. corporations, or 10% of the U.S. workforce. *Guilt by Association* sheds more light on the pro-Israel bias in the Johnson administration.

In the lead-up to the Six-Day War, [Abe] Fortas emerged as a back channel between the Israeli embassy and the White House. He had known Israeli Ambassador Avraham Harman since the ambassador's arrival in Washington in 1959. During Prime Minister David Ben-Gurion's visit to the U.S. in March 1960, Fortas sponsored a breakfast at his home attended by Harman and Johnson, who was then Senate majority leader.

Fortas's biographer conceded: "For several weeks before this crisis erupted into war, the Israeli ambassador was 'in very frequent contact' with Fortas and regularly visited the justice at his chambers or his house." Fortas also attended a critical White House strategy meeting on the Middle East on May 26, 10 days before the war began. When it came to Israel, Fortas was far from a neutral adviser. "When they get back from Egypt," a law clerk in his office overheard [U.S. Supreme Court] Justice [Abraham "Abe"] Fortas say, "I'm going to decorate my office with Arab foreskins."

Organized American Jews were pressuring LBJ as well, as *The Attack on the Liberty* documented.

Many Jewish organizations at the forefront of the antiwar movement opted not to protest, hoping to reduce pressure on the president as Israel sought America's support in its standoff with Egypt. The president, described by one aide as "part Jewish" because of his close ties with that community, found that his years of support did little to shield him from the demands to intervene in the Middle East.

American Jews, however, were firmly against the war in Vietnam.

Despite Johnson's lavish support of Israel, many American Jews refused to back the Vietnam War, a source of frustration inside the administration as antiwar rallies increased and the president's popularity plummeted. Jews had become so prominent in the antiwar movement that it sparked a protest button: "You don't have to be Jewish to be against the war in Vietnam."

American Jews were such a vocal minority that LBJ was forced to note their views.

> Jewish frustration over Vietnam served as a focus of a report for the president that analyzed public opinion. The report, which noted that many Jews worked as writers, teachers, and political and civil rights activists, discussed the possible threat to the president's 1968 reelection. "Vietnam is a serious problem area," the report concluded. "If Vietnam is favorably resolved before the elections, defections among Jews will be minimal; if Vietnam persists, a special effort to hold the Jewish vote will be necessary."

> Many Jews who protested the war in Southeast Asia now urged the president to use force if necessary to help Israel in its standoff with Egypt. Letters, telegrams, and petitions inundated government mailrooms. The State Department processed 17,440 letters during the four days between May 29 and June 1 in what analysts recognized was part of an organized campaign. The analysis showed that 95% of the writers supported Israel, 4.5% opposed American intervention, and only .5% favored the Arabs. Pro-Israel demonstrators crowded the streets. An estimated 125,000 men, women, and children, including several concentration camp survivors, had rallied days earlier in New York City's Riverside Park, singing Israel's national anthem and demanding the United States intervene.

> The president had worked to calm Israeli fears since Egypt closed the Straits of Tiran and mobilized its forces in the Sinai. Johnson assured Israeli diplomats that he would gather a multinational naval force to break the blockade. Progress had proven slow and Johnson feared the Jewish state would launch a preemptive strike, even though he and Defense Secretary Robert McNamara had informed Israel's foreign minister that American intelligence showed Egypt did not plan to attack. The president knew

Israel had mobilized for war. Its military had called up thousands of reservists and requisitioned hundreds of buses, vans, and delivery trucks at an estimated cost of $500,000 a day. Workers piled sandbags in window frames in Jerusalem as residents strung blackout curtains, stockpiled candles, and filled bathtubs with water. Trenches zigzagged across city parks and squares in the city of Elat on the Gulf of Aqaba. Medics converted hotel lobbies into hospitals in Tel Aviv as undertakers transformed movie theaters into makeshift morgues.

LBJ knew well in advance of Israel's land grab what their plans were.

Despite Israel's preparations, Johnson still hoped to avert a war. The president diverged from his prepared remarks on welfare in his speech in New York to reiterate his commitment to peace in the Middle East, comments that drew loud applause. Abe Feinberg whispered to Johnson over dinner that Israel would hold back no longer. The Jewish state planned a preemptive strike. Johnson's efforts had apparently failed; now he waited. He tried to relax Sunday afternoon on the presidential yacht followed by a quiet dinner at the home of Justice Fortas. The president returned to the White House and retired for the evening at 11:45 P.M. The call came at 4:30 A.M. Johnson listened in silence to his national security adviser and asked few questions. He hung up at the end of the seven-minute conversation. Lady Bird asked what was the matter as he dropped back on his pillow. "We have a war on our hands."

The Attack on the Liberty detailed the time D.C. was officially notified of the attack.

At 9:11 A.M. Washington time—36 minutes after the torpedo ripped open the side of the spy ship—the headquarters of America's European Command called the Pentagon with the news.

The Attack on the Liberty detailed the callous disregard LBJ had for what we were going through.

> The president phoned Robert McNamara 10 minutes later, presumably about the *Liberty*, though no record of this conversation has surfaced. The attack was no doubt concerning, but absent more information, the president soon turned his attention back to politicking.

> "Get me in 20 minutes how many states I have been in since I became President," he barked to his secretary in a call on his private line. With five minutes to spare, the president's staff provided a rundown, showing that he had visited every state except Alabama, Mississippi, and North and South Dakota.

At 11:17 A.M. LBJ sent the first hot line message to Moscow— already exonerating Israel—*Body of Secrets* explained.

> We have just learned that USS *Liberty*, an auxiliary ship, has apparently been torpedoed by Israel Forces in error off Port Said. We have instructed our carrier *Saratoga*, now in the Mediterranean, to dispatch aircraft to the scene to investigate.

> We wish you to know that investigation is the sole purpose of this flight of aircraft and hope that you will take appropriate steps to see that proper parties are informed. We have passed the message to Chernyakov but feel that you should know of this development urgently.

> The message arrived in the Kremlin at 11:24 A.M. Washington time; Kosygin replied about 45 minutes later that he had passed the message on to Nasser.

The Attack on the Liberty covered LBJ's attempt to spin the massacre to the press, while my dead shipmates were still warm in their body bags.

> Six minutes after his meeting with *Newsweek* ended, the president sat down with Hugh Sidey of *Time* magazine for an off-the-record interview. During this meeting, the president read a memo from his national security adviser, outlining [Israeli PM] Eshkol's offer to pay retribution to the families of the men killed on the *Liberty*. The president handed the memo to Sidey. "Imagine what would happen," Johnson quipped, "if we had bombed an Israeli ship by mistake?"

> "Well imagine what would've happened if the Soviets had bombed it?" replied Sidey.

> The men laughed.

"I never trust a man unless I've got his pecker in my pocket."
—Lyndon Baines Johnson (August 27, 1908-January 22, 1973)

LBJ's callousness toward *Liberty*'s besieged crew may have another explanation, one as diabolical as the Gulf of Tonkin incident the 36th President of the United States created to engage more directly in the Vietnam War.

A January 27, 2013 article on a blog, *Judy Morris Report*, run by a Libertarian Texan by the same name, goes into some detail on LBJ's "dark side," relying heavily on Peter Hounam's *Operation Cyanide: How the Bombing of the USS* Liberty *Nearly Caused World War Three.*

The real story is that President Johnson, who was being battered in the polls over the Vietnam War and facing a general election loss and even losing the DNC primary, ordered the Israelis to bomb the USS *Liberty* to create a *casus belli* to secure a Gulf of Tonkin-style resolution to explode the world into war because in America everybody loves an outraged and indignant president who will use the full force of the military at the slightest provocation, even a government-planned false flag attack.

The USS *Liberty*, however, encompasses far more than a murderous psychopathic American president resorting to hideously evil deeds to get re-elected. In addition to ordering the total destruction of the USS *Liberty* and sending 294 Americans to a watery grave in the Mediterranean Sea,

LBJ also ordered the nuclear bombing of Cairo, an event specifically designed to create a nuclear war by blaming the entire USS *Liberty* affair on Russia or Egypt.

More horrifying, it's documented that U.S. planes were on emergency standby orders as pilots waited on the runways in their planes armed with nuclear weapons. The nuclear bombing of Cairo was called off only three minutes before the nuclear bomb drops.

That LBJ was mad is validated by his numerous actions that fueled his personal ambitions over the decades, and in the summer of 1967 LBJ was obsessed with one thing and one thing only: reelection. He was in grave danger of losing the presidency and his power. That he would do anything to maintain that power is 100% consistent with the depth of his evil.

To comprehend the severity of the situation, it's imperative to understand the Cold War, the backdrop against which it was played, the prevalent paranoia at the time of the Communist threat and the incredible rise of America's military-industrial complex to the world's sole superpower. Many who knew LBJ well feared that he was unstable, mentally ill, a psychopath or even worse. He was notoriously crude and vulgar.

According to *Operation Cyanide*, the UK's Defense Secretary, Denis Healey, so despised and distrusted LBJ that he wrote this in his memoirs:

Lyndon Johnson was a monster . . . [He was] one of the few politicians with whom I found it uncomfortable to be in the same room. Johnson exuded a brutal lust for power which I found most disagreeable.

The book *Remember the Liberty! Almost Sunk by Treason on the High Seas*, released on the 50th anniversary of the massacre, by Phillip F. Nelson, the accomplished author—and all-around great guy—of *LBJ: The Mastermind of the JFK Assassination* and *LBJ: From Mastermind to "The Colossus,"* presents the case that Johnson positioned *Liberty* there by himself, "for the very purpose of being attacked, and sunk, with every one of the 294 men on board going to the bottom of the Mediterranean Sea. His purpose was to use that event—while blaming Egyptian President Gamal Nasser for the attack—as a pretext for joining Israel in the war, even at the risk of igniting World War III with the Soviet Union."

When the heroic crew saved the ship from sinking, it stopped Johnson's plan to join Israel in the war and thereby saved the world from certain nuclear conflagration. It also prevented his strategy of entering what he felt would be a "popular war" (unlike his other one in Vietnam) in order to give him a better chance to be reelected president the following year. When that failed to materialize, so did his reelection campaign; 10 months later he was forced to announce his decision to not re-run for the office that he had always considered his destiny.

18

Politicians

Many are unaware that the cover-up of the massacre on our ship began in great part right in the halls of Congress, by predominately Jewish politicians, who immediately sided with a foreign nation—Israel—rather than with America, despite the fact they knew almost nothing about the attack.

The Attack on the Liberty revealed this troublesome fact.

> [Secretary of State] Rusk's disbelief that Israeli forces attacked in error contrasted sharply with the first public statements of some members of Congress, many of whom appeared quick to forgive the Jewish state as the first bulletins appeared on the radio and in the afternoon newspapers.
>
> At about the same time Rusk met with the Israeli ambassador, Senator Jacob Javits took the Senate floor and asked his colleagues not to hastily judge Israel.
>
> The New York Republican had long served as a staunch supporter of Israel. The son of Jewish immigrants from Ukraine and Palestine, and raised in the Lower East Side's tight-knit Jewish community, Javits viewed Israel as an "anchor and bastion" of democracy in the Middle East.
>
> Javits had taken his son to Israel nearly five years earlier to celebrate his bar mitzvah there.

U.S. Senator Jacob Javits meets with Israeli Labor Party leader
Shimon Peres in Israel (4/4/78)

Javits told his fellow senators that the "tragic error" saddened him. The attack no doubt resulted from the stress under which Israeli pilots and Navy commanders had fought in recent days, though the senator conceded that fact alone did not excuse the near-sinking of an American ship. "The Government of Israel has already stated that this was an erroneous attack by Israel forces. The Government of Israel has apologized. I am sure that it will do everything that one would expect by way of compensation and other appropriate measures," Javits said. "The incident is one of those tragic fallouts of the dreadful situation in the Middle East, and the terrible pressure placed on pilots and naval people in that area."

Some lawmakers quoted in the morning newspapers appeared to endorse Israel's claim. "With Israel we know it was a mistake," Senator Jacob Javits told reporters. "A miscalculation that could take place any place in the world," added Senator Robert Kennedy. Senate Majority Leader Mike Mansfield told reporters he doubted the attack would spark any lasting complications between the allies. "It certainly wasn't deliberate," declared the Montana Democrat. "It could have happened on either side."

On the opposite side of Capitol Hill, Representative Roman Pucinski echoed Javits's views. Soon after the House met at noon, the Illinois Democrat from Chicago's Polish community—and known to friends simply as "Pooch"—cautioned his colleagues not to rush judgment and jeopardize America's close relationship with Israel. "It was with heavy heart that we learned a little while ago of the tragic mistake which occurred in the Mediterranean when an Israeli ship mistakenly attacked an American ship and killed four boys and injured and wounded 53 others," Pucinski said. "These are the tragic consequences of armed conflict. Such mistakes happen frequently in Vietnam. It would be my hope that this tragic mistake will not obscure the traditional friendship we in the United States have with the people of Israel."

The lawmakers' speeches set the tone for the rest of Congress. No one publicly demanded answers, questioned how Israeli pilots and torpedo boat skippers could have made such an incredible blunder, or called for an investigation or public hearings. The Congressional Record shows that only three other lawmakers mentioned the *Liberty* during the four hours and nine minutes the Senate met that afternoon. In each case, the senators referenced the attack only as a brief afterthought buried in longer speeches dedicated to the Middle East crisis. None of them challenged Israel's assertion that its forces attacked in error. The *Liberty* was not mentioned again during the six hours and 25 minutes that the House met.

Lawmakers failed to appreciate the gravity of the attack. But even in the coming days, as casualty figures climbed and the curious circumstances surrounding the assault emerged, the record shows that most elected leaders remained largely quiet. Those lawmakers who challenged

Israel's explanation for the attack did so behind the closed doors of committee meetings and in hushed tones in the cloakrooms and dining rooms of Capitol Hill. The torpedoing of the *Liberty* did little to dampen the pro-Israel fervor that pervaded Congress.

More than two dozen lawmakers in both the Senate and House—many from states with large Jewish populations, such as New York, New Jersey, and Connecticut—took the floor the day of the attack to applaud Israel for its stunning war effort.

Others rallied for emergency economic aid, urged America to reinforce its commitment to the Jewish state, and argued that Israel should be allowed to keep the territories it captured in recent days.

One senator even inserted Abba Eban's June 6 speech before the U.N. Security Council into the Congressional Record. But the laudatory speeches came even as American sailors aboard the Liberty struggled to put out fires, stop bleeding, and prevent the ship from sinking.

This wasn't the first—or last—time U.S. senators and congresspersons defied a U.S. president to put Israel's interests before America's.

When Edward Irving "Ed" Koch was mayor of New York City, he did just that, as *Dangerous Liaison: The Inside Story of the U.S.-Israeli Covert Relationship*, explains, as well as other Israeli treachery where the U.S. democratic process is concerned.

"If I get back in," said President Carter in the spring of 1980, "I'm going to fuck the Jews."

The occasion was a meeting in the upstairs family quarters of the White House between the president and some of his senior political advisers to discuss his reelection efforts. Unusually for a sitting president, Carter was facing the rough-and-tumble of a serious challenge for the Democratic nomination from Sen. Edward Kennedy. The going was especially bitter in New York, where the president had to deal not only with the senator, but also with the abrasive mayor, Ed Koch.

Koch spoke for the electorally vital Jewish voting bloc in New York, which had come to regard the administration as treacherously disposed in favor of the Palestinians.

The year before, for example, news of a meeting between UN Ambassador Andrew Young and the PLO representative at the world body had sparked outrage among Israel's friends in the U.S., as Mossad had intended.

The Israeli intelligence agency had learned through a phone tap that the meeting was planned. Rather than immediately protesting to Washington, which would have undoubtedly resulted in the meeting's cancellation, the Israelis let it go ahead, bugged the proceedings, and then leaked the news to the press. Young, a friend and long-standing supporter of the president, had to resign.

Now, in March 1980, Carter had discovered that the Israelis were once again covertly intervening in the U.S. The [NSA] had intercepted conversations between Koch and Menachem Begin's office in Jerusalem. The Israeli prime minister was advising the American mayor on the best means of defeating the president of the United States. Given this intelligence, it was hardly surprising that Carter bitterly vowed revenge.

Koch didn't hide his hatred of Carter. In 2008 Koch wrote that he refused to campaign with Carter in 1980 because he felt the president "was hostile toward Israel."

I was popular with the Jewish community and when I would not campaign for him unless he changed his position, he called me to his hotel in New York when attending a fundraiser and said, "You have done me more damage than any man in America." I felt proud then, and even more today, since we now know what a miserable president he was then and the miserable human being he is now as he prepares to meet with Hamas.

In one of the last interviews before his death, Koch was asked what living person he most despised.

"Koch made a lot of enemies in his life—several mayors, upstate suburbanites and two generations worth of Cuomos among them—but his answer was very surprising:"

Former president Jimmy Carter.

N.Y. Senator Daniel Patrick Moynihan, President Jimmy Carter, N.Y. Governor Hugh Carey, and NYC Mayor Ed Koch at the White House (11/ 2/78)

Dangerous Liaison revealed some more shocking information.

Israeli hostility to Carter went back to the early days of his administration, when he had given indications that he might actually be serious about pressuring Israel to make concessions to the Palestinians living under its occupation, and had even made reference to a Palestinian "homeland."

The Israelis were kept well informed of such threatening initiatives from their own highly placed sources. In March 1977, for example, Henry Kissinger invited the Israeli ambassador, Simcha Dinitz, to dinner.

According to an Israeli report of the conversation, Kissinger took his guest aside and stated that as a Jew he could not go on if he did not share certain information. Carter, he said, had told President Sadat of Egypt that the U.S. would get Israel to retreat to the 1967 borders and to agree to the establishment of a Palestinian state. Dinitz asked Kissinger what he thought Israel should do to counter this threat.

"Organized forces in the U.S. and Israel," counseled the man who had been secretary of state less than two months before. "Don't appear too hawkish, but be determined. The trick is to fight Carter's plans in a resolute manner."

In October of that same year the administration displayed a foolhardy insensitivity to Israeli concerns by issuing a joint statement with the Soviet Union on the Middle East.

Clearly, it was taking the former governor of Georgia a little time to understand some of the fundamentals of the U.S.-Israeli relationship.

Moshe Dayan, who had deserted his Labor colleagues to become foreign minister in Menachem Begin's Likud government, was quick to enlighten the American president.

A few days after the U.S.-Soviet announcement, the one-eyed ex-general demanded that Carter state publicly that he stood by all secret agreements reached with Israel by previous administrations.

If this was not done, said Dayan, Israel would consider making them public, which would certainly have been embarrassing all around. Carter's naïve notions about a comprehensive Middle East settlement swiftly fell apart and Begin's initial judgment on the president—"cream puff"—seemed vindicated.

19

Media

From the get-go, the U.S. mainstream media adopted the stance that the attack on our ship was not very important, or that it was our fault.

The Attack on the Liberty detailed the mainstream media's bias and pro-Israel stance.

The news coverage of the attack ranged widely in point of view. Some magazines and newspapers appeared on a crusade while others took a more tempered stand and a few chose to ignore it. Some of the same media outlets that questioned the assault on the editorial pages published news articles that contradicted the paper's position. One of the best examples that illustrated this inconsistency appeared in *The New York Times*. The newspaper printed the Associated Press story that quoted the unnamed Golden. (Many of the *Liberty*'s officers, frustrated by the court's shallow probe, feared the government planned to downplay the attack. George Golden disobeyed orders and talked to the Associated Press. The *Liberty*'s chief engineer told a reporter in a Malta bar that the assault's duration and intensity convinced senior crewmen the attack was intentional. The reporter wrote a story attributed to an unnamed sailor and it appeared in newspapers nationwide.) The same day it published a Reuters dispatch that contradicted the story and claimed the *Liberty*'s officers "rejected the idea that the attack was deliberate." *Liberty*'s officers concluded that the Navy was behind the Reuters three-paragraph story. The *Times* neither investigated nor explained the inconsistency, but rather chose to run the opposing stories alongside each other.

The frustration [U.S. Secretary of State] Rusk felt over the attack—and his disbelief in Israel's assertion that it was an accident—had not been reflected in the newspaper reports now on doorsteps nationwide. Many of the critical questions concerning the *Liberty* focused on America's role in the attack. Newspapers already doubted the Pentagon's cover story and hinted that the ship likely was eavesdropping on the war at the time of the assault. Other stories questioned whether America had informed Israel of the ship's presence. Few if any articles challenged Israel's assertion that its forces had attacked in error.

Defense leaders, who sensed the media shifting blame for the attack from Israel to the United States, grew frustrated. "The main issue was not whether we had notified Israel of our intent to be there," [Pentagon chief spokesman Phil] Goulding later wrote in a memoir. "The real issue could not have been simpler: A United States ship was operating in international waters; it was identified, as are United States ships anywhere in the world, with the American flag, distinguishing letters and number, and name; it was attacked without provocation."

The *Liberty* in contrast sparked surprisingly little controversy for the president. In just 48 hours, the attack had dropped from the front pages of most national newspapers, replaced by headlines about the Middle East war, Vietnam, and debate over a record-breaking $70 billion defense spending bill. Each day as the *Liberty*'s casualty numbers climbed, news stories moved farther back in the pages. The dwindling coverage appeared to reflect reporters' diminishing interest in the story that had once seemed so tantalizing, but had fizzled out following Israel's confession that its forces had attacked in error.

The barrage of press speculation that surrounded the spy ship the morning of the attack had waned to the point that no one even asked about the *Liberty* during the afternoon press briefing Friday [the day after the massacre] at the White House.

Many of the first editorials on the attack now appeared. Most newspapers unquestioningly accepted Israel's claim, even though no investigation had been conducted or a more thorough explanation given. Editorial writers, unaware of the doubts that permeated the closed-door meetings in the White House and on Capitol Hill, had no reason to doubt Israel's assertion. In its editorial, *The New York Times* described the attack as one of the "many mistakes that invariably occur in war."

"The Israelis, flushed with victory, apparently mistook the *Liberty* for an Egyptian ship—a major error in ship identification, since there are no ships under the Egyptian flag with the silhouette and the peculiar and distinctive radio and radar antennas that distinguish the *Liberty* and her sisters," the paper wrote. "Nevertheless, it is clear that accident rather than design snuffed out the lives of some and caused injuries to others of the *Liberty*'s crew."

The Washington Post took a more tempered stance, arguing that the attack "must disturb and depress the whole country." "Israel has made a prompt and complete apology, but this, of course, cannot restore the lives of the dead or make whole the wounded," the paper wrote. "Americans will wish to have, and are entitled to have, a more complete explanation from Israel and from their own government."

Even the *Virginian-Pilot*, the daily newspaper serving the *Liberty*'s home port of Norfolk, failed to challenge the official story. War's chaotic nature rendered such errors "inevitable." "Its confusion, its haste, its inaccuracy have produced numerous examples in Vietnam: Americans shelling Americans and South Vietnamese, bombing raids on military targets killing and maiming helpless civilians," observed the paper. "These same qualities were present in the *Liberty* incident."

The Attack on the Liberty documented the Pentagon's frustration with the mainstream media's pro-Israel stance.

Despite these overtures, the overall lack of criticism of Israel baffled some senior government leaders. The dogged press corps consistently challenged the administration on its Vietnam policy and ambitious social programs.

In the case of the *Liberty*, the press aimed most of its critical questions at the American government. Israel in contrast enjoyed a reprieve. Reporters soon adopted the phrase "accidental attack," a description that frustrated Pentagon officials, who felt it minimized the ferocity of the sustained assault that had killed or injured two out of every three men on board. "There was nothing accidental about it," Phil Goulding later griped in his memoir. "It was conducted deliberately—by aircraft and by motor torpedo boat, by rocket and bomb and torpedo and gun fire. Whether it was a tragic mistake in identity is a separate question, but it was no accident."

The attack had slipped from the front pages of most American newspapers, but media speculation over the *Liberty*'s mission intensified. Press queries swamped the Pentagon as reporters demanded to know if it had been spying. The Pentagon responded by shutting down.

The day the *Liberty* reached Malta, McNamara ordered a news blackout. No one could speak to reporters. If pressed, officials could say only that the Navy had convened a court of inquiry to investigate and planned to release a statement when the court concluded.

Other media outlets discounted the charges or published articles based on Defense Department spin. Such stories often exonerated Israel. "Former Navy skippers in the Pentagon were frank to forgive the Israelis for not seeing or not believing the identity of the *Liberty*, and then attacking it," wrote George Wilson in *The Washington Post*. Pentagon officials told the Associated Press that the attackers likely were unfamiliar with the *Liberty*'s design, though hundreds of identical vessels had sailed for decades. "The Israelis may have thought the *Liberty* was an Egyptian ship masquerading as a U.S. ship," reported Seymour Hersh. "Officers noted that such deceits are as old as sea warfare."

Only deep into the stories did most newspapers address the question of Israeli responsibility. Many articles noted that the court ruled that Israel "had ample opportunity to identify *Liberty* correctly." Other stories quoted the report's finding that the court had "insufficient information before it to make a judgment on the reasons" for the attack. In the 22nd paragraph of its story, *The New York Times* wrote that the court did not interview any Israeli witnesses, a fact most newspapers omitted.

Guilt by Association sheds more light on the machinations of the mainstream media and their masters.

When news of the Israeli attack on Americans reached the U.S., the Israel lobby shifted into high gear along with its Congressional contingent and its media counterpart. [Joseph Ben Zion] Wattenberg [an aide and speechwriter to LBJ from 1966 to 1968] assured Johnson that if he supported Tel Aviv's account of the USS *Liberty* incident as a case of "mistaken identity" and ignored the 208 American casualties, including 34 killed, influential Jews in the U.S. media would tone down their criticism of his policies in Vietnam. In return for his defense of Israel and a presidential cover-up, the shift in mainstream media opinion provided a temporary political respite for the war-weary president who, less than a year later, declined to run for reelection.

Sadly, only a few newspapers expressed any outrage, as *The Attack on the Liberty* painfully pointed out.

Hints of disbelief did emerge, often from small newspapers outside the Beltway. Many puzzled over how Israel's exceptional military could make such a blunder. The facts conflicted with common sense. *The News and Courier* in South Carolina described the attack as "shocking." "It is hard to understand how an Israeli pilot could fail to identify the vessel as American," the Charleston paper wrote. "The Egyptians don't have any similarly configured ships, and all U.S. vessels fly the stars and stripes."

The Times of Shreveport, Louisiana went further, describing Israel's assertion that its forces attacked in error as "far-fetched." "It is not easy in clear daylight to mistake the red, white and blue and the stars of the American flag for the flag of some other nation," the paper wrote. "Mere apology is not enough in a case of this kind. Israel should guarantee stiff punishment for those responsible for the attack."

Mainstream media outlets even prominently ran Israeli propaganda stories, as *The Attack on the Liberty* detailed.

The Associated Press soon published an article written by an Israeli Naval Reserve officer who served on one of the torpedo boats. The first-person account by Micha Limor appeared in newspapers nationwide, including *The New York Times, Washington Post*, and *Chicago Tribune*. Limor wrote that crews tried to identify the *Liberty* with binoculars as two fighters circled the spy ship. The jets fired two rockets then retreated to base. "About 2,000 yards from the ship, a strange spectacle met our eyes. The high masts and the many weird antenna showed that this was a warship. The side of the vessel was blotted out by smoke, and apart from three numbers along her side, which meant nothing to us, we could not discern a thing. We could see no flag on the mast, nor was anyone to be seen on the decks and bridge," he wrote. "We spent several minutes trying to contact the ship and demanding identification. We tried by radio and by heliograph, in accordance with internationally accepted means. But she gave no answer."

Torpedo boats zoomed past the *Liberty* in battle formation and fired across the bridge and bow to demand identification. "Suddenly, a sailor appeared in view and started firing at us with a heavy machinegun from the bridge. We took the challenge and directed cannon fire against him," he wrote. "A moment later he fell, together with the machinegun. Thus there was no doubt that we were faced by the enemy. The prolonged refusal to identify herself, the absence of any flag, the shooting at us, and above all, the weird contraptions on the ship left us without doubt." Limor wrote that Israel hoped to capture the *Liberty* rather than sink it. The torpedo boats circled the ship and repeatedly fired to try to stop it. "This had no effect. No one appeared. No one reacted. The shells caused little damage to the hull and the ship proceeded on her way," he wrote. "You could almost hear the men's teeth grinding aboard our boat. Nothing can annoy a torpedo boat crew more than being completely ignored."

Unable to stop the ship, commanders ordered it torpedoed. "We drew up along the left side of the ship and advanced at full battle speed. Just as in dozens of training exercises we reached the right angle and range—and let go. We thought only a miracle would save the ship," he wrote. "One of the torpedoes hit amidships. There followed an enormous explosion and a huge water spout. And then fires broke out and the ship leaned sideways as if about to sink." Only when Israeli crewmembers plucked a rubber life raft from the water—marked "U.S. Navy"—did the sailors realize their mistake. Limor wrote that after the attack ended, Israeli sailors watched the American flag rise up the mast. "Dozens of shells, rockets and torpedoes were needed to drag a sign of identity from them, said one of my seamen who, like the rest of his mates, was bitterly upset at this surprising turn of events," Limor wrote. "He was right. The showing of the Stars and Stripes at the first stage would have prevented all that happened subsequently."

Limor's story, described by a *Liberty* officer in a letter as the product of a "wild imagination," infuriated the *Liberty*'s men. Fighters did not circle the ship prior to the attack and the torpedo boats were too far away to have witnessed the air assault. The American flag was shot down, but replaced by a larger flag long before the Israeli Navy arrived. None of the torpedo boats fired across the bow, circled the ship, or radioed the *Liberty*. The only markings Limor reportedly saw were the *Liberty*'s hull numbers, which he claimed meant nothing to him. That alone was a shocking statement. How could a naval officer not understand the significance of a ship's hull number? Even Israeli torpedo boats carried similar markings. The Israeli officers should have at a minimum noted the *Liberty*'s markings were not in Arabic, as Egyptian ships are identified. But these gripes were trivial compared to Limor's largest blunder: he attributed the torpedo strike to the wrong side of the ship.

Liberty sailors anxious to challenge Limor's story were barred from talking to reporters. That left many Americans to assume his story was accurate. The Pentagon ended the news blackout after the release of the summary of the court of inquiry, but limited the *Liberty*'s crew— still in Malta awaiting the completion of repairs—from discussing anything outside the summary's contents.

Restrictions on crewmember interviews, published in the *Liberty*'s Plan of the Day, soon evolved into a ban on all press contacts. The one-page memo was read aloud at morning quarters and posted throughout the ship for the crew to read. "Interviews and statements to news media concerning the attack on *Liberty* 08 June are not to be given by individuals. If you are approached by someone wanting an interview or statement inform them that they must contact the Public Affairs Officer," the memo read. "The only information that ships company is allowed to discuss is that already made available to the press. Therefore, there is nothing new that we would be able to tell them in an interview."

20

Shock

I headed back to the mess decks, but seeing that I would be more hindrance than help, I left and began making my way back to the bridge where Captain McGonagle was. Since all of our instrumentation had been blown to hell, we were sailing by the stars, just as our forefathers did in centuries past. Captain asked me what kind of shape the ship was in, and I told him there was no change. Then, somewhat stepping over the bounds for an enlisted man, I asked him how he was doing. His response was short but sweet—"I am fine, thanks Tourney."

I departed the bridge, somewhat comfortable over the fact we were still able to float, and went back to my duties on Sounding and Security. It was dark by then, but I had no idea what time it was. I headed for Main Control, meaning the engine room. The first person I saw when I got there was Lieutenant Golden. He was participating in and directing all efforts to keep the heart of the ship beating—meaning to keep the boilers running. The boilers served as the power source for nearly all the ship's functions, including movement and electric.

Lieutenant Golden, like Captain McGonagle had earlier, asked about the condition of the ship. In particular he wanted to know about the CT spaces that had been obliterated by the torpedo blast. I told him the bulkheads on the forward and stern compartments where the torpedo hit looked like balloons, meaning they were bowed outward from the massive explosion of the torpedo, but they appeared to be holding.

From there I headed to the fire room, one level down from engineering, where the boilers did their work.

As best as I can describe them, the boilers were fireboxes roughly 20-feet-by-20-feet that had a network of pipes running throughout them filled with water that was heated to make the steam that ran the ship's vital systems.

As I entered the boiler room, I was relieved to see my shipmates alive and well, or at least as well as can be expected, considering what they had just gone through. Their nerves had to have been rattled just as badly as mine, if not worse. They, like the CTs, worked below the waterline and it was this very same compartment where I was now standing that Israel had continually targeted, knowing if the cold seawater got into the room, the boilers, and the ship, would be blown to bits. These men remained down there doing their duty as each of the five torpedoes was launched, even though they knew they were at ground zero, the bull's-eye of the ship.

I sat with my brothers-in-arms shooting the bull for a while, staring at them in awe. I knew that none of them—not even one—had abandoned their stations the whole time the ship was under attack. I learned later that during the most vicious part of the assault, Lieutenant Golden, fearing for the safety of his men, ordered everyone in the area to evacuate.

Despite being given a direct order to leave the spaces, Fireman Benjamin Aishe, refused to obey, and remained. In the boiler room one deck below, the other firemen had either not received the orders to evacuate or else had simply disregarded them as well. Knowing they were face-to-face with death and could be killed at any second, they continued their duties without consideration for the danger their own lives were in.

As we sat there shooting the bull—as welcoming as rain during a drought—there appeared amongst us a bottle of scotch. Technically speaking, it was against the rules for us to be drinking anything alcoholic on the ship, however, we justified bending the rules this time on the grounds that we had just been through hell and could use a little anesthesia for our nerves. We passed the bottle around, wondering if we would make it through the night without our "ally" returning. A big question in our minds was why Israel would do something like this to us. The U.S. was not merely her best friend, but indeed her only friend in the world. Friends don't do this to friends. This was pure treachery; the handiwork of an enemy.

Fear was not the only emotion we were dealing with at that time. We were also thankful to be alive and in one piece, at least physically. We were proud to be Americans and proud of the fact that our good ship, *Liberty*, had protected us just as a loving mother would protect the child growing within her. The euphoria we felt just in being alive however also gave us great sadness and disappointment in thinking about all our shipmates who had their precious lives stolen from them. Young men, sons, brothers, nephews, uncles, grandsons, husbands, fathers, all men who had bright futures before them, and whose lives had been erased as if they were the mere scribblings of some child on a blackboard.

We sat there in the boiler room talking about the attack and how glad we were that we survived it. At the same time however, although we did not say so out loud, we all felt an enormous amount of survivor's guilt. "Why me? Why us?" we asked ourselves within the confines of our own minds. What had we done to deserve God's mercy that day in having our life, liberty and pursuit of happiness spared, while others had not?

Again, understandably, we visited and revisited the question as to why no one came to our aid. Whether it was a defense mechanism or just sheer denial on our part, we refused to even consider the possibility it was deliberate. As I already stated, our conclusion was that our government was doing something big—something "hush hush"—which was delaying them from coming to our aid. We didn't realize how right we were in that last assumption.

At that time, we did not have any bad feelings towards our government at all. As an indicator of our naiveté, our assumption was that the mighty USN was busy at that very moment in dealing with what had happened to us. They were "setting things straight" and somebody, somewhere, was surely getting what they deserved. We were happy with this assumption and sure that if the USN and our government had known what was taking place, they would have come to our aid in a microsecond. In our young, idealistic minds, there was no way anyone, anywhere, would get away with what had just been done to the United States. It was, after all, not just an attack on a ship of the mighty USN, it was an act of war against every man, woman and child in America. We were confident our leaders would not let our losses go in vain.

I stayed with my brothers-in-arms as long as I felt was acceptable and then got my ass up and went back to my regular duty.

Despite going through the harrowing attack with no sleep the night before, I was still running on adrenalin. I knew I must be exhausted, but for some reason, my mind and body would not allow it to take hold of me. I thought I wouldn't sleep again for weeks. To call it a long night is an understatement. None of us slept, and for two reasons.

First, we were afraid of the dark. Not like little kids, but rather because we knew that criminals prefer the cover of darkness when doing their dirty work. Those responsible for the previous day's attack might return to the scene of the crime to accomplish what they failed to do earlier.

Second, we didn't know if the ship would even stay together. Although we were not sure of the exact size of the hole in the starboard side of the ship, we knew it was big. In addition to this, there was a ton of work that needed to be done to keep the ship afloat, and with all the losses we sustained in terms of personnel killed or wounded, only a skeleton crew remained to do this monumental task.

Steve remembered that long night.

> That night was the longest of my life. I couldn't sleep; none of us did or could even if we wanted. I volunteered for as many watches as they needed. I recall being offered brandy or scotch on the bridge that evening.

I made my usual rounds on Sounding and Security and Damage Control, which now included both bulkheads encompassing the CT spaces where the torpedo hit. The walls were made of plate steel not more than one inch thick and were sweaty from the cool ocean water on the other side. I could hear the water sloshing around, knowing that if the bulkheads ever gave way, I'd be a goner. I could see cracks in the steel walls caused by the enormous pressure being exerted against them by the Mediterranean Sea, and my biggest fear was that the cracks in the walls would eventually get larger and larger until finally they gave up the ghost and surrendered to the awesome power of the sea. The walls looked like they were alive and breathing as they heaved in and out with the movement of the ship and the pressure of the water. I got shivers standing in such close proximity to them, knowing the only thing standing between me and my maker was a plate of steel that was ready to cry uncle and give up the fight at any second.

Making my rounds, I made my way to the bridge yet again, where Captain McGonagle was alert and in charge. Francis Brown, my good friend who had his brains blown out while steering the ship, had been taken away. The floor was caked with dried blood, giving it a sandpaper-type surface, meaning rough and tractable, the opposite of what it had been when I slipped and fell. I made a report as to what damage I had encountered and what needed to be done about it and he asked about the condition of the crew. I told him everything that could possibly be done was being done.

No doubt by this time, he had gotten word that his right-hand man and XO, Lieutenant Commander Armstrong, had passed away. I doubt though that Captain was aware of the fact that I was one of the last people to see him alive. I did not think it necessary at that time to relay the story to him about how I had given his XO his last cigarette before he left this world. It made me think about those old movies where someone convicted of some capital crime was about to be executed and was given his last meal, last rites and last cigarette.

I left the bridge and continued on with my rounds. As I descended the stairs from the bridge, my eyes caught something off to my peripheral right—faint sunlight. The sun was coming up over the eastern horizon, just as it had done millions of other times before, during periods of both war and peace. I welcomed the return of daylight the way a kid welcomes toys on Christmas morning. Even if our world had been turned upside down, the sun was coming up again, just as it had the day before and just as it would tomorrow. This meant there was a power higher than both man and the devil still in control of things.

21

Doc

O nce the helicopter left, Captain gave orders to head out to deeper waters. Praying we would no longer be dealing with any further attempts on our lives, we got busy trying to save the wounded.

The task at hand now was to find a place to put all the injured. They were packed as tight as sardines in a tin can, leaving little room for us to even walk around. It was a sea of casualties—bleeding head wounds, bones protruding from arms and legs, injuries all made indescribably worse by the projectiles hurled at us by Israel.

One sailor I'll never forget was a fellow named Quintero. As he lay on one of the dining tables, I stopped by to check on him. To my horror, I saw he had taken a .50 caliber machinegun bullet that ran along the top of his head from the front to the back, digging a trench through the crest of his skull.

He was alert, and we talked a few minutes. I asked him if there was anything I could get for him—some water or anything to make him more comfortable. He lifted up his hand to reveal he was missing his thumb, as if to say, "If you happen to see this thing lying around, pick it up for me."

Since we were headed out to deeper waters, I left the mess decks to check out other areas of the ship that needed repair. I went to the weight-lifting room, directly above the CT spaces where the torpedo hit. I entered the room and saw that what was a perfectly level steel deck floor before was now turned into something resembling some weird modern art. There was a giant hole in the middle with writhing tentacles of steel protruding upwards, and I stepped up to the edge of the hole and looked down and saw only ocean below and no ship at all.

I took the 20-second walk to the Log Room where Ensign Scott was to tell him about the hole, and that we needed to plug it up and that I needed some help. A few other guys showed up and I told them to get some mattresses, which we used to plug the hole. Then we went to work plugging other holes to keep the sea out. The plugs were made of wood, sometimes as wide as 15 inches in diameter and tapered like a sharpened pencil. We wrapped cloth around the points and then pounded the dowels into the holes of the ship. With close to a thousand of them, we were busy well into the night.

Rick and I went back to the CT spaces where the torpedo hit and found the scuttle hatch was open and the waterline a mere 18 inches below the hatch, so I sealed it. Maybe some Good Samaritan came along to see if there were any souls left to be saved in what was now a giant, watery grave. We left the area and headed towards shaft alley, which housed the mechanism for turning the ship's propeller. Part of my regular duties on Sounding and Security was to check the packing around the shaft that kept the ocean out. It was fine; one of the few things on the ship not damaged in Israel's massacre, and so I left the area.

We headed back to the mess decks, and when we arrived, the sun had already set. The sheer mass of human suffering moved me to such emotion that my knees got weak, and my impulse was to break down in tears, but I dared not. There were men in front me, broken men, and I was not about to show disrespect for their suffering by crying like a baby when I was on both feet and with no mortal wounds to my body.

In boot camp I had learned basic first-aid. Now however, looking at everything that lay before me, it was obvious that this training would do me—as well as the men lying before me—no good. I went from broken man to broken man, asking what I could do to make him feel more comfortable. As I was doing this, all at once I heard a voice off to the right call me—"Tourney."

I turned to discover that the source of this was Lieutenant Commander Phillip McKutchen Armstrong, the ship's Executive Officer (XO). He was lying on a dining table and by all appearances must have sustained only superficial wounds, because there was very little blood. In addition, he was alert, active, and didn't seem to be in any pain.

He asked me for a cigarette, since he knew I smoked at that time. I lit one, put it in his mouth for him, and we sat and shot the bull for a few minutes and he asked me a series of questions.

"How many wounded?" "How many dead?" "What time is it?" "How's Captain doing?"

I answered as best as I could and he asked for another cigarette. I lit one for him, as well as one for myself. We sat and smoked together, continuing our conversation. He never moaned or groaned or complained about anything; not his wounds, physical pain or anything else. His entire demeanor was one of concern for the crew and the ship, making our little sojourn with each other a pleasant break for me.

For those brief few minutes during the conversation between us, things were semi-normal. He was an officer and I was his subordinate. He had the bearing and confidence necessary if an officer is to lead his men, and this made me feel good.

While this conversation was taking place, in perfect stereo I could hear the sounds of agony all around me as men lay waiting, either for the comfort of morphine or the comfort of death. Thinking that Lieutenant Commander Armstrong was OK, I told him I had to get moving, and headed for the First Class Mess to see if there were blankets or anything else I could find to make the suffering of my wounded shipmates more endurable. There was nothing to be found, and a few minutes later I went back to Lieutenant Commander Armstrong to check on him to see how he was getting along. To my great shock and sadness, he was dead.

A 37-year-old married father of five, he was a graduate of the USNA in Annapolis, Maryland. He served his country honorably in life and with dignity in death. Like any good American serviceman, Armstrong died in his uniform, unlike many of our politicians, whose only uniforms are the lies, false promises, and platitudes they give when trying to get elected to an office they do not deserve to hold.

I was summoned to the Ward Room, the officers' mess hall. As I entered, the first thing I saw was Doctor Richard Francis Kiepfer, the only doctor on a ship carrying close to 300 men.

Joe explained why the *Liberty* had a doctor on board, when typically only corpsmen are assigned to these ships.

Under Captain Weiland, the ship was sailing off the west coast of Africa, and one of the sailors had appendicitis, and the captain, because apparently it was critical, pulled into a foreign port down the river to get that kid to an embassy and airlifted out. He didn't bother to get clearance from the country.

Shortly thereafter, a doctor was assigned to the *Liberty*, and it happened to be Dr. Kiepfer. Normally on board—and what they had at the time—were corpsmen, who are perfectly able to do some kind of surgeries in a battlefield condition, but they weren't able to handle a simple appendectomy. As a result of that, we would've lost a lot more than 34 if Kiepfer hadn't been on board.

Captain Richard Francis Kiepfer

Like any college grad, "Doc" was an officer, holding the rank of lieutenant. He was in his khaki uniform that U.S. naval officers wear, but curiously, he also had a life vest around him. I thought at the time that this was because he was afraid the ship would sink from the torpedo hole. I found out later this was not the reason.

I assumed the blood I saw on his pant legs was from wounds he had been treating. Like my previous assumption concerning the life vest, I found out later this also was not the case.

When I had finished my quick study of Doc Kiepfer, I turned to see one of my fellow enlisted men, Seaman Gary Ray Blanchard, lying on a table right next to me. Although his front showed no signs of any wounds, he was lying in a puddle of his own blood that seemed to get bigger by the second.

His first words to me were to ask that I remove his socks, saying his feet were on fire. I did as he asked. His next words were to ask if he was going to make it. I could do no more than shake my head.

Years later I always hated myself for that. Why didn't I lie to him, or at least, try to change the subject? They say honesty is a virtue, but if I had to do it over again I would probably not be as "virtuous" as I was that day. My only hope is that the shaking of my head put him in the frame of mind he needed to be in to make peace with his Maker before the final curtain.

Doc came over and unbuttoned Blanchard's shirt. I figured he was going to examine his wounds, although I could see there weren't any—at least in the front.

A second later, when I saw that scalpel in Doc's hands, I knew what was coming. He started at his chest bone and cut him open all the way to his crotch. As fast as he opened him, Blanchard was on his way to a better place. I had been holding a battle lantern for Doc so he could see what the hell he was doing. Doc, seeing that Blanchard was gone, put two or three stitches in him to hold his guts together and moved on, because there was so much more work for him to do.

Don recalled his time in the make-shift hospital.

I returned to the mess deck, and that night Doc Keipfer grabbed me and told me to lay down. And they stuck a needle in me and ran a tube to a stanchion that somebody he was gonna operate on. And all I remember is him cutting the guy open saying, "Look, his kidneys are shot out, there's nothing I could do for him," and he sewed him back up and went on to the next person.

I remained in the Ward Room until I was no longer needed. At that point, Ensign Scott told me I could go back to my "regular" duties. If anyone aboard that ship deserved the Medal of Honor, as with Lieutenant Golden, it was Doc.

I learned later why Doc was wearing the life vest. It wasn't because he was afraid we would sink. Rather, it was because he had taken a razor-sharp piece of shrapnel across his midsection and was using the vest to hold his insides in. He stood there, literally with his guts wanting to spill out all over the floor, and rather than take care of his own needs he took care of the more seriously wounded. Doc is one of those guys who—if this had been another time and another battle—would have had books and movies made about him. Every school kid in America would know about him the same way they know about George Washington.

Doc did receive the Silver Star Medal, the third-highest military decoration for valor, awarded for gallantry in action against an enemy of the United States. The award stated, in part:

> With complete disregard for his own personal safety, he exposed himself to overwhelmingly accurate rocket and machinegun fire by going to different stations and compartments to administer first aid after sick bay became untenable and evacuated following a rocket hit. He treated men for pain, shock, and took emergency measures to control hemorrhage and later performed a chest operation. After the torpedo hit, he organized personnel for removing the wounded in case of an order to abandon ship. He again went to different General Quarters stations to administer first aid and made trips through some of the damaged areas to the medical storeroom for needed supplies. He organized teams of men to wash wounds and instructed less seriously wounded personnel in preparation of antibiotics for injection. He conducted a major surgical operation, giving the anesthesia (spinal) himself, with a Hospital Corpsman as his assistant and a seaman and fireman as circulating assistants. Although wounded himself, Lieutenant Kiepfer treated patients in excess of thirty hours without relief or rest. His

aggressiveness and coolness under fire was exceptional in an hour of awesome peril, thereby saving many lives and easing the pain and suffering of many others. His initiative and courageous actions were in keeping with the highest traditions of the United States Naval Service.

A USS *Liberty* supporter visited with Doc in December, 2007, and wrote an article about what he—stationed aboard *Liberty* six weeks before the massacre—had gone through that day.

While operating on a sailor to control his bleeding, Doc received 11 shrapnel wounds to his abdomen, a gunshot to his leg, burns and a broken knee cap. He remained on his feet caring for the crew for the next 28 hours.

Doc explained in his own words what happened.

A rocket struck above the ceiling of sickbay and the light over my head and the operating table protected me; both acted as a life saver for me, otherwise I would have gotten hit in my shoulders, side and back. I was knocked against a wall and waves of red and white pain throbbed through me.

I knew I had to finish with the guy on the table—if I walked away, I wouldn't have returned. All I could think about was keeping limbs attached to sailors. From the moment the attack began, I felt a greater presence within me that was physically holding me up. I thought it was the spirit of all the Navy docs who had gone before me. I felt physically held up by my invisible assistants and with all that adrenalin coursing through me and some carefully titrated morphine that I self-injected, I was able to do what I did.

It was not until I finished that operation did I even examine myself. The fragments that penetrated me were so hot they cauterized my wounds. The pain was intense, but after applying surgical dressings to my wounds and putting on a life vest to control the bleeding, I gave myself a shot of morphine and remained on my feet and working for the next 28 hours.

Just before the torpedo struck, I was summoned to the bridge and went through the mess decks from sickbay, where a number of wounded sailors were. Captain McGonagle was the only man still functioning there, the lookouts were dead, the helmsman—the guy at the steering wheel—was dead and I saw the blown apart remains of our Navigator, Mr. Toth, two decks below me. All I could do was administer morphine to the still living and get them onto stretchers to evacuate them. I had two corpsmen working with me and knew I needed more surrogates, for the wounded were shoulder-to-shoulder the full circumference of the passageway.

While I was on the deck, I got hit by a .50 caliber machinegun bullet to my leg that came from the torpedo boats. I was bleeding into my shoes and not until the next day when I was able to lie down did the bleeding slow down. You know the story of *The Incredible Hulk* and mothers who lift cars off of their kids? When you are angry and hurt you can do amazing things.

If you got 100 people into my skin that day, probably all of them would have thrown up from the hell that erupted on the *Liberty*. Men were groaning and crying for their mothers, but it was just background noise for me. I was slip-sliding as I crossed the bloody deck to get to the Captain who had been hit. McGonagle was leaning back in the Captain's chair, bleeding from many orifices; some natural and some new ones. I applied battle dressings, started an IV, gave him some morphine and sent an enlisted man to find as many officers as possible to come up to the bridge and assist him and to watch him for shock. The Captain said, "If I sit up, I pass out, but as long as I stay in this position, I am OK."

People I had eaten lunch with were dismembered all around me, burned, dead. To this day, every time I have a phone conversation with Phil Tourney, who held the light while I was operating on Blanchard, he tells me he can still see the look in my eyes.

I spent almost two weeks with Doc in the 1980s, and learned a lot more about this man than his simply being a brilliant surgeon. After his tour of duty was done aboard *Liberty*, he was in a military jet which had malfunctioned right after take-off. He ejected from the plane, and although he was able to save his life, it cost him the use of his arm, something a surgeon obviously needs, as much as a rifleman needs his eyes. At the time he was a captain in the Navy and well on his way to becoming an admiral, but the loss of his arm dashed those hopes, which was a terrible blow to him.

22

Pump

O f the many miracles taking place that day, one of them was the issue of the coffin pump. What a name. The coffin pump was responsible for bringing water into the boiler during an emergency when the regular pumps were not working.

Louisiana native Gary W. Brummett was a 20-year-old Third Class Petty Officer Boiler Technician (BT).

> I got on the *Liberty* 'cause my damn brother was a plankowner of the *Liberty*. He was a CT.

Gary explained why the coffin pump played such an important role in keeping the *Liberty* afloat.

> I was a repair petty officer in B Division, along with J.P. Newell. J.P. was a third class like I was, but he was senior to me. He was our best BT we had on board.

> Sometime early on June 7, we had a pump that had gone down, an auxiliary feed pump to the boilers. J.P and I worked on it for 22 hours, and we had taken it apart and put it back together, oh hell, six or seven times. And the last time we went to take it apart, I failed to bleed down the superheated water in the drain, and when I broke the flange loose I got sprayed with it, and burnt myself from the tip of my nose, my lip, down my chest, around the private parts of my body, and down one leg and in my

shoe and burnt my foot. So we had to stop and take a little break; I had to go to sick bay and get greased up.

J.P. and I got back to the quarterdeck, it would've probably been three o'clock in the morning, four, somewhere in that neighborhood. Now we had been up at this point in time roughly 30 hours, and we stopped and had a cup of coffee. And J.P. knew I was in pain and discomfort, and he told me, he said, "Just go to the compartment and take a shower and go to bed. I'll put the pump back together," which he did.

Now, we got to sleep late that day 'cause we had put in so many hours, and we probably didn't get back up till around 10 o'clock that morning.

I was not awake when the first recon flights came over the ship, when Israel started reconning the *Liberty*, but I was still in the rack. I remember the bridge calling out for the duty photographer, five or six times, to lay to the bridge to take photographs of these planes that were reconning us.

Some say that they didn't recon us that much, but that would not be the truth, because they did. Probably every 45 minutes, Israel had eyes on us, looking at us. And by their own admission, at 10:55 A.M., on the morning of June 8, by using *Jane's Fighting Ships*, they had identified the USS *Liberty* as a signal intelligence vessel. They knew who we were, and we knew they knew who we were.

One of the CT officers on board, who Gary didn't want to name, gave him important information about what Israel knew.

He told me that they were told that any Israeli communications that you hear, to make a note but don't copy. OK, if you're not gonna copy something, why in the hell are you gonna make a note of it? I think to hell that we were copying it. Our government said, "Well, no, we didn't have any Hebrew linguists on board." I think to hell we did. I've been told that by someone out of research. Our engineering officer said there was two.

We had GQ at 1300 hours, and that secured at about 1345. And the captain came on the 1MC, which is the public address system on the ship, and he stated that there was hostilities on the beach at 12.6 nautical miles. We were in international waters. We were nowhere near the Israeli coast.

I can remember going up on the port side of the ship, and you could see two of the minarets at El Arish. J.P. and I stood up there for about five minutes and looked at that, and then went back to the engineering spaces. We had gotten down to the hole in the fireroom and we put on a pair of coveralls, which turned out was a good thing.

We were sitting down on the catwalk on the machinist's mate's level when the first missile hit the ship. And I remember that just like it was this morning.

I jumped up, as J.P. did also. And I'm trying to figure where in the hell that steam line was that just blowed up.

Time slowed down, or went in slow motion at this point it seemed like.

I smelled what seemed like burnt gun powder. On a cold morning hunting, you fire a shotgun, a rifle, you notice that smell. And about the split-second I smelled that burnt gunpowder, the GQ alarm went off on the ship, I thought "Oh, holy shit, we're under attack."

Everybody has a job and a place that they go, a repair party that they're in. I was in Repair 3A, which is made up solely of engineers. You usually had a two-man team for everything; me and a fellow BT named Robert Clyde Kidd, now deceased. We went up to the O1 level port side; we had some hatches to close and dog down. There was an explosion; I don't know if it was a missile hit the ship, I don't know if it was those gas cans that were in a rack on that side of the ship blew up, which they did blow up at some point in time.

I was closing a port hole and it knocked me down. It didn't hurt me, it just scared the mortal crap out of me. Kidd had closed his port holes, and I had one left as he come through the hatch, and I was on the floor and he said, "Are you OK?" I remember getting up and looking at myself and I wasn't bleeding. And I said, "Yeah, hell I'm OK." Well we had one more hatch to close and we come out into the passageway, and there was a guy begging for help. He was covered in blood; I don't know who he was. I think we told him to go to the mess decks 'cause they set up a triage there.

Here was a point in time right here where I lost some time. It may've been 30 seconds; it may've been a minute. It didn't vanish from my memory but I don't think we tried to help the guy or administer first aid—I know we didn't do that. We were too intent on getting our job done.

We got the last hatch dogged down and we went back to the mess decks through an inner passageway. We didn't go out topside because you could hear the rockets hitting the ship, and all the other ordnance that they were putting on our ass at that point in time.

We got back to the mess decks and they were bringing the wounded in there. And I don't recall who gave the order, but we were only on the mess decks for a couple of minutes, and somebody told the engineers to go back to your workstations. Well, my workstation was in the fireroom, which would've been a story-and-a-half below the waterline. Hell, that doesn't seem too significant, but when a torpedo's coming at you it gets significant.

When I got back to the fireroom, Newell, BT3 Albert E. Rammelsburg and BT2 Eugene Owens were trying to get the boilers online. The rest of the BTs were trying to pressurize the port boiler up.

Our main feed pumps were two giant reciprocating pumps. They were what's called a positive displacement pump. The machinist's mates, Chief Brooks and Mr. Golden, for whatever reason, which I always thought it was short-sighted, they dropped a thing called a DA tank, that's de-aerated water, water with oxygen taken out of it. You can superheat it, up to I think 400 or so degrees Fahrenheit; it doesn't turn to steam, it's in a closed vessel. And this water's very hot. Well, these pumps that are pulling this water are just hot as hell. You can take a hot suction with a cold pump, but you can't take a cold suction with a hot pump. And when we tried to do that after they dropped our DA tank and we had to switch over to a distilled tank to draw water for the boilers, it locked those pumps up. Well, when it locked those pumps up, all of a sudden, we're about out of water for the damn boilers. I remember one of the BTs hollerin' that we need some water.

Getting back to that coffin pump. I didn't know if this damn pump was gonna work or not. First thing I did was I broke out a three-inch firehose and run over there and I was spraying the bottom of our reciprocating pumps trying to cool the suction end down to where's they'd take a cold suction, but that wasn't workin'. And R.C. Kidd, he came over and I gave him the firehose and I told him, I said, "Let's see if this goddamn pump works." And it was called a coffin pump of all things. And I remember turnin' it on, or cuttin' it on, cuttin' the steam to it, and it's a high-speed centrifugal pump. And when I cut it in, it kinda scared the hell outta me, 'cause all I got was a high-pitched whine, which meant I was pumping air, I wasn't gettin' no damn water. But what it was, this pump hadn't been run, it hadn't been bled down, or nothin'. And after about maybe 10 or 15 seconds, I could hear this deep hum, and that we had actually fixed that pump with all that work we had done to it, and we did get water to the boilers. 'Cause without that, the title to that movie *Dead in the Water*, that's exactly where in the hell we would've been. We would've been dead in the water. That ship would not still been movin'. 'Cause without steam— this is something you see and hear so little of about the *Liberty*. Everybody's job was important, ours no more than anyone else's. But steam flushed your commodes, it cooked your food, washed your clothes, it run the turbo generators which powered up all your electrical circuits. Without steam, nothin' worked on board that ship.

So, we come right down to one goddamned little nickel and dime pump that saved the day.

23

Saratoga

Thanks to Terry's actions, an SOS was able to be transmitted. Glenn was one of the first on board to know that help was on the way, when the radiomen received a message from the aircraft carrier USS *Saratoga* (CVA-60), the only known vessel to pick up *Liberty*'s cries for help.

> Within 15 or 20 minutes after they started communicating, *Saratoga* said, "Help is on the way." That's probably half-an-hour after the attack started.

USS *Saratoga* (CVA-60)

Saratoga, or *Sara*, was named after the American Revolutionary War Battles of Saratoga—September 19 and October 7, 1777, which historians consider to be "a great turning point of the war, because it won for Americans the foreign assistance which was the last element needed for victory."

Sara was the second of four *Forrestal*-class supercarriers built for the USN in the 1950s. Supercarriers—an unofficial term—"are the largest warships ever built, larger than the largest battleships laid down by any country," carrying around 80 fighter jets.

As of 2017 the U.S. has 11 active supercarriers, a huge number— considering there are 41 active aircraft carriers in the entire world— the total combined deckspace of the USN's carriers is over twice that of all other nations combined. *Sara* served the U.S. from 1956 till 1994.

Sara played a huge part in the fate of my ship, or to be more accurate, one "lowly" sailor aboard her did. The story of how *Liberty*'s SOS was picked up is as unbelievable as the fact that I, and many of my crewmates survived.

John W. Lipscomb, North Carolina born and Georgia raised, joined the USN in 1966 and was stationed aboard *Sara*—from October 1966 to October 1968—as a radioman in the communications department.

John remembers that day clearly.

> On June 8, 1967, I was on Radio One, and my job was to monitor the voice circuit, a pretty low priority circuit, 'cause it was "in the clear" [unencrypted] and we never really used it. I heard something; it sounded like static but it also had a pattern to it.

> One of the boys, Chuck Burns, came outta crypto and came over to get some coffee—he had to walk past the desk there to get to the coffee machine—and I stopped him and I said, "Listen, what do you think of this?" And he said, "It just sounds like static," and more or less kept on walking. And I said, "I don't believe it is."

The reason John didn't believe it was static is an incredible part of this story.

> I had a lot of experience with radio before I joined the Navy. I was with the civil air patrol, I was in Air Explorers [part of the Boy Scouts], I was around aircraft radio all the time, and I did a lot of amateur radio, and I was just kind of a radio nut.
>
> And my house was covered in antennas where I was trying to pick up shortwave radio, to train that ear to listen for that signal way off.

If John wasn't there at that exact time, our cries for help while the massacre was taking place would have never been heard.

John modestly explained this point, that if he wasn't there, no one would've heard our cries.

> It is possible because I was the only person who heard them. They weren't picked up by any other ship. It is possible that if I had not stayed with it then they would not have been heard because none of the base stations, none of the other ships, nobody else could hear them; only our radio was picking them up.

John was sure there was a pattern.

> So that's when I went over to the receiver and sort of fine-tuned it in a little bit, and you could hear it although it was garbled, and it was garbled because number one they were off frequency a little bit, which I fine-tuned it in, that became not a problem.
>
> But the problem that we had all along was that they were being jammed. There was a constant carrier, just like somebody holding a microphone button down nearby, it distorted their voice a good bit. But by that time, by the time that I had tuned them in and actually found them,

we could understand what they were saying without too much problem.

I was able to pull in a signal, still very scratchy, very hard to decipher, but someone was saying, "Any station this net. This is Rockstar. We are under attack. Any station this net. This is Rockstar. We are under attack." And it repeated. Rockstar was the call sign for the USS *Liberty*.

And I answered him, "Rockstar, this is Schematic," and called for the watch officer to come in. [Rockstar] came back and told me they were under attack. By then the radio room was full of everybody else in the division; there was probably 20 or 30 people hanging around.

John, "a lowly seaman," was asked to step aside.

After just a few minutes of me taking the message from the *Liberty* and forwarding it on, [Ron Minion, a second class radioman] actually relieved me at the desk—on the orders of one of the officers—and then I was a spectator from them on. They had some questions because I had authenticated."

John explained what "authentication" was.

The authentication was each ship had a book and there was a phrase and a challenge phrase that went with it. Like I would say, "Request you authenticate Oscar Mike," and they would look in the book under Oscar Mike and the word for them would be Whiskey Sierra, and they would say, "Authentication's Whiskey Sierra." And then that way you knew that you were actually talking to who they said they were. When Ron took over, one of the higher ups, a chief or an officer, or somebody told Ron to get 'em to authenticate and that's when I stepped back in and said I had already had 'em authenticate.

Well they had already asked them to authenticate before I jumped in, but the guy on the other end did not authenticate. He got a little upset with it, and said, "I've already authenticated," and so they let that go, they didn't push the authentication anymore.

It was time to let the skipper know.

We called up to Captain Tully and told him that we had a distress call. Instead of sending it up through the pneumatic tubes—the bunny tubes we called them, the way we normally sent messages to the bridge—he requested that it be hand-delivered to him by a runner. So one of the guys took the message and carried it all the way up to the bridge to Captain Tully.

It took a while to get the captain the message that way, which still has John stumped.

We were all the way forward of the ship, and it was a long, long trek to run that message up there. I don't know why he didn't allow it to be sent up through the bunny tubes. It would take probably 10 minutes to walk it up to the captain, whereas the bunny tube would take probably 30 seconds.

John had never experienced Captain Tully requesting a message—especially a distress call—to be hand-delivered.

To my knowledge this was the first time.

Bunny tubes were the preferred source of delivery.

They were always used. Messages were always distributed through the bunny tube.

Liberty was still screaming for help, but now they had another problem.

> We received several other messages from Rockstar. They were under attack, and the radio operator on the *Liberty* said that they were being bombed and strafed by aircraft. Then shortly after that they said that there were three motor torpedo boats that were attacking them.

Sara swung into action.

> We received a message to launch aircraft, which we did, and we received a message from the *Liberty* that they had been struck [by a] torpedo, and were listing badly and requested immediate assistance. We could hear the machinegun fire, we could hear explosions and the radio operator on the other end was frantic. He was asking me where was the help. We didn't know at the time in the Radio Room that the jets had been recalled. So we went on for several hours communicating back and forth.

The Attack on the Liberty detailed what one of the radiomen, 22-year-old Second Class Petty Officer James V. Halman experienced while using the high-frequency radio network, which was monitored by the Sixth Fleet.

"Any station this net," Halman called out at 1:58 P.M. "This is Rockstar." Halman didn't know it, but he would be unable to transmit anything until Terry did his magic.

> "Any station this net, this is Rockstar," Halman called out. "We are under attack. Be advised we are under attack."

> The USS *Saratoga* was steaming approximately 500 miles west of the *Liberty* at the time fighters strafed the spy ship. The aircraft carrier USS *America* [(CV-66)] sailed in formation, along with the cruiser USS *Little*

Rock [(CLG-4)], which carried Vice Admiral William Martin, the commander of the Sixth Fleet. Halman's distress call crackled over the airwaves. The *Saratoga*'s radio operators, likely stunned by the emergency message over the high-command network, struggled to decipher Halman's distress call. Two minutes after Halman made his first call, the carrier responded. "Rockstar, this is Schematic," answered the carrier's operator. "You are garbled. Say again."

As shells rocked the *Liberty* and smoke poured into the radio room, Halman fingered the transmit button and repeated his distress call. "I say again. We are under attack," Halman shouted. "We are under attack."

The *Saratoga*'s message came back the same. "You are still garbled," the operator replied. "Say again."

"Schematic, this is Rockstar. We are under attack. We are under attack," Halman yelled. "Any station this net, this is Rockstar. We are under attack. Do you read me?"

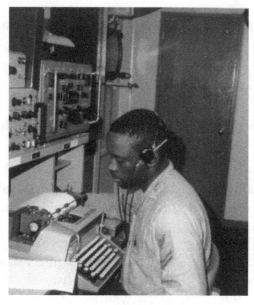

James "Vern" Halman

Israeli jamming of all frequencies also prevented a clear signal from being transmitted.

> Six minutes into the assault, the *Liberty*'s radiomen switched transmitters but still could not get a clear message out. CPO Wayne [L.] Smith darted down to the transmitter room on the main deck near the rear of the ship. There Smith discovered that the frequency dial was one kilocycle off. He adjusted it and the radio operators tried again. Problems persisted. Each time the planes strafed the ship, the radiomen found the frequency interrupted by a sound like feedback. The noise over the receivers was so loud that one of the men would later tell the Navy's investigating board that the sailors concluded the transmitters had malfunctioned. The men switched frequencies only to find the same feedback noise on all of them. Halman and the other radiomen concluded the attackers had jammed the *Liberty*'s communications. Only between attacks could the operators receive signals.

> The radio log shows that at 2:08 P.M.—10 minutes into the assault—Halman called for help again. The fighters by now had strafed the *Liberty* multiple times. Fires raged on deck and wounded sailors flooded the sick bay, wardroom, and mess deck. The chaotic and frightful reality aboard the ship reflected in Halman's desperate call for help. "Schematic, this is Rockstar," the radio operator called out. "We are under attack. We are under attack. We are under attack."

> "Roger," the carrier's operator finally replied.

> "Schematic, this is Rockstar," Halman radioed one minute later. "We are under attack and need immediate assistance."

> "Roger," the carrier's operator answered. The *Saratoga*'s radioman asked the *Liberty* for an authentication code, a secret variable letter combination that ships use to verify

the identity of others. RM2 Joseph P. Ward crouched next to Halman and fed him the authentication code from a book. The carrier's radioman responded five minutes later. "Authentication is correct," the operator replied. "I am standing by for further traffic."

Saratoga forwarded the SOS to the commander of the Sixth Fleet and the Navy's European and Middle East command in London.

"Following received from Rockstar. I am under attack. My posit 31.23N 33.25E," the carrier's message read. "I have been hit. Request immed assistance."

This broadcast was completed at the exact time the torpedo hit the *Liberty*, and two minutes later another message was broadcast.

"3 unidentified gunboats approaching vessel now."

The carrier followed that message at 2:45 P.M. with the relay of a five-word distress call. "Under attack and hit badly."

Nine minutes later, the carrier forwarded the first confirmation that the *Liberty* had been torpedoed. "Hit by torpedo starboard side. Listing badly. Need assistance immediately."

Vice Admiral William Martin, the commander of the Sixth Fleet, sailed on the cruiser *Little Rock* as the attack unfolded. The three-star admiral's flagship had joined the carriers *Saratoga* and *America* for maneuvers off of Crete. Over the open airwaves, Martin heard the desperation in the voice of *Liberty*'s radioman. At 2:50 P.M.—15 minutes after the torpedo killed 25 [men]—the admiral ordered his carriers to turn into the wind. "*America* launch four armed A-4s to proceed to 31–23N 33–25E to defend USS *Liberty* who is now under attack by gunboats," Martin instructed. "Provide fighter cover and tankers. Relieve on station. *Saratoga* launch four armed A-1s ASAP same mission." The Sixth Fleet sent a message to the *Liberty* at 3:05 P.M. to assure the defenseless ship help would arrive soon. "Your [FLASH] traffic received. Sending aircraft to cover you. Surface units on the way."

The *Saratoga*'s communications officer personally delivered the news of the attack to Captain Joseph Tully, Jr., on the bridge of that carrier soon after radiomen picked up the *Liberty*'s distress calls. Unlike the *America*, the *Saratoga* had a strike group ready within minutes. Tully would later write that he immediately turned into the wind and launched fighters only to have his superiors order him moments later to recall the fighters and wait for the *America*. Tully wrote that he instantly readied a second strike group. Commander Max Morris, the *Saratoga*'s navigator, who later would rise to the rank of rear admiral, confirmed Tully's account of the launch and recall in a letter to his former commanding officer. The *Saratoga*'s deck log does not reflect the launch, but does show that at 2:41 P.M. the carrier began a series of course and speed changes that could indicate flight activity.

Deck crews raced to prepare the fighters. The *Saratoga* had been ordered to launch A-1 Skyraiders, a propeller plane with a slow speed of only about 350 mph but a range of 3,000 miles. The *America* in contrast had been ordered to launch A-4 Skyhawks, a jet that flew nearly twice the speed of the A-1 and at an altitude of almost 50,000 feet, but had a range of less than 1,000 miles.

Ordnance crews retrieved rockets and missiles from the magazines below. Intelligence officers briefed pilots on weather conditions and used maps of Egypt to highlight port facilities, antiaircraft batteries, and surface-to-air missile sites. The *Saratoga* messaged Martin at 3:22 P.M. that it planned to launch its four A-1s at 4 P.M. The *Saratoga*'s deck log shows that the carrier increased speed

197

to 25 knots at 4:01 P.M. and started the launch sequence one minute later as fighters zoomed down the flight deck. The *America*'s deck log failed to record the launch, but [Don] Engen [captain of the *America*] wrote in his memoir that planes lifted off soon after the *Saratoga*.

"We are on the way," the *America*'s flight leader announced over the departure frequency.

Rear Admiral Lawrence Geis, commander of the Mediterranean's carrier strike force, repeated Martin's launch order at 3:16 P.M. and instructed pilots only to protect the ship. "Defense of USS *Liberty* means exactly that," Geis ordered. "Destroy or drive off any attackers who are clearly making attacks on *Liberty*. Remain over international waters. Defend yourself if attacked."

Martin outlined more detailed rules of engagement in a message at 3:39 P.M. "You are authorized to use force including destruction as necessary to control the situation. Do not use more force than required. Do not pursue any unit towards land for reprisal purposes. Purpose of counterattack is to protect *Liberty* only," Martin's message stated.

Martin waited for his fighters to reach the *Liberty*. The *Saratoga* had estimated its propeller-driven Skyraiders would take approximately three hours to cover the distance to the battered spy ship. Martin had told his superiors that he expected the faster jets to arrive in half that time.

We all couldn't wait for help to arrive.

Ohio native John Edward Nuss was 17-years-old when he joined the Navy, and he was onboard the *Saratoga* when they received our SOS.

I filled out my "wish list," and I said I wanted an aircraft carrier off of the West Coast, I want to go to boot camp in San Diego, and of course the Navy recruiter was all agreeable to everything. Come down to the time for me to leave, went down to the induction center, and they said, "You're going to the Great Lakes Naval Training Center." And I get my orders, and I'm sent to the USS *Saratoga* out of Mayport, Florida. And I said, "Well, I got one outta three wishes. At least I'm in the Navy."

John began as a Fireman Apprentice.

I ended up as a BT Third Class, which is a Boiler Tender Third Class.

John explained his job onboard the *Saratoga*, eight stories belowdecks.

We had pump rooms where we would help maintain the balance of the ship, by pumping oil from certain tanks, from certain sides of the ship, to keep it level.

We were responsible for all the drinking water, cooking water, and shower water. But our main concern was the boiler water, and there were eight boilers on the ship. They were 1,200 pounders. Superheated, we could increase our pressure to 1,500 pounds in order to launch planes off of the flight deck.

John remembered the day of the attack.

I got off the midwatch, I went and had some breakfast and was coming back down to the work area, and they blew general quarters, and I headed for Central Control. When I got down there, all the hatches were shut, and we really didn't know what was going on. They said it was not a drill; I do remember that. And all of a sudden they called for full steam ahead and the whole nine yard deal that people see in the movies.

I know they had launched planes. And it wasn't too much longer before they called them all back.

Where I was at, in Central Control, the guys were on our headsets, they said, "Launching now." I knew every time they were launching a plane. Every plane that was shot off, I knew. I wanna say 15, but it's been so long.

John remembered how soon the planes were launched after they went to GQ.

It was within an hour.

Israel's attack didn't just disrupt our ship.

It was over 48 hours of general quarters, a little bit under 72, but it was pretty much close to three days. We could get 15, 20 minutes of sleep here, 15, 20 minutes of sleep there, with your headphones on, on a metal deck plate at times.

The skipper of the *Saratoga*, Joseph M. Tully, Jr. hailed from a famous military family. His father, Brigadier General Joseph Merit Tully, who led the Fourth Cavalry Group into Normandy on D-Day two hours before the main assault force landed, passed away about four years before they attacked our ship.

Joe, Jr. explained—in a statement—what happened when he launched his planes to come to our aid.

I was Captain of the USS *Saratoga* on June 8, 1967. *Saratoga* and the USS *America* were aircraft carries in the Sixth Fleet on station in the Mediterranean. We had been at a state of readiness for a month because of the Middle East tension.

My communications officer raced to the bridge with a distress call from USS *Liberty*. I called Admiral Martin

(Commander of Sixth Fleet) aboard the USS *America* and informed him I was launching aircraft in support of *Liberty*. I scrambled 12 F-4 fighter bombers armed with .50 caliber machineguns and 500-pound conventional general purpose bombs and four fuel tankers. I launched my planes within five-to-15 minutes and figured they were about 15-to-25 minutes away from USS *Liberty*.

I noticed that the USS *America* had not launched any planes. I queried by signal light "Why have you not launched aircraft?" I never received an answer. Before my planes were out of sight Admiral Geis recalled them.

Later we received orders from USS *America* to be ready to launch in 90 minutes. I told them I was ready to launch now. The second launch included nine planes from USS *America* and USS *Saratoga*. These aircraft were also recalled. I am still puzzled by what happened.

Captain Joseph M. Tully, USN (Retired)

Official Navy photo of Captain Joseph M. Tully, Jr.

John saw Captain Tully aboard *Sara*.

I saw him on several different occasions. As a matter of fact he was even in the oil shack one time. Regardless of all the gold he was wearing, he was really a good, down-to-earth guy. He was a nice guy. He'd come in and talk to us. He said, "You guys are doing a good job." He was a very sincere man, and he did look out for his crew.

I think I seen him probably four or five days later in the mess deck area he was walking through. And he said, "How's the oil shack doin'?" I said, "Just fine sir, couldn't be better."

I met Joe Tully several times, and he never forgot what happened to our ship. That poor SOB, it killed him. Of course he had cancer. He got pushed out of the Navy. He was a carrier captain. His next step was a star. That's just the way it is. Most carrier captains become admirals. He disobeyed orders. He sent the rescue aircraft out anyway, even though Admiral Geis said don't do it. And they got recalled. And it wasn't his fault, but he felt it was, and it broke his heart. He was a broken man.

The man who knew it wasn't static, John, is still hard-hit from the jets being recalled.

Pretty much all of us in that radio division that were in that room that day and witnessed the horror and the cries for help that we weren't able to answer. It's haunted me; it's been a really tough time. It's been 50 years.

It's something that most Americans don't know about, it's something that was covered up by our government.

I've been in therapy for 20 years and I continue to be in therapy, because 34 men died out there that day and hundreds injured, and it's been a really, really tough time, and it still is.

I have a lot of feelings of guilt—and that's one of the things I've been working on in counseling that I'm getting through the VA now—that I failed them, especially the 25 that died when the torpedo hit the ship. If we had gotten planes out earlier then we could've stopped those torpedo boats.

I was a 20-year-old kid, I was E-3, I had no rank and no knowledge of how the chain-of-command worked or anything, and to me, they're asking for help, we sent a message up to the captain, and I thought planes woulda been launched automatically, but apparently they had to go through the chain-of-command, and then there was a big cover-up by Johnson and McNamara.

I feel a lot of guilt about it. The guy was asking me for help, and at one point I told him help was on the way, but help wasn't really on the way. And when we did get the message to launch the planes, they never made it to the *Liberty;* the *Liberty* never saw our planes. They were recalled. It was tough.

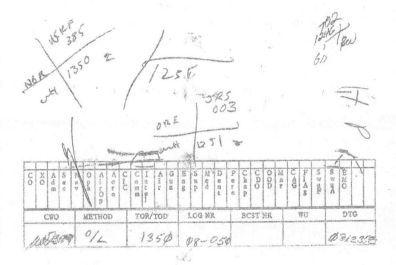

BKD-OPPO-JAX-2964 (Rev. 11-96)   USS SARATOGA (CVA-60)

DTG _0812 35 Z_   DATE _8 JUN 67_

FROM
USS SARATOGA

ACTION
CINCUNAVEUR

INFORMATION
CT6 60.1 / CTG 60.2 / Com Sixth Flt

(Do not use this space)

081235Z

FOLLOWING RECEIVED FROM ROCKSTAR
I AM UNDER ATTACK MY POSIT 31 23N 33 25E. I HAVE BEEN HIT.
REQUEST IMMED ASSISTANCE   TOR: 1220Z

C O	X O	A d m	S e c	N a v	O p s	A i r O p s	A A e r o	A C I C	C I C o m m	I n t e l	A i r	G u n	E n g	S u p	M e d	D e n t	P e r s	C h a p	C D O	O O D	M a r	C A G	F I A S	S w b f	S W u A	E M O
CWO		METHOD		TOR/TOD		LOG NR		BCST NR			WU			DTG												
		O/L		1350		08-050								0812352												

GSD-8772-JAK-3084 (REV. 11-65)   USS SARATOGA (CVA-60)

DTG _Ø8125Ł2_   DATE _8 JUNE Z_

FROM   PRECEDENCE   DRAFTER
USS SARATOGA   ImmED

ACTION   CLEARED
CINUSNAVEUR   RELEASED
                                                        Jm Tully

INFORMATION
XX COMSIXTHFLT/CTG 6Ø.1/CTG 6Ø.2

(Do not use this space)

UNCLAŁ — Z —   Ø81245Z

THE FOLLOWING RECEIVED FROM ROCKSTAR:
UNDER ATTACK AND HIT BADILY
TOR: 1238Z

                        NGR | KRF
                        1300| Cb

VICL | DRE
wtd | 1301 Z

C O	X D	A d m	S e c	N a v	O p s	A e r O p	A e r o	C I C	C o m m	C I n t e l	A i r	G u n	E n g g	S u p	M e d	D e n t	P e r s	C h a p	C O D	M a r	C A G	F I A S	S u p f	S E M O

CWO	METHOD	TOR/TOD	LOG NR	BCST NR	WU	DTG
	Ø/L		053			Ø81251Z

205

CONFIDENTIAL

621

II/WI

```
W    CR 072
     ZZ RUEDNAA
ZNY CCCCC ZOV RUTPH
FH-2
V    AAA151VV    NYC695
     ZZ RUTPP
DE RUTPRC 078  151912Z
ZNY CCCCC
Z 081250Z JUN 67
FM COMSCKTHFLT
TO RUTPP/USS SARATOGA
RUTPP/USS AMERICA
INFO RUTPP/CTF SIX ZERO
RTPP/CTG SIXSNE GJ PT TW 3
BT
CONFIDENTIAL
1. AMERICA LAUNCH FOUR ARMED AA'TKTO PROCEED TO 31-23N 33-25E TO
DEREWFXLAN ERTY WHO IS NOW UNDER ATTACK BY GUNBOATS.  PROVIDE
FIGHTER COVER AND TANKERS.  RELIEVE ON STATION.  SARATOGA LAUOLH
FOUR ARMED A-1'S ASAP SAME MISSION.
GP-4
BT
```

INF 01 05 21...... 05 2..... 05 3..... C.......

Declassified and approved for
release by NSA and the U.S. Navy
on 01-12-2007 pursuant to E.O.
12958. as amended ST 51667

CONFIDENTIAL

USS SARATOGA (CVA-60)

DTG: 08/25#　　　DATE 8 JUN 67

FROM SARATOGA　　PRECEDENCE IMMED　　DRAFTER

ACTION CINCUS NAVEUR　　　CLEARED / RELEASED

INFORMATION COMSIXTH FLT / CTG 60.1 / CTF 60.2

(Do not use this space)

THE FOLLOWING RECEIVED FROM ROCKSTAR

WE HIT WERE HIT BY TORPEDO STARBOARD SIDE LISTING BADLY REQ ASSISTANCE
IMMEDIATELY

JTCC JRS 006 / CB 1307Z

NGR KRF 368 / CB 1302Z

-6's A

IPJQ

1305Z

C O	X O	A d m	S e c	N a v	O p s	A i r / O P	A e r o	C I C	C o m m I n t e l	A i r	G u n	E n g	S u p	M e d	D e n t	P e r s	C h a p	C D O	O O D	M a r	C A G	F l a g	S W U F	S W U A	E M O

CWO	METHOD	TOR/TOD	LOG NR	BCST NR	WU	DTG
365	O/L	1307Z	08-050			081254

GNO-2PPO-JAX-3664 (REV. 11-65)   USS SARATOGA (CVA-60)

DTG   Ø81715Z   DATE   8 JUNE 1967

FROM USS LIBERTY	PRECEDENCE IMMED	DRAFTER
ACTION CNO		CLEARED
		RELEASED

INFORMATION
CINCUSNAVEUR/USCINCEUR/JCS (ØRG)/CINCLANTFLT/COMSIXTHFLT/COMSERVLANT

(Do not use this space)

UNCLAS
SITUATION FOLLOWING AIR ATTACK
1. AT TIME Ø81205Z WHILE SHIP ON COURSE 283 DEGREES SPEED 5 KNOTS
POSIT 3135.5N 3329E SHIP ATTACKED BY UNIDENTIFIED JET FIGHTERS
BELEIVED TO BE ISRALI. APPROX SIXSTRAFFING RUNS MADE ON SHIP. APPROX Ø8122
THREE TORPEADO BOATS ONE IDENTIFIED AS ISRALI APPROACHED SHIP ON STBD
QTR AT HIGH SPEED. HULL NUMBER OF ONE WAS 206-17. APPROX Ø81427Z TOOK TOR-
PEDO BOATS UNDER FIRE WITH 5Ø CAL. MACHINE GUNS AT RANGE OF 2ØØØ YDS.
TORPEDO BOATS LAUNCHED TORPEDO AND STRAFFING ATTACK. ONE TORPEDO PASSED
APPROX 75 YDS ASTERN. APPROX ONE MINUTE LATER SHIP SUSTAINED TORPEDO
HIT STBD SIDE. SHIP HAS 1Ø DEGREE STBD LIST. WATER TIGHT BOUNDERIES
ESTABLISHED AND HOLDING. AFTER ATTACK TORPEDO BOATS CLEARED TO EAST
ABOUT 5 MILES. CLEARING AREA AT 1Ø KNOTS.
2. PHOTOS OF AIRCRAFT AND BOATS TAKEN. AFTER ATTACK COMPLETED, TWO
ISRALI HELO ORBITED SHIP. AT ABOUT Ø81255Z RANGE 5ØØ YDS
ISRALI INSIGNA CLEARLY VISABLE. PHOTOS TAKEN. SEVERAL PROJECTILES HAVE
BEEN RECOVERED FROM TOPSIDE AREAS. NUMBER DEAD ESTIMATED 1Ø. NUMBER
OF SERIOUSLY WOUNDED ESTIMATED 15. TOTAL WOUNDED 75. NUMBER MISSING
PRESENTLY UNDETERMINED.
3. SHIP UNABLE TO CARRY OUT MISSION. WILL SUBMIT PERSONNEL CASREP, ASAP.
SEPERATELY.
4. EXTENSIVE SUPERFICIAL DAMAGE TOPSIDE. LOWER DECK FORWARD DESTROYED
5. COMMUNICATION CAPABILITIES LIMITED. WILL PROVIDE FILM AND
PROJECTILES RECOVERED ON REQUEST. SHIP WILL REQUIRE DRY DOCKING AND
EXTENSIVE REFITTING.

COMM NOTE: WRITTEN UP FOR INFO ONLY

CO	XO	ADmc	SNecv	NOps	OAirOP	ACeto	CIComCmatel	AGir	EGun	SMacgp	DMecat	PCerps	CCHanp	OCDOD	MOnr	CAGAG	FIALGg	SSwpWf	SEMWOA	

CWO	METHOD	TOR/TOD	LOG NR	BCST NR	WU	DTG
WDS	VOICE	173ØZ	S-194	N/A	DEW/17452	Ø817152

24

America

The crewmen of the *Davis* and *Liberty* started moving the most seriously wounded from the mess halls and passageways up to the main deck. Shortly thereafter, the brand-new aircraft carrier USS *America* maneuvered itself into the area, keeping some distance between her and us, just in case it was necessary to launch fighter jets.

USS *America* (CV-66)

What I found out much later was that *America* did launch jets, almost a day before, to come to our aid.

Don Engen, captain of the *America*, in his 1997 book *Wings and Warriors: My Life as a Naval Aviator* recalled what happened aboard the carrier.

Thus the notification about *Liberty* came at the exact wrong time for *America*, thus adding a certain amount of additional complexity. I found Rear Admiral Geis in his war room and informed him that unless otherwise directed I was stopping the training exercise to strike below those weapons and to arm the air group airplanes with more flexible and appropriate loads of ammunition. He was so busy that he hardly answered me, but his staff agreed. Along the way, Rear Admiral Geis, as CTF60, directed *America* and *Saratoga* to launch a specific number of airplanes against whoever was attacking *Liberty*. In *America* there ensued about an hour's effort to move some bombs below and bring up others and to launch four A-4Cs fully loaded along with F-4B escorts. That group was judged to be the correct size for a response— not too large and warlike, but still large enough to protect *Liberty*.

A-4C Skyhawk   F-4B Phantom

As our airplanes departed the task group, I heard the flight leader announce on the departure frequency, "We are on the way. Who is the enemy?" Our knowledge was such that no one knew yet who had attacked *Liberty*.

Within minutes the national command authority— President Johnson—was on the radio telephone from the

White House direct to Rear Admiral Geis directing that the aircraft be recalled. The president told Rear Admiral Geis that the Israelis had admitted they had mistakenly strafed and torpedoed the ship. The Israelis had said they had believed *Liberty* to be an Arab intelligence ship.

Donald Davenport Engen

Donald Davenport Engen entered the USN in 1942, and was trained in dive-bombing. He mastered take-offs and landings on aircraft carriers and took part in the invasion of Guam, where he sank a Japanese freighter. In 1944, during the Battle of Leyte Gulf, he helped sink a Japanese aircraft carrier (which saved countless lives since the carrier could carry out no more kamikaze missions) and was one of 32 pilots awarded the Navy Cross, as well as the Air Medal and the Distinguished Flying Cross for his service in the Pacific. Although Don was released from active duty in 1946, he continued serving in the U.S. Naval Reserve, and in 1950 took part in the first jet combat missions in the Korean War, where he was awarded two more Air Medals. He went on to serve as a test pilot, eventually commanding a squadron at the Naval Air Test Center, Patuxent River, Maryland, now Naval Air Station Patuxent River. In 1962 Don was appointed commander of a carrier air group, in 1963 he served as operations officer aboard the USS *Coral Sea*, and in 1964 received his first command as captain of the USS *Mount Katmai*, leaving in 1965 to attend the Naval War College to prepare for command of the *America*. On July 21, 1966, Don took command of *America*, and the month following the Israeli massacre on our ship, he relinquished command of the *America* in Valletta and returned stateside. In 1968 he headed the Aviation Plans Branch for the CNO until 1970, and in 1971 was appointed commander of a carrier division and awarded the Gold Star to the Legion of Merit. In 1973 he was appointed Deputy Commander in Chief U.S. Naval Forces Europe and his final command was Deputy Commander in Chief U.S. Atlantic Command, and in 1978 Don retired with the rank of Vice-admiral. In 1982, he was appointed to the National Transportation Safety Board (NTSB) and in

1984 was appointed Administrator of the Federal Aviation Administration until 1987. In 1996 he was appointed Director of the National Air and Space Museum (NASM) at the Smithsonian Institution, the fifth most visited museum in the world, a role he held until his untimely and suspicious death on July 13, 1999.

Joe had a friend arrange a meeting with Don Engen at the NASM on June 19, 1998.

> I spoke personally, eyeball to eyeball, with Don Engen, who on June the 8th was commanding officer on board the *America*. I guess we talked for over an hour. Just one-on-one, no interruptions, the phone never rang, it was just the two of us, and we were talking with each other, not to each other, so it was really nice.
>
> He told me, "I've waited a lot of years to apologize to you guys. Please convey it to your crew. I'm sorry." I said, "What do you have to apologize for?" He said, "We were in the middle of a GQ drill and we had the wrong aircraft loaded with the wrong munitions topside. And when we went to GQ we had to get those planes down, unarmed and rearmed and then get them back topside. It was a Chinese fire drill. We were taking jets down the up elevators. Men were carrying bombs away to get the right ones on the planes."
>
> He told me that when they were finally able to launch to come to *Liberty*'s aid, they let Washington know, and the minute they did, Robert McNamara came on the voice network ordering Engen to recall the aircraft, just as he had done with the *Saratoga*.
>
> And Don was ready to comply, when Admiral Geis took the microphone from Don and told McNamara, "Sonny, you're neither big enough nor bad enough to have me recall aircraft going to help a Navy ship with sailors in peril." And Don said the next voice he heard, the next voice everybody in that space heard, was Lyndon Baines

Johnson saying, "Get those goddamn planes back or you'll be pushing pencils the next day. I will not embarrass an ally over one ship and a few men." And the admiral recalled the aircraft.

The president of the United States was willing to sacrifice the ship and the crew and he didn't wanna embarrass Israel.

Although I never met Don Engen personally, I was scheduled to share a phone call with him for the making of the documentary *Loss of Liberty*. Don was going to testify about what really went on aboard his ship, the *America*, and the day before that, he was killed in a freak glider accident. That interview was to be with Tito de Nagy Howard, the filmmaker, and myself on a conference call, but obviously it never happened.

Don was in the rear seat of a Nimbus 4DM glider piloted by long-time friend, William S. Ivans, when a wing snapped off at about 5,000 feet over Nevada, plunging it to the ground around noon, about 15 miles east of Lake Tahoe, where Don was vacationing with his wife.

Don and Mr. Ivans were officers in the Soaring Society of America, an organization of gliding enthusiasts. The president of the Society said both men were top pilots in "an extremely well-built aircraft. So it had to be a very unusual set of circumstances that stressed the aircraft."

An NTSB officer said, "To get a break-up, you need some serious forces, whatever it was."

I don't care whatever they say, I feel he was suicided, just like the other great men who tried to expose the truth about the *Liberty*.

The evacuation of the wounded had finally begun, some 18 hours after Israel's initial attack. Helicopters from the *America* were coming over, would hover above the *Liberty*—there was no place to land because of all our antennae—as life stretchers were hoisted up to the helicopters with cables. Taking as many as the choppers could hold, the wounded of the *Liberty* were ferried over to the *America* and taken to the hospital aboard the carrier.

In *Wings and Warriors*, Don Engen recalled the assistance his carrier gave to my ship.

> During the evening of June 8 *Liberty* was directed by Vice Admiral Martin to steam as best as the ship could north out of reach of any further attack, and he sent USS *Davis* and USS *Massey* to escort the intelligence ship. Commander John Gordon, senior medical officer in *America*, remained on board to prepare our 80-bed hospital to receive the wounded. Lieutenant Commander Peter A. Flynn, second most senior medical officer in *America*, and an accomplished surgeon, and two medical corpsmen were sent in *Davis* to help *Liberty*'s heavily taxed ship's doctor and two corpsmen.
>
> At 1030 on June 9 two *America* helicopters rendezvoused over *Liberty* and began transferring the more seriously wounded to *America*, where Commander John Gordon and his doctors and corpsmen were well prepared for their arrival.
>
> After the helicopters touched down on the flight deck, the patients were carried in Stokes litters directly to nearby bomb elevators already prepared to take them down five decks to the hospital. At 1130 *America* rendezvoused with *Liberty*, and we put our boats in the water to facilitate damage assessment and the transfer of the dead. I took *America* slowly down the port side of *Liberty* from bow to stern and about 200 yards away.

Billy was evacuated to *America*.

> The next day they took us off the ship; all I know is they got me somehow up on the main deck. I believe the captain and Mr. Golden came over to me and said my guys had done real good. Then that was the last I had seen of them until we had our first reunion.

214

Dave was flown to *America* as well.

I went back to sick bay from there, and they patched me up a little more, and flew me to the hospital in Naples, and to Frankfurt and then to Washington. When I was in the hospital in Naples, and the first thing I did was to go down to the morgue and see the morgue officer, and I asked him how many people drowned. And he said, "None." It's not a good thing to say that they're all dead, but I'd rather they're killed by the torpedo than drown down there.

Joe shared his memories of that day.

The hardest part of that whole thing for me was the airlift in the basket up to the helicopter and the ride to the aircraft carrier. It was so bouncy, that even though my leg was stabilized, it was a godawful ride. And I was still having trouble breathing, and they laid me down flat. So basically I was drowning in my own fluids.

The *America* crew came out and moved the stretchers down to the hospital area. We were each assigned a corpsman. One by one, they took us into surgery. They set my leg, and where the bones had come out there was a big gap and they couldn't get it closed. Turned out my fractured skull was down the front of my face and they set my broken ribs and re-inflated my lung, and I could finally breathe normally again.

The doctor came around, and the first time he came to check on me, he handed me a washcloth. I said, "What's that for?" He said, "Well, I'm gonna change your dressing, you might wanna bite down on it 'cause it's gonna hurt." Now, I was 24, I was doing a couple of hundred sit-ups. When I crossed the equator and had to shave all my hair off, I looked like Mr. Clean. I looked at the doctor, and I said, "Well, sir, you go ahead, I don't need it." He said, "OK, I'm gonna pull the bandage out." It was all down in that open wound, and he knew, I didn't know, the gauze had clotted and it was kind of attached to me. He said, "One . . . two," and before he said "three" he pulled it out. It felt like somebody had taken a blowtorch to my leg. I didn't scream, I might've shed a couple of tears, but man, I wanna tell you what. Do that to me a couple of times and I'll tell you anything you wanna know. From that point forward, anytime I'd see the doctor, I'd quickly put a washcloth in my mouth; he appreciated my sense of humor.

George E. Sokol, a Connecticut native who entered the Navy at the age of 17, was serving aboard *America* as a 19-year-old Third Class Aircraft Structural Mechanics, Hydraulics, conducting maintenance and repairs on all the aircraft in his squadron, which was performing maneuvers off of Crete. More than 50 years later, George still remembers exactly what he was doing when he first got word that my ship was being attacked.

I was coming from the berthing compartment walking down the hangar bay, and the hangar bay fire doors were almost completely closed because six nuclear bombers were there and they were being protected by Marines. As I went through those doors, I heard the first words of the announcement. What I heard was something like, "NAVY SHIP UNDER ATTACK. THE UNITED STATES SHIP LIBERTY UNDER ATTACK BY UNKNOWN AIR AND NAVAL FORCES. GENERAL QUARTERS, GENERAL QUARTERS. THIS IS NO DRILL."

Then what really scared the hell out of me was "SET CONDITION ZULU."

Material Condition Zulu is one of three different conditions aboard a ship. Zulu, the most serious one, has all hatches dogged, and it is used in combat and during storms.

George explained why that frightened him so, and how Israel's evil, irresponsible attack brought the world close to Armageddon.

> Aircraft carriers were supposed to be able to take a nuclear hit if it's at least five miles away. Condition Zulu is basically airtight security because we were expecting a nuclear attack. The saltwater wash-down system, which goes all over the ship, in case there's a nuclear attack, was pressurized and ready to go, to wash the fallout over the side. I spent two-and-a-half hours believing we were at war with Russia, preparing myself to die.

> One of the things that burns my ass about what happened to the *Liberty*, is that I just found out recently that when the *Liberty* was hit we were only 300 miles away from her.

America, George explained, was capable of moving fast through the water.

> When we did cruises, we went to high speed, and they told us we hit 57 knots.

> They kept us at bay for eight hours before they let us do anything. We could've been there in five hours, but instead of letting us go to speed, they kept us at normal cruise speed which is around 30 knots. Men died because we weren't allowed to do our job.

Incredibly, George received the information in 2015 on *America*'s distance from *Liberty* from a radioman aboard the *Davis*, Gerry Surette, who was capturing radio transmissions and positions. It took this fella almost 50 years to provide this important information, a reflection of how thorough the cover-up was, and is.

George explained what would've happened if *America* was allowed to launch their A-4 Skyhawks, with a top speed of almost 700 mph, and their F-4 Phantoms, with a top speed of almost 1,700 mph.

217

The torpedo probably never would've made it.

George described when he first saw my ship.

I could see this flash of white, like a strobe, out on the horizon. And as I watched it, all of a sudden, under that flash of white, I saw the ship. So that flag was there, and that was on the horizon over 20 miles away, and we could see that flag right from the flight deck. So there was no doubt there was a flag on that lady. It was flashing like a strobe, the white stripes. You couldn't miss it.

George recounted when *America* pulled up to *Liberty*.

We were maybe 200 yards away, no further, and I was on the flight deck, on the port side, right at the elevator. When I saw her, the way I described it to my parents in a letter, was from bow to stern, from the waterline to the mastheads, it was blown to hell. The whole bow of the ship right up to the bridge was black and brown. There was still blood on the decks, coming off the sides from the scuppers [a hole in a ship's side that allows for ocean or rainwater drain off]. It tore me up. I felt like I swallowed a tennis ball and I wanted to cry. My eyes felt like they had an extra 10 pounds of air on them. And all I could think of was, "We did nothing."

What George saw on board *America* when a wounded *Liberty* crewman was transferred aboard, illustrates how intent our own government was—and still is—on covering up what happened to my ship.

This kid's there, a *Liberty* crewmember, who just got off a helicopter, he's got a battle dressing around his head, and about two inches behind his right ear, there's a circle about the size of the old, real silver dollars. And there was gray matter coming through it. I'm not sure if the guy was totally conscious.

This other guy was kneeling next to him, screaming at this kid, loud enough so I could hear it. And he goes, "YOU DON'T TALK TO YOUR SHIPMATES, YOU DON'T TALK TO YOUR FAMILY, YOU DON'T TALK TO YOUR FRIENDS, YOU DON'T TALK TO THE GUY AT THE BAR ABOUT WHAT HAPPENED. IF YOU DO YOU'LL BE COURT-MARTIALED OR WORSE."

George still remembered many details of the guy who was screaming, believing he was a civilian from either NSA or the Office of Naval Intelligence.

He was about 5'6", 5'7", kind of stocky, and wearing khaki pants with brown loafers with a fringe and tassels. He had a cream-colored shirt with a pinstriped aqua check pattern on it, and he had sandy-brown or light-brown hair. I could still see his face to this day. When he got through screaming at this kid, he looked at me and said, "Did you hear that?" I answered in the affirmative. Then he said, "Stay away from the press."

The civilian had taken note of George's identity.

He had my name and my unit from the flight-deck jersey I was wearing. Two hours later, I walked into the airplane shop, and everybody, except for the petty officer in charge, Henry "Toad" Burdette, walked out of there like I had the plague. Toad just said one thing to me, he said, "Steer clear of the press," and he turned around and left the room. I don't know what the hell they said to these guys, but I was like *persona non grata* for the rest of my time in the Navy.

With my wounded shipmates safely aboard *America*, George, as well as many others, felt guilty they provided no assistance to the *Liberty*.

I couldn't look in their face, I was ashamed.

Sadly, George passed away October 1, 2017, all alone in his home. God bless you, George, for all you have done to bring the story of the *Liberty* massacre to all you met.

All the seriously wounded had been taken off the ship and we double and then triple-checked the shoring until we were confident it was as good as it was going to get. I marveled at how quickly time was passing. The day before, while we were under attack, every minute seemed to pass as slowly as an hour.

Everything that could be done had been and the other ships— *Massey* and *America*—had to get moving and back on their schedules. As *America* prepared to depart, carrying our wounded with her, the crew aboard gave three cheers for *Liberty*—"HIP, HIP, HORRAY! HIP, HIP, HORRAY! HIP, HIP, HORRAY!"

The sounds of the men's voices echoed across the Mediterranean and crashed against the side of our battered ship.

My throat swelled up with emotion like someone had punched it. Seeing a sea of men across the way, donning their blue work uniforms and white hats while cheering for us poor SOBs is a memory I will never forget as long as I live.

Don Engen recalled that moment in *Wings and Warriors*.

> I will never forget that sound. It made the hair stand up on the back of my neck and made me proud to be in the Navy.

We then thanked the crew of the *Davis*, who then jumped ship and went back, but as far as we were all concerned, we were no longer two crews but one, especially since around 18 of their crew remained with us to assist.

As soon as the *Davis* crew left, a voice came over the intercom, telling ship's crew to prepare for departure and the boilers were fired up. No sooner had this taken place, than I felt the ship under me begin to move as the screw started to turn.

Because of the gaping wound in our side, we had to move slowly. Although Captain must have known where we were headed, the rest of us on the deck did not. I knew we must be headed for some dry dock for repairs, as there was no way in hell we could make it across the Mediterranean and then across the Atlantic to America. However, as I was soon to find out, the fix had been put in place and the cover-up of the massacre was already well underway.

25

Angels

Right before daybreak, I stood on the main deck taking in the scene, when I was approached by Ensign Scott.

"The old man wants the ship cleaned up," he said.

I knew exactly what he meant without him going into the details of it. He wasn't talking about a spit shine. He was talking about hosing off the remains of the murdered *Liberty* crew from the decks and bulkheads.

The ship's deck looked like the floor of a slaughterhouse. Pieces of flesh, bone, hair, organs, and everything else imaginable were glued to it with dried blood. Rick and I found what undamaged firehoses we could and started hosing off the deck.

The hose had what was called a "suicide nozzle" on it, named thus because it was tapered in such a way that the water came out in an extremely concentrated and high-pressure stream, used for removing stubborn stains. Two men were needed to operate the hose because it was literally like wrestling a giant python and something one guy couldn't do alone.

We began the gruesome, heartbreaking task of washing the remains of our friends off the deck as if they were pieces of unwanted debris, knowing the fish would be all too happy with the treats they would be getting. As we were cleaning one of the guntubs, we found a shoe with a foot still in it. We did not wash this overboard but rather put it aside to be collected later.

As much as we hit the bloodstains with that hose, they would not come up. The previous day's intense heat, both from the sun and from the fires caused by the rockets and napalm, had baked the blood into the deck permanently.

"Napalm turned the deck into a 3,000-degree inferno," wrote James Scott in *The Attack on the Liberty*.

As Rick and I performed this ungodly work—which took around 90 minutes—tears streamed down our faces. We had once known these pieces of flesh as men. They had been our friends and our brothers and I prayed that God would forgive me for what I did in treating the remains of these brave men so disrespectfully. We worked inch-by-inch, trying as best as we could to return *Liberty* to something close to the condition it was in before June 8, 1967 at approximately 2 P.M., when the State of Israel tried to murder us all.

Around 30 minutes after Rick and I were done, we were approached by another helicopter, but this one had the clear markings of the United States of America.

It hovered on the starboard side, and we were both thrilled.

Piloting the chopper was 26-year-old New York City native Robert H. Hamel.

Bob joined the USN after he bumped into a naval aviator recruiter who took him "up in a P-34 over the Statue of Liberty," where he "signed up the next day."

Bob served his country for two decades—from 1963 to 1983—ending "up as the CO of a Sikorsky H-3 anti-submarine helicopter squadron," volunteering because he "was very strongly opposed to the advance of communism anywhere."

> I chose helicopters over patrol planes and I had done a tour in Vietnam on the USS *Roosevelt*.

Bob flew the Kaman SH-2 Seasprite, a ship-based chopper primarily used for anti-submarine warfare missions, which was introduced in the USN in 1962 and retired in 1993. From 1959-1969, 184 Seasprites were manufactured.

Bob was part of Helicopter Combat Support Squadron 2 (HC-2), known as the "Fleet Angels." established in 1948 and disestablished in 1977 "due to budget constraints."

Bob explained how he came to be "the first rescue vehicle to get there."

Kaman SH-2 Seasprite

After the Vietnam tour, I have to assume my squadron wanted to reward me, so they flew me over to the Med to replace an aviator who was releasing from active duty on USS *America*.

On 8 June I flew an unusual 7.1 hours. Before we took off on one of these flights they put a few Marines on us with M14s and a cameraman, which was pretty unusual, and we were now taking pictures of a *Komar*, and all of a sudden this one boat just hit it max RPM, rooster-tailed, did a 180, and took off.

A *Komar*, which was NATO's reporting name—meaning mosquito—was a Soviet missile boat from the 1950s and 1960s. Officially called Project 183R class, a *Komar* was the first class of missile boat to sink another ship, using guided missiles. The ship, destroyed by an Egyptian Navy *Komar*, sunk on October 21, 1967—around 4.5 months after the massacre aboard my ship—was the Israeli destroyer *Eilat*, mentioned at the end of Chapter 15.

We got recalled to the ship [*America*] and we found out USS *Liberty* was attacked.

I was a budding intelligence officer, as my extra duties, and I was sitting in the intelligence spaces for weeks just trying to pick up how this stuff went, and I saw the war developing in the Mideast. We saw who we believe started it and we learned a lot of stuff that I still don't know if I can even talk about.

I recall loading the A-4s and the F-4s with ordnance. Now this was routine for me from Vietnam; I had never seen it done in the Med. It was quite remarkable and I recall remarking to my copilot that there's gonna be a war; we're gonna get involved in it in the Mideast. And we all thought the Russians were getting ready to do something.

Onboard *America*, Bob witnessed some planes launching and returning.

America launched several flights of A-4s and F-4s. After the planes were recalled, "one of the pilots got out of an F-4, threw his helmet on the deck, and kicked it over the side.

Another helmet smashed to *America*'s deck by an angry pilot

Now I'm aft in the helicopter sitting in the arresting gear, refueling or something, wondering "what the heck's going on," because nobody briefed us about anything. We were the mushrooms, kept in the dark and fed you know what. And these guys came back and some of them were still armed with bombs, and that was a no-no in Vietnam from what I can remember. You got rid of that stuff before you landed aboard the ship.

Back at the ready room—the reporting place on the ship for pilots—that night we were talking about the attack, and before I sacked out that night, I was told to come down for a briefing the next morning. It had to be 0400 or 0500, because when I took off it was dark. So I went and got the briefing and they said, "You're going to take off and you're gonna follow instructions from a radar plane." I was told nothing else.

We launched in the dark, and of course I knew I was heading toward the Sinai; I had a compass. And we followed vectors from this radar plane, and about sunrise—and I will never forget this—as the sun came up I saw the smoke over the horizon. And we saw a ship, listing severely, and a wisp of smoke was going up into the sky and it was dead in the water.

Approaching *Liberty*, taken from Bob's helicopter

Another, taken from Bob's helicopter

The sun was up now and we circled around this thing and I didn't know if it was gonna blow up or what. I was a little leery about getting too close, but then I knew, it looked like a piece of Swiss cheese, and we could see the gore and the blood. We circled around it a few times.

Circling *Liberty*, taken from Bob's helicopter

There was no radio communication from anyone to me; I was totally on my own. I'm still mad about not getting briefed about this before I took off. I approached, I think it was the bow, my nose was pointing aft and I put my left gear and tailwheel on the deck and my right wheel had to hang over the side, because there was no room to do anything else. I maintained a contact hover on the ship, and I was looking at the guntub, and the tub was, again, Swiss cheese. And as the ship would gently roll, the guts and gore would go. I was hoping I wouldn't puke. I was holding it and wondering, "What the fuck is going on?"

As we're sitting there waiting for something to happen, for someone to talk to us, I saw a man's head stick out from the superstructure of the ship at deck level, and he was peeking around the superstructure. I was totally astonished. I told my copilot to wave to this guy and tell him to come up here. And the copilot waved to him, and the guy kind of like combat ran and crawled up to us and snuggled up next to the helicopter.

Obviously he was distressed—and I will never forget this either—and he said to my copilot, "Are you here to help us?" And the copilot of course relayed that in the microphone to me, and I went crazy with my expletives, I will not repeat right here, but basically I said, "Well what do you think we're here for?" We were in a clearly marked Navy helicopter, and again, I was mad because I had no prior information from anyone in the fleet about what in the heck to expect. So we told him, "Yes, of course we're here to help you." He said, "Will you take off several of our wounded?" I said as many as we can haul. We had a weight restriction obviously. So he and another man, and I think one of my crewmen got on the deck and helped them bring in the wounded, and I think we had six or seven. There was no wind that day and I was in a precarious situation, so I could not take more than what I considered 1,000 pounds of weight, 1,200 pounds of weight, something like that. And I didn't wanna make things worse and put these guys in the water.

So we got them on board and we lifted off, and of course I'm gonna take 'em back to *America*. I had no idea there was another carrier over there, I had no idea there was a submarine out there. I didn't know anything except I knew where my carrier was.

So heading back, I told my crew chief to put the most lucid, wounded sailor from *Liberty* on his helmet; put his helmet on the man because he'd be miked up. I wanna know what happened. On the way back to *America*—he was a senior enlisted man, I believe—I said, "Tell me what happened." He said they were on holiday routine, 12-13 miles off the coast of the Sinai, and they actually had their beach chairs on the deck, they were flying a holiday flag, and most guys were on holiday routine: reading books, writing letters, and then watching the airshow. I said, "What airshow?" He said a bunch of jets were flying over and doing banks and turns all kinds of stuff, and said it was quite interesting. We knew what was going on on the Sinai, but we figured that these guys were attacking targets. I wrote down I was 12.6 miles off the coast in international waters; I guarantee that. I said, "Well, what happened?" He said then they started to fly low, and we saw the Star of David and we waved at them and they looked at us. We figured they were just coming by to say hi and then all of a sudden the deck started to explode. And he did indicate to me this so-called airshow went on for an extensive period of time.

I flew them back to *America*, and apparently I did a lot of flying that day, because I've got seven flights on the ninth, and they total about six, seven, eight hours, which was a lot.

Bob has several more "descriptive photos that have never been published."

26

Davis

The deck was full of men. Some of them were milling about and some of them were lying down trying to sleep. They were scared to be belowdecks in case the ship went down. I stayed on the main deck to watch the miracle of sunrise when I noticed an unidentifiable ship on the horizon at our stern. Later, I found out it was Soviet and that it had been following us throughout the night. Then I saw two other ships coming up behind that one, moving fast. In due time I could see they were both U.S. destroyers. They closed the distance between us quickly and the next thing I knew, were almost on top of us. As the USS *Davis* (DD-937) and the USS *Massey* (DD-778) made their arrival, the Soviet ship left.

USS *Davis* (DD-937)

The destroyer was named after George Fleming Davis, who at 33-years-old was given command of the USS *Walke* (DD-723), a destroyer, in November, 1944. A little over a month later, while conducting minesweeping operations, *Walke* was attacked by four Japanese kamikazes.

Though two of the suicide planes were shot down, the third plane hit *Walke*, enveloping her bridge with burning gasoline. Commander Davis, though burned horribly, remained standing, commanded the ship, directed damage control, and led the destruction of the fourth kamikaze. He then relinquished his post and died a short time later. Davis was posthumously awarded the Medal of Honor and buried at sea.

Despite the fact it had not saved us from being attacked the day before, the crew of the *Liberty* was excited to see the red, white and blue flag of our beloved homeland being displayed on the other ships as they approached. Someone's voice came over the ship's intercom announcing that a destroyer was coming alongside us. The water was like a sheet of smooth glass—not a ripple to be found.

Bob remembered the day help finally arrived.

> On the morning of the 9th—USS *Davis* and the *Massey*— and I remember being topside and I could see the shape of the USS *America* at the horizon; the ship was so big you could see it. I felt some relief that somebody was finally coming to our assistance, and I still could not believe, and we were saying it to each other, "What the hell? Where's our help? Who's coming to help us?"
>
> That's something that I'll never get over. I'll never get over the fact that they sent nothing, no one. No planes to help us, nothing. And for 18 hours we floated around trying to get away from that area that we were dead in the water. We didn't know what the Israelis were gonna do.

The *Davis* came up alongside us until we were separated only by inches. They threw over about half a dozen lines and we caught them and tied the two ships together. As soon as they were wed, a plank was put in place and about 30 or 40 men of the Davis started boarding our ship.

The emotions of the *Davis* crew ranged from fury to devastation. Men cursed like sailors and cried like babies. Over and over we heard from them the apologies; that they would have given their family jewels to have been here to stop the carnage. Some of the *Davis* crew ran their hands over the holes in the ship's surface, shaking their heads in disgust and outrage. No one lost control though. As ambassadors of the United States of America, they remained orderly and professional, just as their training in the USN had imposed upon them.

Despite the fact there were no more bombs and bullets raining down on us, our situation was still just as dire as it had been during the massacre. Because of the torpedo blast, the ship was in such a state that it could break apart and sink at any minute. Since the crew of the *Davis* was there to help out with evacuating the wounded to the *America*, I was put back to work in bandaging the ship in any way possible. We got help from some of the damage control personnel serving aboard *Davis*, which was a really good thing. We had just been through 18 hours of hell, so naturally, we were all exhausted.

Davis personnel brought over shoring equipment and other supplies we needed earlier but lacked. Lumber was brought on board the *Liberty* piece by piece.

We went belowdecks to assess the damage done by the torpedo and stood there, examining the walls as they bulged from the pressure of the seawater on the other side. It was—literally—an emergency situation. If those walls gave way, it would flood a barely-afloat ship with even more water and the fact was we couldn't take on even one more drop if we expected to stay above sea level.

What this meant then was bracing up those steel walls before they finally gave out, and doing it fast. There was no time for architects or structural engineers to do a long, drawn-out study of the situation and draw up blueprints.

All of us had grown up learning something about building and had heard the old phrase "measure twice, cut once" from our fathers and grandfathers many times.

We did this, but in a hurried fashion. Working side-by-side with men whom we had never met but who seemed like lifelong friends, we started the construction of our masterpiece. Timbers went high and low and diagonal. We made as many triangles as we could, since the triangle is one of the strongest shapes you can use in construction. We worked at a very fast pace, yet remained cautious and methodical.

In many ways it was like doing field surgery on someone who had just been hit—you had to stop the bleeding fast and get the wound covered before he bled to death, but you didn't have time to worry about making it pretty.

We could feel the warmth of the Mediterranean Sea on the bulkhead, as water dripped through the fractures in the wall caused by the torpedo explosion. We were aware—and terrified—of the fact that at any moment the wall could give way, resulting in us being swept into watery graves, just as our fellow crewmen had been the previous day.

As we worked, the *Davis* guys wanted to know about the massacre. The confusion on their faces was obvious when we described the Star of David flag on the MTB. They asked us again and again, "Are you sure it was Israel? Maybe it was the Arabs pretending to be them."

We assured them it was not the Arabs who had done this to America. A few guys were slow in coming to grips with the ugly truth that the culprit was indeed America's "only ally in the Middle East."

It is safe to say that the crewmen of the *Davis*, realizing that America had indeed been stabbed in the back by her "ally," now took it just as personally as we did.

Our work was directed by the Engineering Officer from the *Davis*, Lieutenant Paul E. Tobin, Jr., along with John Scott. Incredibly, Tobin was awarded a Bronze Star for his work in salvaging the *Liberty*, while many of the men who had actually been aboard the ship fighting off Israel's vicious assault received nothing. This is especially insulting when one looks at what the medal is awarded for: heroic achievement, heroic service, meritorious achievement, or meritorious service in a combat zone.

Our team was by no means the only one doing damage control. Since virtually every inch of the ship had been cut to pieces by Israel in some way, we had plenty to do. We all worked, busy as bees, doing field surgery on the battered ship *Liberty*. The operation lasted most of the day.

Larry J. Broyles, Sr., a member of the rescue, damage control and repair team aboard the *Davis* who boarded *Liberty*, has vivid memories of that day.

> I can still see all the dead, wounded, dying, mangled crewmembers and smell the death. When we opened sealed compartments we found many drowned fellow shipmates.
>
> I also vividly recall seeing the mess deck full of wounded and disfigured bodies and pans and pots full of flesh and pieces of bodies lying on the decks in several places and all the green bags with bodies and pieces of body remains placed in the reefers.
>
> Phil Tourney was one of the crew that was put in the forward hole to help shore the ballooned bulkhead that had cracks and leaks. *Davis*'s engineer gave us the order to shore the bulkhead or sink before we got underway to dry dock. The *Davis* crew and a couple of *Liberty* crewmen worked all night shoring that bulkhead with no escape route should the bulkhead give way. Our team shored up that bulkhead and came out of the hole the next morning at the light of day after the all-night shoring job was completed. Several of us thanked God for keeping us safe as we performed our duties. Believe me, we were especially glad just to breathe fresh air.

27

Geis

Dave Lewis was aboard *America*, having been medevaced off *Liberty* the day after the attack.

His company was requested by Rear Admiral Geis, who was in charge of the carrier group consisting of *America* and *Saratoga*. They met for about 30 minutes and discussed one thing.

> I was in sick bay. I'd been there a couple of days until they decided to lance my eyelids and [to find out] if I could still see. I was still covered with paint. It wasn't until the next day that the doctor called me in and said, "You've gotta stare straight at the scalpel and don't flinch. I'm cutting the paint off your eyeballs."
>
> When I could see, I found out that Admiral Geis had left word that I was to report to his cabin. His orderly came and picked me up and took me there. It was either the 11th or the 12th of June.
>
> He started off the conversation by saying that he's gonna have to swear me to secrecy, but he couldn't die without somebody knowing what had happened.
>
> He said the reason he requested me specifically was because I was the senior representative from the *Liberty* on board *America*.
>
> He said that as soon as they got the SOS, he launched aircraft. Apparently the ones that he launched were the ones

from *Saratoga*. At the time of the attack, the U.S. was having a nuclear weapons drill, throughout the military. And that's probably why he didn't launch any from the deck of *America*.

He said he launched aircraft, and almost instantly, McNamara came on the line and said, "Recall the aircraft."

So he reconfigured the flight of aircraft from *America*, with aircraft that were incapable of carrying nukes, and relaunched them, and McNamara again ordered them recalled. And he challenged the order.

He said people are dying out there. And that's when Lyndon Johnson came on and he said he didn't give a damn if the ship sunk, he would not embarrass his ally.

Dave was sure LBJ didn't mention Israel.

LBJ did not say Israel. It was obvious he knew who it was several hours before he was informed who it was. Geis said when they were recalled the first time, he figured some idiot back in Washington thought he had launched nuclear warheads, and that was the reason they were recalled.

Dave felt the same.

I was wondering what that idiot was thinking, McNamara, in order to do that, or Johnson. Nobody had come forward with any reasons at that point in time why they would have.

Dave said Geis didn't apologize.

No, he was just agonizing over what had come about and wanted someone to know that it wasn't his fault. He didn't want to go to his grave without somebody knowing that he had tried.

Dave explained why he broke his silence.

It was at our 20th reunion that I was talking to Admiral Moorer, who was retired then, and I mentioned that Admiral Geis had sworn me to secrecy. He said, "Well, Admiral Geis passed away last year, so you're no longer sworn to secrecy." And that's when I told people what Geis had told me.

Pro-Israel partisans attacked what Dave had revealed after 20 years.

I was accused of hallucinating and all sorts of things until the radioman in Port Lyautey came forward and admitted that he patched the call through from McNamara. The gentleman was scared to death when he heard who was on the line, so he got off the line.

Port Lyautey, now called Kenitra, is a city in northern Morocco. During the Cold War, the U.S. Naval Air Facility there served as a stopping point in North Africa.

28

Yellowstone

At the same time *Saratoga* was attempting to aid our ship, another U.S. Navy vessel was coming to our rescue. We didn't know this at the time, but found out just a short time ago. In fact, if it wasn't for the wife of a Navy vet, we, and the world, may have never been made aware of this hidden chapter of the attack on my ship.

Robert Thomas Erpelding, a Michigan native who enlisted in the Navy in 1966 at the age of 18, was serving as a deckhand aboard the USS *Yellowstone* (AD-27).

Bob explained his connection to the *Liberty*.

A couple of years ago my wife, Laura, said, "Did you ever know about the USS *Liberty*?" And I said, "No." She told me a little bit about what she had heard, and I said I was in the Med the same time. And then the bell rang. That's when I said, "Something was going on there."

She's the one that pushed me to contact Phil Tourney, but I kept telling her, "I don't have a story." It's not like I was involved in anything.

But Bob did have a story, a huge story.

The *Yellowstone*, nicknamed "Queen of the Tenders" and "Old Faithful," was a destroyer tender named for Yellowstone National Park, the second U.S. Navy vessel to bear that name.

A destroyer tender provides maintenance support to destroyers and other small warships. Due to technological advances, destroyer tenders no longer serve in the U.S. Navy. The last destroyer tender was the USS *Shenandoah* (AD-44), which was commissioned in 1983 and decommissioned in 1996.

USS *Yellowstone* (AD-27) alongside some submarines and destroyers

Bob recalled the day he heard our ship was attacked.

We were in Malta, and scheduled to go to Naples later, probably a week or two later, I think. They passed the word the ship was gonna get underway immediately. They got us underway, and we were going flank, about 14 knots probably.

It was my understanding we got about 10 to 15 miles from *Liberty*, and they told us to shut down and turn around. And we didn't think anything of it at the time. But we didn't go back to Malta, we went to Naples. I never thought about it. I served on a couple of ships afterwards.

> Knowing the Navy and the way the government works, they sent us back to Naples because *Liberty* was coming to Malta and they didn't want us to see it.

This is another heartbreaking episode of the cover-up of the massacre on my ship.

The "Queen of the Tenders" was just a few nautical miles away, and could have provided much-needed aid for our men and ship, but our own government ordered the *Yellowstone* to steam away from us instead of rushing towards us, forcing us to wait almost a full day for help to arrive.

Thank you, Laura and Bob, for coming forward with your story, which sheds more light on this shameful chapter of U.S. history.

29

Papago

B esides *Davis*, we had as guests in our little corner of the sea USS *Papago* (ATF-160), a USN tug boat built during WW2, serving the U.S. Sixth Fleet as a rescue, salvage, and towing ship, now providing escort and communication support for *Liberty*. *Davis* and *Papago* trailed behind us closely and yet at a safe distance, ready to help if something went wrong.

USS *Papago* (ATF-160)

Papago, with their 68-man crew, let us know debris had floated out of the hole, and in the interest of not losing anything else, someone decided it might be best to do something. The ship came to a stop and some *Papago* divers put a type of net over the hole and secured it with ropes that went completely over and under the ship. As soon as we started moving however, the nets tore and the ropes broke.

We had to stop again and take the whole thing off because of the danger of the nets and ropes getting caught in the propeller, something that would have brought our journey to a halt real quick. So, debris, and undoubtedly bodies and body parts, continued to escape through the massive hole.

I found out later *Papago* fished three corpses out of the sea. As James Scott explained in *The Attack on the Liberty*, the scene was something out of a horror movie.

> At 9:41 Sunday morning, *Papago* sailors spotted the first body floating in the sea. The men alerted the bridge and the tug slowed to idle. Navy diver Ensign John Highfill slipped into his wet suit, climbed overboard, and stroked out to the body on the sea's surface. Far out in the Mediterranean, the water was warm and clear.
>
> Highfill noted that the body floated face down. When he approached within 10 feet, he paused, unsure of what the body might look like. The sailor had been in the water for three days, first trapped in the *Liberty*'s flooded compartments and now floating freely in the sea. Highfill held his breath and ducked beneath the surface to look.
>
> The scene stunned him. A piece of shrapnel had hit the sailor in the back of the head. The exit wound had caused his face to explode. Peering through his mask, Highfill saw what looked like the man's brains and skin hanging down in the water. It reminded him of jellyfish tentacles. He eyed the rest of the sailor's body and noted the man's left arm was missing, leaving only a piece of jagged bone.
>
> Highfill had no other options: he reached out and grabbed the bone. The diver turned and paddled back, towing the sailor by his bone. When he reached the *Papago*, deck crews lowered a metal litter. Highfill floated the body onto it and at 9:55 A.M., the body left the water. That afternoon

at 1:36 P.M., the *Papago* pulled alongside the *Liberty* and transferred the remains.

Papago searchers spotted a second body at 6:39 P.M. that evening floating down the starboard side of the tug. Many of the sailors had just settled into the tug's mess deck to watch Jane Fonda and Lee Marvin in the 1965 western comedy *Cat Ballou*.

When the bridge again called man overboard, sailors slipped into life jackets and headed topside. Petty Officer Third Class Kit Rushing watched from the upper deck as Highfill swam out and retrieved his second body of the day.

The crews lowered a litter into the water and then hoisted the body out at 6:53 P.M. The body thudded onto the deck. The dark skin led Rushing to conclude the dead sailor was black.

Only when a *Papago* corpsman bent over and unfastened the man's dungarees did the young radioman realize he was wrong. He stared down at the man's bright white stomach. Oil coated the parts of the body not covered by his uniform. In the water, the challenge magnified. "You couldn't grab anything except the hair or the collar and swim with them," Highfill recalled years later. "Everything was just greasy."

The corpsman on deck yelled the dead sailor's name to the bridge, where a signalman flashed the information to the *Liberty*. Sailors retrieved a body bag and zipped the remains inside.

Crews hauled the body to the ship's refrigerator, where vegetables had been cleared to make room. Searchers spotted the third and final body at 4:44 P.M. the next day. Eighteen minutes later, divers retrieved the body, this one unidentifiable.

Missouri native Ronald A. Thomas, a 20-year-old Third Class Engineman and *Papago* crewmember, made contact with me on November 28, 2015, and explained what he remembered about the attack, the first *Papago* sailor to do so.

> We were in the Mediterranean in 1967 towing targets when we got the SOS that the *Liberty* was attacked, and we set out full speed ahead to come to their aid. It took us about 20 hours to get there.
>
> It was a devastating scene to behold. That torpedo hole was so big; about 40 feet in diameter. The ship was listing in the water, to the starboard side I believe, about 15 degrees. We had to lay back and pick up bodies out of the water.
>
> Oh, lord, it was terrible. I remember just crying to myself when we picked up the first person. We weren't expecting nothing like this to happen; we were out there just to tow targets, and all of a sudden we're at war.

Ron told me what the *Papago* crew did with the bodies of my fallen shipmates.

> We took all our food out of one freezer and put the bodies in body bags and put them in there. It was a hard thing to do. There were body parts and pieces. We pulled up to the side of the *Liberty* to render aid and to hand over some of the bodies that we picked up. Lord have mercy, just thinking about it brings back a lot of memories. Oh, it was just terrible.
>
> A few days after we got to dry dock, we handed over all the bodies and classified materials that we had picked up out of the sea. It was very difficult, I remember that. It was terrible. I've never seen such devastation in my whole life.

Ron explained the cover-up that took place on *Papago*, eerily similar to what had happened to me.

> A few days before we left *Liberty*, they had all of us sailors from *Papago*, a few of us at a time, they took us over into town, back in this room, and told us that we were never to talk about this, ever. What we saw and what we did we could never tell anybody, or we would be court-martialed, fined, thrown in prison, whatever, just to put a deadly scare on us.

I asked Ron, looking at *Liberty* as he did, if there was any way in the world that he believed that it was some kind of an accident, considering the damage they did.

> Oh, no, it was very deliberate. All those rocket holes and all that napalm, and blood running down the side of the ship, oh, it was terrible. I just knew we were going to war.
>
> When we entered that area, I remember the captain coming over the PA system saying, "We don't know how we're gonna come out on this." He said, "Pray to your God." It was awful, that's all I can say. What I saw was very devastating and it affected me very much, and it still does today.

James M. Makris, a 20-year-old New Hampshire native, and a friend of Ron's, was a deckhand aboard *Papago*, assigned there in the summer of 1966.

> I remember going to GQ when we first heard about the attack, and we changed direction and headed right to them. I was on deck. I was a lookout. The *Liberty* sent out an SOS and all the ships that were in the Mediterranean at the time received it, and certain ships were deployed directly to their assistance, and we were one of them.

We weren't the fastest ship on the ocean, however, being a sea-going tug, so we got there later in the day. The initial rescues had been done, and it was just a matter of us picking up the pieces afterwards, which we did. We were responsible to pick up classified material that had floated out the side of the ship from the torpedo strike, as well as body parts were floating out and incomplete people.

On the fourth day after the sailors' bodies became deteriorated and bloated up, they started floating out of the torpedo hole.

As all this was happening, we were being drilled by any of the superior officers on the ship to put the cameras away, don't take pictures, don't talk about it, don't ask questions. Just do what you're told. It was a constant reminder. If anybody had pictures, you were supposed to turn in your pictures to the superior officers.

I served two years on the *Papago*, and there was so much turmoil still going on a year after the incident, that they were transferring people to different ships to try to split them up.

Jim explained the cause of the turmoil.

Because they wouldn't let you talk about it.

It was a trying time for anybody to see that. We followed *Liberty* to Malta where she went into dry dock for repairs, and we stayed in Malta for roughly six weeks, and then *Papago* went on from there to escort *Liberty* back to the States.

While we were there with *Liberty* for six weeks, it was an eye-opener for me, seeing all the damage that was inflicted on her. The rocket holes, the strafing of the deck, the rocket holes in the side of the ship, the torpedo hole.

It was just amazing how any ship could withstand that kind of attack.

Jim recalled seeing the floating bodies.

I didn't see that body at first, until it was all the way out of the torpedo hole. Later, I don't know if it was the second or the third one, I was also on lookout, I spotted one of the bodies bobbing in the waves. The waves were not big, but they were probably three or four feet, anyway. You could see something coming up to the top and then following the wave action, which turned out to be another body.

I can't even begin to think how many people were involved with getting the dead sailors out of the water, because we had a deck crew of at least a dozen men, and everybody was there helping.

When the first body was recovered, I was on lookout. I helped retrieve them. Bodies would float up and we would try to get it in a net. I remember one particular individual where only half the body was coming up. The other half wasn't there.

And this man's skin came off in my hands. He had already been dead for four days. And he was one of three identifiable people that we recovered by following *Liberty*. There were others that were recovered right away, by *Davis*, I think, or one of the other ships.

Jim voiced his thoughts on the attack, whether he believed it was a case of mistaken identity, as Israel claims, or if it was deliberate.

There's a lot of people that don't believe that Israel would ever do such a thing. We were monitoring the Six-Day War and Israel didn't want us there and they attacked us. And we should've blown 'em off the map at that time but we didn't.

Navy brass inspect *Liberty*'s damage in Malta

30

Kidd

We were attacked on a Thursday, and four days later we were paid a visit by two-star Admiral Isaac Campbell Kidd, Jr., whose father, Rear Admiral Isaac Campbell Kidd, was killed on the bridge of the battleship USS *Arizona* (BB-39)—along with 1,176 others—during the Japanese attack on Pearl Harbor. After a Japanese bomb detonated ammunition on the ship, the *Arizona* exploded and sank, and still lies at the bottom of the Hawaiian harbor. Kidd, the highest ranking casualty at Pearl Harbor, became the first USN flag officer killed in action in WW2, as well as the first killed in action against any foreign enemy.

Captain Isaac Campbell Kidd, photographed aboard USS *Argonne* (AS-10), circa 1931

Kidd was brought over by the USS *Fred T. Berry* (DDE-858) and we assumed he had come aboard the ship to show his support for the crew and what we had endured.

USS *Fred T. Berry* (DDE-858) Grand Harbor, Valletta, Malta, 19 days after the massacre aboard *Liberty*

The *Fred T. Berry* was named after USNA graduate Fred Thomas Berry, a U.S. dirigible commander born in 1887, who began training in dirigibles, and was lost at sea in the 1933 crash of the airship USS *Akron* (ZRS-4). The airship was destroyed in a thunderstorm off the coast of New Jersey, killing 73 of the 76 crewmen and passengers, making it the greatest loss of life of any airship crash.

USS *Akron* (ZRS-4)

Kidd assembled the officers and senior enlisted men first and began interrogating them about what happened. I was not privy to how these interrogations progressed. In fact, I never assumed I would be involved in any questioning since I was just a junior NCO. As far as I was concerned, the officers and senior NCOs were all together talking about it. Being the brains of the operation meant they would do their thing while we enlisted men did ours. That's just the way it is in the military. As far as officers were concerned, we enlisted were like children—we should be seen and not heard.

I continued with my Sounding and Security detail which included reporting to the bridge every hour and giving a report to Captain McGonagle concerning the ship's condition. I made my way to the bridge to give my report and immediately upon arriving I saw that something was wrong. Captain McGonagle's demeanor was completely foreign: he was short, curt, off-balance, irritated and anxious.

My first thought was that having a two-star admiral on board after the ship was attacked had him on edge, as if he thought that might result in something negative coming his way or toward his career.

McGonagle had joined the Navy during WW2, and prior to coming aboard *Liberty* he had done multiple shore duties as well as commanding several ships. When he had taken command of *Liberty*, he was already a full commander; the equivalent of a lieutenant colonel in either the Army or Air Force. The rumor aboard ship was that he had been passed over twice for promotion to captain—the equivalent of full colonel in the aforementioned branches—indicating that the Navy was planning to retire him and that this would be his last ship.

Now, the change in his demeanor made me very uncomfortable, especially at a time when I was still in a certain amount of shock because of what we'd just been through. Like a kid who sees an unexplained change in the behavior of his mom or dad, there was an unease that came over me. I ran into some of the other officers and senior NCOs and noticed they were different as well; "sullen" is the best word to describe them, and after that, "bitter" and "confused."

The next day, Monday afternoon, I was summoned to sick bay. I reported as ordered and saw that four or five other sailors were there already. My first thought was that maybe we had done something wrong and had gotten a call to report to the proverbial principal's office.

Ten minutes later, the door swung open and in marched Admiral Kidd, a medium-sized man with a double-chin. A voice called out,

"OFFICER ON DECK!" and we stiffened up and stood at attention as was routine. Kidd shut the door behind him and spoke in a kind fatherly voice.

> Relax fellas, you have no reason to fear me. In fact, I'm going to take off my stars.

Admiral Isaac Campbell Kidd, Jr.

He took them off and tossed them on the metal table, resulting in a high, metallic "ping" sound. As soon as his stars were off, he was—officially speaking—not an officer anymore. Continuing in his fatherly demeanor towards us, he spoke humbly.

> Gentlemen, I am trying to piece together what happened, and I can't do it without you. I know you know I'm a flag admiral, but right now I am here to congratulate you and to let you know that your testimony is very, very important to me and my staff. I know that since the attack

you fellas have had a lot of time to reflect about what happened and this is what I want to dig out of you. I'm not an admiral anymore, I am just like you—a third class petty officer or a seaman recruit. Feel free to speak up with anything you think is important. Also, this is off the record, so I want you to speak freely.

With great relief, we all started to breathe normally now, feeling that the weight of the world had just been taken off our shoulders. A flag admiral talking like this and treating you as an equal was nothing I experienced before.

He asked if any of us were in damage control, and I raised my hand, and he informed me I would be the last to be questioned.

He dealt with each of us individually. In his hand was a pen as he wrote things down on a yellow legal pad like lawyers use. His first question was whether or not we had seen any markings on the recon aircraft surveilling us the morning of the attack. All answered in the affirmative. Then he questioned each of my shipmates one at a time.

What about the attacking aircraft, were there markings? Did you see the MTBs? Did you see MTBs machine-gunning life rafts? Are you sure the U.S. flag was flying?

They all answered that there were no markings on the planes, that an MTB was flying the Star of David and that they machine-gunned the life rafts and that yes, they were all sure the U.S. flag was flying.

I started to get excited because he was asking all the questions that a cop would ask right before he went after the bad guys.

Then, Kidd came to me. Seeing how well he had treated the other guys encouraged me and made me feel like I should tell it all, which I did. I told him exactly everything I had seen, which was a lot, considering my duties in Sounding and Security and Damage Control. I described everything I had witnessed—the surveillance flights, the attacks, the fires, the wounded, the life rafts being shot up, the U.S. flag flying and everything. Throughout my description, he never interrupted me once.

When I had finished, the feeling was great. We all had opened up our hearts and souls to this man, who for all intents and purposes was like a father to us at that moment. How proud we were that we could confide in him, just as sons feel who know their dad is there looking out for them.

Then, without warning, his face changed; it went from pale to red, almost as if he got an instant sunburn, and his attitude changed as well, and he asked us one last question.

Is there anything else anyone wants to say?

Buoyed on by the fatherly way he had treated us and letting my sense of trust in him guide me, I raised my hand with a single question.

Sir, why didn't we get any help?

I saw immediately that this did not sit well with him at all.

Without answering my question, he walked over to the stainless steel table onto which he had tossed his stars an hour or more earlier and put them back on his collars.

The pins slipped easily into the same holes from which they had come, indicating he had done this many times before. As soon as the stars were in place—perfectly, just as they had been when he had entered the room—he spoke directly and I would say, threateningly. Dr. Jekyll had now become Mr. Hyde.

> Ok fellas, now I'm an admiral again and I want each and every one of you to understand something. We're talking about national security here, not your personal feelings, not what you did or did not do. I could really give a shit about any of that.
>
> You listen to me once, because this is the only time you're ever going to hear it. You are NEVER to repeat what you just told me to ANYONE—not your mother, your father, your wife—ANYONE, including your shipmates. You are not to discuss this with anyone, and especially—

ESPECIALLY—not with the media, or you will end up in my little prison, or worse.

As he said the word "worse" he scowled. His face turned into a mask of hatred and rage. He presented it to each of us personally, one at a time.

On June 8, 1967 I had come face-to-face with the devil over the course of the massacre and now I was looking into the eyes of the devil yet again in the person of Admiral Isaac Kidd. Who else but Satan himself could have moved a man to do what he had just done— not just to us, but to America?

It may sound like drama on my part, but now, 50 years later, I know in my gut that he hated the fact we were standing in front of him alive and breathing.

He started out of the room, stopping to look back at us. We were standing there in the same relaxed mode which he had encouraged us to adopt when the interrogation began. Now he seemed to be offended that we had not come to attention as he was leaving.

"ATTENTION ON DECK!" I shouted, fearing that if we didn't stiffen up, he might kill us and throw us overboard right there.

He opened the door himself—gently. But before leaving, he turned his entire body in our direction and stared at us for as long as 15 seconds. I thought I might piss in my pants, I was so scared. Then after finishing his glare, he stepped through the door and slammed it, so hard that the steel-on-steel sounded like a bomb had gone off in the room.

We stood there at attention for a few seconds, unable to speak or think. We didn't know if he was coming back through the door or maybe listening outside, waiting to catch us disobeying the orders he had just given us regarding our silence.

As we stood there, still hearing the reverberations of Kidd screaming at us and slamming the door, you could have heard our hearts breaking. We wailed out from within our souls, knowing and yet not knowing that the rest of our lives would be a nightmare.

I didn't know it at the time, but bringing us in small groups was a deliberate maneuver on Kidd's part. He wanted to scare us and knew it would be easier if we were few in numbers. Had we been in there with 20 other guys, we would not have felt so helpless.

After Kidd left, I walked over to the door he had just slammed shut and beat my hands against the steel bulkhead as hard as I could. They exploded with pain, but the pain was refreshing because it let me know I was still alive. What I was saying with my fists that I could not say with my mouth was, "FUCK YOU, ADMIRAL, SIR! MY LIFE AND THE LIVES OF MY SHIPMATES MEAN SOMETHING, SO FUCK YOU, SIR! GET IT?!"

And in that instant I lost all respect for authority. I lost my respect for the Navy. From then on, although I would salute as required, what I would be thinking within the confines of my own mind would be, "KISS MY ASS, SIR." As far as I was concerned they were—all of them—accomplices to cold-blooded murder, and the worst part was they knew it. This is not the mark of a leader; it is the mark of a coward and a traitor. It was not just Admiral Kidd, but also his boss, Admiral McCain, and his bosses, Secretary of Defense Robert Strange McNamara and President of the United States Lyndon Baines Johnson.

I thought about Mom telling me the story of her people, the American Indians, who had been forced to walk their trail of tears and whose lives were cheap and expendable, and now I realized that my life, too, was cheap and expendable.

It was on that day, when realizing that my country was gone and had been taken over by a foreign, hostile force, that my heart broke and marked the beginning of my own trail of tears which has lasted to this day.

Glenn recounted his time with Admiral Kidd, something that has never been released publicly.

It was either late morning or early afternoon on the 12th that we had this muster. I would have to say that 90% of us were still in shock, but we mustered on the deck of the ship. They kept saying over the 1MC, "EVERYONE ON THE SHIP, MUSTER ON THE FORECASTLE OR THE AFT DECK."

Officer George Golden was doing a head count, trying to make sure that everyone who was still alive on the ship was gonna hear this address from Admiral Kidd. They said the admiral was gonna speak to everybody but we had to make sure we had everybody on the ship.

After 20 minutes they finally decided they had everybody who could walk on the ship.

The admiral approached us and he spoke.

"I'M GONNA YELL REAL LOUD SO EVERYBODY CAN HEAR ME."

Then he took his stars off his collar and continued.

"I'M GONNA TELL YOU GUYS THAT I DON'T EVER WANT TO HEAR ANYONE TALKING ABOUT THIS, BECAUSE IF YOU GUYS TALK ABOUT THIS, I'LL MAKE SURE YOU'RE COURT MARTIALED, AND IF YOU'RE IN CIVILIAN LIFE I'LL MAKE SURE YOU'RE IN PRISON. YOU SHOULD NEVER, EVER TALK ABOUT THIS TO ANYONE."

It took less than five minutes. I didn't see him again until we got to Malta, where I saw him walking around on the ship several times.

31

Malta

When we were two days away from our destination, the scuttlebutt was we were headed for the island of Malta, into dry dock.

The Malta Dockyard in Valletta, the capital, has an incredible history.

The island of Malta

The Sovereign Military Order of Malta, founded in 1099 in Jerusalem during the Crusades, established dockyard facilities to maintain their galley fleet, using marble blocks from one of the Seven Wonders of the Ancient World to construct these docks. In 1800, Malta became a British protectorate, and a dry dock was planned. Begun in 1844 and opened three years later, it was extended to form a double dock in 1857. Five more dry docks were constructed from 1861 to 1909, and in 1959, the dockyard was handed over to a civilian firm.

After the firm was evicted by the Maltese government, the dockyard was closed as a naval base, with the Royal Navy withdrawing completely in 1979. A workers' council then managed it from 1987 to 1996, repairing civilian ships.

I didn't know it at the time, but Malta was chosen for a specific reason.

As Don Engen, captain of *America*, explained in *Wings and Warriors*, Malta was the perfect location to keep Washington's and Tel Aviv's crimes under wraps.

> Valletta was chosen as the port to assess damage and to administer those repairs needed to return to the United States, principally because it was remote and the British still had not left the major shipyard there.

This would be our first time there. The only thing we knew about it was that it was a small island in the Mediterranean that was very Catholic. To say we were looking forward to putting our feet on solid ground is an understatement. Our anticipation made the hours creep by even slower.

We knew we were headed there for repairs, and we also knew once we docked we would be going down into the CT spaces and getting the guys out, or at least what was left of them.

Out of the original crew of 294—after all the dead and wounded had been airlifted off—only about one-third remained. The few left whom I trusted—Brummett, Smith, Aimetti, and Demori—and I would get together and talk about what Kidd had done to us. We always made sure to be careful with what we said, where we said it and who was around.

Kidd had literally put the fear of—I don't want to say "God" here, because I know God had nothing to do with this evil thing—something in us for sure. One of the many things we agreed on was the feeling that we had all been treated as if *we* were the criminals instead of the people who had attacked us. I have heard stories about women being raped, and how the newspapers and others would suggest it was their fault because they were "provoking" the attack with their dress and demeanor. Now to a certain extent, I understood a little bit of how it felt to be a woman who experienced such a thing.

Remember, relatively speaking we were just kids at the time. We didn't understand all this business involving geopolitics and complex strategies. As young enlisted men, ours was a very simple worldview. There was good and there was evil and if you didn't want bad things to happen to you, you made sure not to do bad things.

Furthermore, we were America. We had fought the bad guys and won every time. The idea that our government—and more importantly the president, the progeny of George Washington himself—could conspire with the enemy, or be the enemy, was unthinkable, making this perplexity all the more difficult to handle in our young minds.

Ironically or not, my two best friends aboard the ship, Aimetti and Demori, were both full-blooded Italians. Italians are well-known to have an easily-pushed "pissed-off button." In the case involving Kidd, their anger was easy to see. More importantly, it was infectious and therefore easily passed on to other crewmembers.

After Kidd did his "thing" to us, we knew we had fallen into something big, but we did not know how big. Now, half-a-century later, we know a lot more than we did then.

We certainly don't know the whole story, but the one thing we learned above all else is that what Israel wants, Israel gets, and everyone else—including the American servicemen killed on June 8, 1967 (as well as those who have been killed fighting Israel's wars in the Middle East today) can just go to hell.

As we sat there, the three of us, letting our anger boil up to the surface, we made a pact that if possible, we would stay with the ship and see her home.

The rest of the trip to Malta was uneventful. Then, on Wednesday morning, like something out of an epic movie, we could see land far off in the distance. That we had made the 1,200 miles trip in six days without going down was just another of the many miracles that took place surrounding this whole thing. Minute by minute, the ship got closer and closer as the island got bigger and bigger. The next thing we knew, we were preparing to enter dry dock, The gates of the dock opened like the inviting arms of a beautiful woman, we were guided in and the doors closed behind us.

USS *Liberty* in Malta

It was a special day for Glenn.

> One of the best birthday presents I ever got was when we arrived in Malta on June 14, my birthday, and I got my feet on solid ground. That was a wonderful feeling.

Our superiors had warned us not to talk to anyone in Malta, nor to wear our uniforms when we went ashore, even so far as saying if we had our uniforms on for official business, to remove our USS *Liberty* patches that were sewn into them.

Divers from *Papago* got suited up and jumped in the water next to us. They stretched a large canvas across the torpedo hole to prevent debris, dead bodies and body parts from floating out. Underneath the ship, huge wooden blocks were placed so that when the water was drained from the dock, the ship would rest above the floor with enough space for a man to walk underneath if he hunched down.

The Maltese dock workers, who we referred to as "yardbirds," because they worked in a Navy yard, put 12-inch-by-12-inch wooden timbers up as braces against the side of the ship to keep it from tipping over once she came to rest on those blocks. When all the preparations were made and double-checked, they started the pumps and the water began receding. The ship sank, but not that far because of the huge wooden blocks placed below us. Finally, there was no more water around us.

The canvas over the torpedo hole began to bulge with the debris it was holding back. We could see the slimy mixture of water and fuel oil pouring out. I watched, leaning over the side of the ship as they released the canvas.

Because of the fact that the debris included highly classified documents and communications equipment that were the property of the NSA, the CTs were sent down there to retrieve them. Luckily, I did not see any body parts down there. However, just because I did not see them does not mean they weren't there.

For the first time, we could see how big that hole was. I stood there, speechless as I considered its size. We all stood in an almost perfectly straight row at the ship's edge, leaning over the steel railing—saying nothing—in awe. How we had managed to stay afloat with something that big should be counted as one of the wonders of the world, yet we were forbidden from even mentioning it to anyone, and once we saw that torpedo hole it made the picture of what Israel did to us complete.

There should have been cussing at the sight of the size of that hole, but by that time we were simply worn out. As a result, our mood was very subdued. I could not make out what they were saying down there on the floor of the dock, but by their body language I knew they were just as amazed as the rest of us.

The workmen rechecked the timbers holding the ship in place. Once they were sure everything was safe and there was no danger of the ship falling over, the gangplank was lowered to the floor of the dry dock so that men could go down and inspect the damage.

Like a line of ants marching in unison, I saw them come down, all wearing the khaki uniforms of U.S. naval officers. Hours went by quickly and darkness soon overcame us, and I rested uneasily that night. Most of the other guys insisted upon sleeping above deck because of the smell below.

32

Rome

The next morning, I prepared for a full-day's work. I dressed up in a clean uniform despite the fact I knew I would be up to my elbows in some pretty dirty work.

As soon as I got dressed, in walked Lieutenant Golden, who informed me I had just won an all-expense paid trip to Italy for a few days, courtesy of Uncle Sam. There was no reason and no warning, and they sweetened the deal by telling me it wouldn't count against my leave time. I assumed it was as an "atta boy" for all the hard work I had done before, during and after the attack.

The truth is, and this is the God's honest truth, it took everything I had in me, all my training and discipline to keep from saying, "NO SIR. I AM NOT LEAVING THIS SHIP." But I knew this was not an option and was not about to dishonor or disrespect Golden. I loved and respected him like I loved and respected few people on the planet.

I followed my orders and got on the plane waiting for me. I headed to Italy, wondering if I would ever see my ship again.

The trip to Naples was quick and therefore I didn't have much time to reflect on what just happened to me. I think at that time I was still in a state of shock, so thinking was not really an option anyway.

As soon as the plane landed and I exited in Naples, I wished like hell I could get back on that plane and go back to the ship where my duties were. That was where my "family" was, and my "family" had just suffered a terrible tragedy, and being a "family man" I felt I was needed at home.

I went with a buddy of mine who was one of the ship's corpsmen, basically a nurse. He was one of only three guys I knew of aboard the ship who was Jewish and who made his Jewish heritage known by wearing a gold Star of David necklace. He told me while we were in Rome he was terrified he would be thrown overboard after we learned it was Israel who attacked us. I told him it wasn't his fault, and the topic never came up again in Rome.

I had very little to eat since the attack, but now in Rome, one of the world's headquarters for delicious food, I sat down to what I was sure would be a good meal.

Dressed in civilian clothes—and not our uniforms, as we were usually required to be—we found a nice outdoor restaurant with tables and chairs on the sidewalk. Italian music was playing and in general the people there lived their lives as if at that moment there wasn't a care anywhere in the world to be considered. I ordered a plate of pasta—fettuccine, I think—with some tomato sauce and lots of meatballs.

As I mentioned before, I always had something of a magnetic pull towards the Italian people, as my best friends Rick and Dulio can testify, and here in Italy it was no different. I found Italians to be incredibly friendly and hospitable, especially since as an American I stuck out like a sore thumb.

Literally starved, considering I had nothing substantive to eat in almost a week, I wolfed down the food like I was going to the electric chair. Then I sat there, stuffed from a wonderful meal nursed along with a glass of Italian red wine.

For a few minutes I forgot who I was and what I had just gone through. In that moment, I was like any of these other people who didn't have a care in the world. My stomach was full, there were beautiful women all around me everywhere I looked, and no one—that I knew of—was trying to kill me at that moment.

And then in a flash, the dream came to an end and reality came crashing down, just like our ship had when the torpedo hit, lifting us up out of the water and then back down again like a meteor striking Earth.

And I remembered I was a sailor in the USN, assigned to the ship USS *Liberty* that had just been attacked by the state of Israel—rockets, machineguns, napalm, torpedoes, my best friends with their limbs and guts literally blown all over the place, me fighting to stay alive while trying to save them, Admiral Isaac Kidd coming aboard and warning me that if I breathed a word of this to anyone he would see to it that life as I knew it would be over. And like a tidal wave, the guilt washed over me. Who was I to be enjoying myself like this, as my shipmates lay moaning in agony aboard *America*, fighting for their lives?

Then suddenly, without any warning, the memory of the smell of death and fuel oil came over me. There was no slow build-up of this thing, it literally hit me like a tsunami and I knew what was coming. I started to get up to head to the bathroom, but as I stood, I could feel the food I had just thoroughly enjoyed making its way back up. I thought I was going to pass out. Trying to concentrate on not falling over meant I could not devote any resources to keeping my chow down, and so, with mortifying embarrassment, I threw up all over the place.

I don't want to be too graphic, but it was like a firehose. I threw up all over the table and it even hit some of the people nearby. I fell back down into my seat, defeated in front of all the diners who had chosen to eat outside, about 10 packed tables. I felt bad for myself, but I felt bad for those around me, too. Who wants to eat when some guy has just shit through his mouth all over the place?

The maître d' and a team of assistants from the restaurant came up to me with a wet towel and a pitcher of cold water. The maître d' washed my face and mouth with the same care and respect that a nurse might give to a wounded man. The assistants cleaned up the whole mess I made by grabbing the corners of the table cloth, pulling it all towards the middle and picking everything up in one motion to carry it out.

I couldn't speak Italian but the maître d' spoke some English, so I asked him to please apologize to everyone for me. Through my delirium I told him as best I could that it was not his fault—it was nothing he had done with the food and that I would be willing to pay for anyone's dinner ruined by my accident. His response was gracious, one of the characteristics I've always loved about Italians: "You are a patron here sir, our guest, and there is no reason for you to be embarrassed."

I wanted to pay for everything, but they would not let me. They wouldn't even let me leave a tip. There was not an unkind word or glance hurled my way from anyone, despite the fact I had just ruined quite a few peoples' evening with my little performance.

The smell of my vomit was powerful, no doubt, but was still not enough to overcome the smell of my dead shipmates that would not leave my nostrils or my memory.

We headed back to our room; I wanted nothing but sleep. More than sleep though, I wanted to wake up aboard *Liberty* again, because that was where I belonged. As beautiful as Rome was and as much as I loved Italians, I simply didn't belong in paradise; at least not right now, or perhaps never. I belonged with my shipmates, and every minute I spent away from them added to my fears that I would not see them again. I couldn't help but think that every minute I spent away from them was a sin I would have to answer for later, before God or someone else.

Several days later, to my great relief, I was finally getting on a plane for Malta. When I got on board, I prayed I was heading back to my ship and not somewhere else. I started fearing that Admiral Kidd might have pulled a fast one and now they were going to send me from the paradise of Rome to the frigid hell of Antarctica. I prayed and prayed, and getting no response from God, I decided to ask the captain of the plane directly, since in those days the cockpits were open to the whole cabin. I let him know I needed to get back to Malta, where my ship and my "family" were.

He was an American pilot, and in the same confident, relaxed demeanor typical of American pilots, his response to me was, "Don't worry about it sailor, that's where you're headed."

33

Recovery

Only later did I learn why I was sent to a foreign country where few spoke English. After the plane landed in Malta, I took a cab from the airport to the dry dock, carrying nothing except my bag. As I approached the ship, I could see the wounds she sustained, and with each step the wounds got bigger and uglier. I stood in awe of the damage and actually had to remind myself that I had been aboard that ship when all this had taken place.

I reached the point where I was ready to board. I did the regulation saluting of the flag at the stern and then turned towards the CPO who was the OOD at the time and said, "Request permission to come aboard, sir."

Permission was granted and I stepped on board, glad to be home. The first thing I wanted to do was get together with some of the guys and talk, and I hooked up with Jim Smith.

As soon as I got together with Smitty, he gave me an earful. While I was gone they had gone through the gruesome task—as he described it—of body recovery/identification of the fallen heroes in the CT spaces. As he recounted it, men were trapped behind bulkheads and wrapped around steel beams in a scene not unlike what happens in the American Midwest after a tornado blows through and tears everything up. He said the bodies—despite having been young and virile—looked like they had aged 80 years. Their skin was bleached white and their heads were hairless. Some of them were without clothes as a result of being trapped inside a giant washing machine for almost a week while being sloshed back and forth in the warm salt water. He ended it by saying some of the men's bodies were intact and some were in pieces.

At the time, Smitty was the only one I knew who had been involved in the horrible task of body recovery/identification. Years later I would befriend Ron Kukal, who was in charge of the whole gruesome business. What details I had not learned from Smitty that day, I learned from Ron. What he told me would make the most nauseating Hollywood movie look like an episode of Captain Kangaroo.

Sifting through the wreckage in dry dock

His job was to piece together the arms, legs, hands, heads, eyeballs, ears and everything else in the attempt at rebuilding what had once been a man. It was greasy, oily, smelly and horrible. He talked about trying not to dishonor our fallen shipmates by stepping on their body parts.

His job was to try—TRY—to put them back together in such away so their loved ones back in America could give them a respectable burial.

Ron has experienced some memory loss, perhaps due to his proximity to the torpedo blast or as a way to not remember what he saw.

I know that I did it but I can't tell you the specifics very well.

Ron explained how he got assigned to body recovery/identification.

> After the attack when we were headed to Malta, they
> made the decision to recover the bodies, and one of the
> officers, and I don't remember which one it was, caught
> me in a passageway and said, "You're gonna be on the
> body recovery team. And you'll be the enlisted man in
> charge, the senior ranking noncom down there."

Ron admits he wanted nothing to do with it.

> I did everything I possibly could to try to get out of that;
> everything. I didn't wanna do it.

The operation to recover and ID the bodies began about a week
after the attack.

> After we got into dry dock and they drained the water out
> and got the ship stabilized, we went down below. I think
> the first day of body recovery might've been the 14th or
> 15th of June. We started about 7:30 in the morning and
> I think we knocked off around 4 o'clock, somewhere in
> that area.
>
> I was on the deck where a lot of the bodies were and
> another deck down, there were more bodies, so everybody
> was bringing them up to me and I was trying to put them
> together like a jigsaw puzzle.
>
> We had to recover our own men; 25 down below and
> nine topside. Many of them were in pieces and putting
> them together to make a recognizable man was next to
> impossible.
>
> Had it not been for the names that were imprinted on their
> shirts and trousers, I don't think we could have done it at
> all.

We had a lot of parts that we couldn't identify and all of them were placed inside a body bag and sent to Arlington National Cemetery.

The recovery itself lasted three days. And that's a guess.

Don was a CT, so he was part of the body recovery crew, where early on he made a gruesome discovery.

Somebody picked up a piece of equipment and I remember seeing an internal part of a body like a liver or something like that.

Bob remembered to ghastly recovery operation.

The only people that could go down—collect the bodies from the torpedoed spaces—were people with a Top Secret clearance, and I was one of those guys. I wasn't so badly wounded that I couldn't go down and work and I just did so what I was told to do.

I went down and started collecting first the bodies and putting them in body bags and bringing them topside. I remember helping zip Bobby Eisenberg into a body bag. I just remember his eyes were wide open, and his eyes were blue. That was the worst experience of my life.

And I remember one body—whether it floated there or whatever—a big man was on top of a vent, and he was really lodged up there, there was no way to get that man down but to roll him off. It was horrendous.

I don't remember how long we worked down there.

Don had stepped into a house of horrors, coming upon my friend—or, a part of him—Phil Tiedke.

Well I just couldn't believe I found his arm, and of course it was all ballooned up because it had been soaked in salt water for a week. He was a bodybuilder, so the relative structure of the muscles, even though it was ballooned up, you could tell he had been a bodybuilder, a weightlifter.

Many years later, Don paid his respects to the man whose arm he found.

About six years ago, somehow I had found out, I don't remember who from, that someone had found Tiedke's obituary and it said he had graduated from Downey High School. Well Downey, California is just north from where I live about 20 miles. So I kept emailing the high school and emailing the high school. It took me almost a year, and finally I got somebody from the high school to answer me, and they said, "We have no record of a Phil Tiedke at this high school, but there's another Downey High School in Modesto."

So then I got a hold of the one in Modesto and found out, yes, that's where he went to high school. I also got a hold of the cemetery that it mentioned in the obituary, so about six months before my wife died we went up and I talked to one of the teachers at the high school, and then Eva and I went and visited his grave.

The Attack on the Liberty detailed some of the efforts of the body recovery team.

California native, 26-year-old officer Lieutenant JG [junior grade] Lloyd Painter, searched the torpedoed compartments for bodies.

Painter aimed his flashlight upward. Electrical wires and cables that once powered this secret intelligence hub now sagged from the ceiling. He froze. Wrapped in the wires, one of the dead officers, eyes open, stared down at him. Painter recognized his former colleague even though the remains were bloated from days in the salty seawater. Painter moved his flashlight down the length of the body. Only the head and torso remained.

The searchers easily located some of the dead. Other remains proved more difficult to find as the bodies often lay buried beneath piles of heavy debris or stuffed between steam pipes, the only clue a protruding hand or foot or the intense smell. Six days in the salty seawater had left the dead grotesquely swollen and distended. The skin had bleached white . . . and the hair largely had fallen out. "You'd puke, then go back at it," recalled Second Class Petty Officer Robert J. Schnell. "It had to be done."

Second Class Petty Officer Dennis Eikleberry spotted feet protruding from a pile of twisted metal. Eikleberry, who had been in a room across the hall when the torpedo exploded, let his eyes wander up the body, past the legs, torso, and arms.

Instead of a head, Eikleberry found only a long piece of skin that looked like string. Another body he found resembled hamburger meat. The smell was horrendous. "When they picked him up by the belt and the breastbone," Eikleberry recalled, "his arms fell off."

Though many of the bodies were largely intact, some of the recovered remains consisted of only decaying tissue and intestine littered amid teletype papers, tapes, and work manuals, much of it unrecognizable. "Not just arms and legs," recalled Seaman Don Pageler, "inside pieces of bodies and all sorts of stuff."

Recovery of the bodies concluded by the following day. The men continued to sift through piles of classified records, much of it little more than soggy mush, before zipping it inside 168 canvas bags for future sorting.

The canvas bags stayed on *Liberty* all the way to Virginia, where NSA employees sifted through them.

A team of NSA analysts visited the *Liberty* two days after it arrived in port to inspect the canvas bags stowed below deck. The agency demanded an inventory if possible of all surviving classified materials. The bags, stacked several high, held the remnants of key cards, manuals, and magnetic tapes that crews had shoveled up in Malta.

Liberty sailors with classified clearances slipped on coveralls, masks, and gloves inside the darkened compartment that morning. The men opened the duffle bags and emptied them one after the other onto the deck. A rancid smell filled the air. Some manuals contained legible material, but many others had been reduced to an oil-soaked pulp. One of the men spotted a finger.

"It was a nightmare," recalled John McTighe, a young Navy lieutenant who worked at the NSA. "It was just mush."

A final report on the effort was bleak.

Twenty remains have been shipped to Naples. It may not be possible to identify all 20. Bodies of five of the 25 originally reported missing have not been found. It is reasonable to assume that the five not found were lost at sea.

34

"Investigation"

I found out in the conversation with Smitty that while I was away in Italy, an "investigation" into the attack had occurred. As he was telling me this, things began clicking into place in my mind as to why I had been sent to Italy with no warning. It didn't make a whole lot of sense to send me hundreds of miles away just for the same R & R I could have gotten right there on the island without Uncle Sam footing the bill for airplane tickets, motel rooms, food and expenses. Furthermore, why would some lowly third class petty officer get the red carpet treatment somewhere else?

The only logical explanation was that they didn't want me there in Malta while this "investigation" was taking place.

As it turned out, I was in Rome the same six days the "official investigation" of the attack took place by the same khaki-wearing naval officers I had seen going up and down the gangplank a week earlier. As they were doing their investigation, there I was, one of the key witnesses to the attack, lollygagging in Rome, just as they wanted me to be.

I am sure now that it was my testimony to Kidd that was responsible for my Rome "vacation." I let him know exactly what I had seen and how I felt about all of it; especially the machine-gunning of the life rafts by the MTBs.

I am sure it was the life raft thing that did it more than anything else, because this was a war crime, according to the rules of the Geneva Conventions. My testimony concerning the life rafts was the only part of what I had told him that had not elicited any follow-up questions from him.

The Geneva Conventions—four treaties and three protocols—establish standards of international law for humanitarian treatment in times of war.

As Israel was—and still is—a party to the Geneva Conventions, it was—and is—bound by its obligations.

The Second Geneva Convention deals with the sick, wounded, and shipwrecked members of armed forces at sea, and multiple war crimes were committed by Israel that day.

The treaty consists of 63 articles, and just two of the articles illustrate how Israel violated the Convention: All parties to a conflict are required to protect and care for the wounded, sick, and shipwrecked, according to Articles 12 and 18.

Of the many "smoking guns" surrounding the events of that day, the shooting of the life rafts was a big one, and one not easily explained away. Israel's defense for the last almost five decades has been that the attack on our ship was all a case of "mistaken identity," an "accident."

As Dave said, "This was the best-planned accident in the history of the world."

The brains behind this operation knew this excuse might fly, except for the fact they had shot up the life rafts. No matter how much production they put into peddling the story about "mistaken identity," it would all be pushed into the background if revealed—by eyewitness testimony no doubt—that these bastards shot up our life rafts. No professional military does this. As I pointed out, it was a war crime, akin to shooting down men who have thrown down their arms and surrendered. The people who were putting together this cover-up knew they would never be able to make this thing believable if the life raft business was made public, and this was the reason why I was "Romed" for a week.

An investigation that "would take at least six months to conduct" was over and done with in just six days.

The bombing of the USS *Cole* (DDG-67) in 2000, with 17 murdered and 39 wounded, was investigated for nearly three months. *Cole* was ferried back to the U.S. in full view for the world to see her battle damage, and in 2007, a U.S. federal judge ruled that the Sudanese government was responsible for the bombing. No cover-up, no threats to the crewmen, nothing to hide, simply because it was not Israel who was implicated.

USS *Cole* (DDG-67)

By contrast, *Liberty* suffered 34 killed and 171 wounded—which would later rise to 174 since three survivors were overlooked for their Purple Heart awards—but its crew has been dealt only scorn and insults.

The Attack on the Liberty reveals the official "investigation" was a farce.

> Despite two days of often-gruesome testimony that would fill 158 pages of transcripts, the court failed to answer the central question: How and why did the attack happen? The Navy had tasked court members to examine all relevant facts.
>
> The final transcript, however, revealed a shallow investigation, plagued by myriad disagreements between the captain and his crew. Reconstructing the assault had proved challenging. No one wrote in the quartermaster's notebook for 51 minutes during the most intense part of the attack.

The bloodstained log jumped from the arrival of Ensign Patrick O'Malley on the bridge at 1:55 P.M. to [Ensign David George] Lucas's identification of one of the torpedo boat's hull numbers at 2:46 P.M. Thirty-four men had either been killed or mortally wounded in the interim.

The court recognized this weakness. After the first day of testimony, it asked McGonagle to gather with his officers and crew and assemble a concrete timeline to present to the court the next day. Even then the men's testimony clashed. Many of the officers said the court appeared afraid of uncovering information that might prove the Israelis deliberately targeted the *Liberty*. [John] Scott photographed the first reconnaissance flight at dawn the morning of the attack.

He believed he gave the court a "critical piece of information" that showed Israel had detected the *Liberty* almost nine hours before the attack. The court appeared uninterested, asking instead whether Scott had attended damage control school and whether he found it useful.

The court's final report dismissed his testimony, stating that reconnaissance flights began hours later than he said. Declassified Israeli records show the plane Scott observed was in fact the reconnaissance flight that first identified the *Liberty*. "It was all perfunctory," Scott later said of the court's interview. "The questioning was not probing or in-depth. It was all superficial."

Other officers who testified described the court as "shallow," "cursory," and focused on "process rather than product." The transcript shows that some of the witnesses testified for only a few minutes, if even that long.

The court asked [George] Golden, the *Liberty*'s chief engineer, only 13 questions, including such basic information as his name, how many years he had served in the Navy, and the cost of his waterlogged tape recorder.

Court members asked [CPO Carlyle F.] Lamkin, who fought fires on deck as the planes strafed the ship, just 11 questions and [CPO] Thompson only eight, ranging from whether he had attended damage control school to whether he was aware that a court had been convened to examine the attack. [Lieutenant JG Malcom McEachin] Mac Watson, another of the *Liberty*'s officers, was asked only five questions.

The court ignored other important details. No one followed up on [Lloyd] Painter's testimony that the *Liberty* sailed 17.5 miles from shore moments before the attack, a fact that clearly established that the *Liberty* was in international waters and well beyond the territorial limits of either Israel or Egypt. Another fact absent from the discussion was that the *Liberty*, attacked off the coast of Egypt, never approached within 38 miles of the Israeli coast.

The court also failed to explore the testimonies of Wayne Smith or Lamkin that the attackers jammed the *Liberty*'s communications, indicating possible foreknowledge of the ship's identity. James Halman, the radioman who made the calls for help, was available to testify, but the court never summoned him. The jamming convinced Halman that the Israelis knew the *Liberty* was an American ship.

Other crewmembers said the court deleted testimony unfavorable to Israel and the Navy from its published report. Lucas submitted a container of unburned napalm jelly that he scraped off the front of the *Liberty*'s superstructure after the attack.

Nowhere in the court's printed transcript or in any of its findings is that mentioned, though court members did ask the ship's doctor if he treated any napalm burns.

Painter's testimony that the torpedo boats machine-gunned the life rafts—witnessed by other crewmembers and recalled years later by Captain [Ward Boston, Jr., the Navy's Chief Legal Counsel for the Court of Inquiry]— also is absent from the court's final transcript. [Charles J.] Cocnavitch said he was ordered to report to the wardroom, sworn in, and asked about the abandon ship order he heard passed over the sound-powered phones. None of the radarman's testimony appears in the court's final record, nor is Cocnavitch even listed as a witness.

More importantly, the court failed to challenge Israel's story despite a directive "to inquire into all the pertinent facts and circumstances leading to and connected with the armed attack." The American government never forced Israel to produce its pilots, torpedo boat skippers, or commanders to testify. Likewise, the government never demanded that Israel submit its ship logs, flight books, or recordings of its pilot communications, all reasonable requests between allied nations.

The only evidence submitted on Israel's behalf were telegrams from Ernest Castle, the American naval attaché in Tel Aviv. These telegrams repeated Israel's claim that the *Liberty* was unmarked, acted suspiciously, and resembled an Egyptian cargo ship a fraction of the *Liberty*'s size. When shown one of these messages, McGonagle refuted it.

Kidd confessed years later that his superiors had handicapped the investigation. Israel had been off-limits. "Our Navy's Inquiry was tasked to paint but one part of the picture," the admiral wrote in a letter to one of the *Liberty*'s officers. "Any dealings with any other Nation or any like sources beyond our own people were precluded." Inside the *Liberty*'s wardroom that picture became clear to the testifying officers.

Many believed that the court was more interested in whether the *Liberty* and its crew had erred than what actually prompted the attack.

"The court didn't seem interested at all in who attacked us and why," recalled Painter, who described the court as a "sham." "It was all about whether we had done something wrong."

Despite contradictions in testimony, the witnesses agreed on one fact: the *Liberty* flew the American flag. Scott testified that he looked up at dawn to check the wind direction and saw the flag flying. Painter told the court he observed the flag later that morning and again right after the torpedo attack as he prepared life rafts in response to the abandon-ship order.

Golden recalled that after lunch, while sunbathing with McGonagle, he observed two recon flights circle the ship. When the latter plane buzzed the *Liberty*'s smokestack, Golden couldn't help but notice the flag.

"Was it extended?" the court's lawyer asked.

"Yes, sir," he replied. "There was a slight breeze blowing."

"And it was standing out where it could be seen?" the court pressed.

"Yes, sir," he answered. "Not completely the full length, but it was standing out."

Watson also told the court he saw the flag flying during lunch that afternoon. Like Golden, the young officer noted the wind was blowing while he tracked a recon flight as it zoomed over the ship's radar mast.

"Extended?" the court asked.

"Yes, sir," Watson replied.

Wayne Smith testified that during the attack he sprinted from the main radio room to the transmitter room in part so that he personally could check to make sure the flag was hoisted. Lucas recounted spotting it on the mast during the attack.

Even McGonagle, whose testimony differed from his men on other points, agreed with his crew that the *Liberty* flew the American flag. The skipper testified that when he first observed the torpedo boats approaching from about 15 miles away—long before the torpedo hit the ship—he ordered the signalman to hoist the *Liberty*'s largest flag.

[Lieutenant James George] O'Connor, who was en route to a military hospital in Germany to have his blasted kidney removed when the inquiry took place, later provided one of the clearest accounts of the flag at the start of the attack. He told officials at the NSA that an explosion knocked him to the deck of the flying bridge during the first strafing run. When he fell, he looked up to check the flag. "That question was in my mind," O'Connor recalled. "The American flag was up there and it was flying."

"It was not obscured by any smoke or any of that stuff?" NSA officials asked.

"No," O'Connor replied. "The flag was ahead of where the smoke stack was. We hadn't taken that many hits at that point."

"And there was enough wind to have it—"

"It was standing straight up."

Doc Kiepfer summed the "investigation" up nicely when he said:

Never before in the history of the United States Navy has a Navy Board of Inquiry ignored the testimony of American military eyewitnesses and taken, on faith, the word of their attackers.

USS *Liberty:* Torpedo hole above and below water views

35
Lipstick

Orders came down to patch our ship up and hide what had been done to her so that no one—back home or anywhere—would be any the wiser when we got home. In effect, we were forced to participate against our will in the cover-up of the deliberate, murderous attack on our ship.

To see the beating the *Liberty* took was beyond belief. The order came down from high up, and we were told to stop counting the rocket holes after we reached 850. Over 5,000 armor-piercing shells had pierced the skin of my ship, some holes running clear through her.

Repairing the ship basically meant cutting her into pieces, something that did not make any of us happy. Of course we knew the torpedo hole needed to be fixed—that was a matter of life and death—but as far as we were concerned, the rest of the holes needed to stay. Our feeling was that these holes were sacred wounds that needed to remain as a testimony to what was done. Erasing them was just another slap in the face to us and what we had endured.

If we had our way, we would have sailed the ship with all her battle wounds—as the *Cole* did into Pascagoula, Mississippi—into the harbor of the most populated city in America, with TV cameras as far as the eye could see, so that everyone would know what happened.

Deservedly so, the *Cole* got a memorial a year after she was attacked. We, the crew of the USS *Liberty*, are still waiting for our memorial, after nearly 50 years.

We tried protesting as much as we could without crossing any lines, but the mood from above was, "Shut up. Quit complaining. Patch the holes. Do your job. Captain says we're taking this ship home clean and mean."

And so, in the end, like gangsters working frantically to erase any evidence of their evil deeds by cleaning up the scene of a crime, we put the ship through an extreme makeover of sorts. The boys upstairs wanted to make damned sure that when *Liberty* came sailing back home, Israel's fingerprints had been wiped clean from the body.

With each hole I cut out of the skin of the *Liberty*, I felt I was degrading my dead and wounded shipmates, like I was part of the cover-up and was selling out both myself and America. I watched as each hole was removed and covered with a clean plate, welded in place, sanded and painted, to destroy all evidence of the vicious, unprovoked attack.

To make matters worse, Captain McGonagle's demeanor throughout all of this was straight-laced and one of total business. He had changed completely, almost as if he were one of those people in the movie *Invasion of the Body Snatchers*. In his case however, instead of his body being snatched it was his soul. As far as his demeanor went, it was like winter had arrived in the middle of summer. Now, our former captain was gone and replaced with someone more to the liking of Washington and Tel Aviv. I can only imagine what McGonagle got from Kidd after what we had received. It obviously destroyed him every bit as much as it did us. I found out later that Captain McGonagle was not who I thought he was.

To soothe our troubled souls, we headed ashore and frequented the local watering holes located in "Scum Alley," part of the town where all the bars were. Being that we were docked and not at sea, our work days were cut in half, which meant we were basically clocked out by mid-afternoon, and could start drinking early, a long-time Navy tradition.

Before leaving the ship, we were reminded again sternly by our superiors that we were not to talk about anything to anyone, and especially not to any media.

To our surprise, there were not many prostitutes in Malta. As I said, it was a very religious country with churches or shrines on just about every corner. They obviously did not tolerate the world's oldest profession as other places we had visited did.

Both enlisted men and officers from the *Liberty* would sit together in the bars, and it was there where military decorum took a back seat. There was no "Yes sir/No sir" business. Having gone through everything together the way we had, we were on a first-name basis with each other. We huddled together, not wanting to be around anyone but "our own." We were suspicious of any new faces coming around wanting to get friendly and share our personal space. We were sure we were being watched. A few times at the bar, someone we didn't know, speaking American English, would ask us what happened to our ship. Our answer was stock—"Go ask someone higher up than us. We don't know. It's beyond our pay grade."

We assumed these guys were American Jews who wanted to know what we knew, or were perhaps seeing if we were following Kidd's orders concerning the code of silence.

They needed to know whether or not we were willing to remain loyal to a treacherous, disloyal government or whether there were "leaks" that were going to cause them trouble later. Even though we were nothing more than dumb enlisted men, we were smart enough to know that if we started talking too much, each of us would start running into "mishaps" that would silence us permanently.

Work progressed quickly. The Maltese yardbirds were everywhere like rats. Their work was fast and frantic, just like the investigation that ruled the attack was all a case of "mistaken identity" on the part of the Jewish state.

The clean-up—cover-up—continued day-by-day, and with each passing day we knew we were getting closer to going home. All the dead were gone, as well as all the CT's equipment. The fuel oil was cleaned off, except in our minds of course where it would remain a permanent part of the sights, sounds and smells burned into our memories.

The CT spaces of *Liberty* were originally a cargo hold used to ferry military equipment such as tanks, jeeps, ammo, food and clothes during WW2 to American troops in the Pacific theatre, as well as the Korean War. Later, partition walls had been constructed for the CTs.

Now, following the attack and "extreme makeover," it was restored to its original state, with the walls being knocked out by the torpedo blast. All the rubble was removed and the area was converted once more into one big room. The space was completely washed down. We worked with scrub brushes, buckets of steaming hot water, bleach, soap and everything else we could find. However, no matter how much we scrubbed the place it didn't matter; the smell of death and oil remained as if we had done nothing. When it became obvious we couldn't wash out the blood, the higher-ups—worried about anything pointing to Israel's mass murder—decided to camouflage it by painting the room "deck red," as we called it.

Patching the torpedo hole was the most difficult task because of its size: approximately 22-feet-by-39-feet. The "ribs," the skeleton upon which the steel plates making up the ship's outer wall rested, had to be replaced, since they had been blown all to hell by the Israeli torpedo. I-beams were put in place and then steel plates were put over them like plywood sheeting on a stick house.

The stench of death and fuel oil remained. Neither new paint nor new steel was a match for the massacre's memory. The walls of the room, like a giant tomb, were impregnated permanently with the smell of my shipmates' rotting corpses, and all our efforts at removing this smell were a waste of time. It was almost as if the ghosts of these men refused to allow such a thing to take place.

As I said before, those in the ship's engineering department were furious over the fact that things were being patched up before heading home. When we got together in Scum Alley amidst those we trusted, this was the main topic of discussion.

Then, just as expected, the orders came down from McGonagle: "PREPARE FOR DEPARTURE!"

The locks were filled up with seawater again, and the yardbirds started removing the timbers holding the ship in place one-by-one. Once the timbers had been removed, we could see there were battle scars remaining we could not get to because they had been covered by the timbers. Paint was immediately rolled over them in yet another hurried, hasty attempt to put some rouge over a bruise.

And then, before we knew it, the ship was afloat once again.

Once afloat, I went down to the CT spaces with some "khakis"— or officers. We had flashlights and checked every weld for leaks.

The Maltese yardbirds who had done all the welding were true artists. During the weeks they had done their magic, I would watch their skill with amazement, as they would do it all practically onehanded while remaining meticulous with detail.

Now, the proof of their skill was obvious—not one leak, not one drop of seawater was visible, even after I had spent close to two hours down there, inspecting, inspecting and then re-inspecting. Now that the yardbirds' work was done, they left the ship.

At this time, I didn't know exactly how many of the ship's crew remained, but around 90% of the men in engineering volunteered to take her back home to America. There were a few CTs and a few boatswain's mates.

The locks opened and we were pulled out into the bay by a Maltese tug boat.

"The *Liberty* sailed for home at 7 A.M. on July 16, once again passing the Ricasoli lighthouse at the entrance of Valletta's Grand Harbor," wrote James Scott in *The Attack on the Liberty*.

Leaving dry dock filled me with many different emotions. In the first place, it had been our refuge. There were no rockets, machineguns, napalm or torpedoes to deal with. It was the place where we licked our wounds and began the process of recuperation that continues to this day. The people of Malta were some of the most gracious, kind and generous folks I've ever known, and I made good friends with many of the yardbirds and townspeople there.

Looking back at Malta as we left, we were filled with a sense of appreciation for its beauty. As anyone who has spent his or her life at sea will tell you, it's impossible to take your eyes off land as you head out. Just as Malta had grown larger and larger when we had approached her weeks earlier, now she grew smaller and smaller, until she was nothing but a mere speck. At last, she disappeared completely. We were now officially at sea and headed back to America.

36

McGonagle

Although most of us considered Captain a hero for what he did to save the ship, information surfaced from a variety of different sources that raise serious questions about why he did many of the things he did after the massacre.

A book written about the massacre by someone who attempted to prove it was all a case of mistaken identity and to make Israel look good revealed the first piece of evidence. While there is absolutely no truth in the "mistaken identity" story, there are parts of the book that may contain technical information related to the attack that are quite valuable. And although the author—who will be discussed in greater detail in a following chapter—attempted to use all the information he acquired to prove his point, that he failed to do so does not discount all the alleged facts he uncovered.

One of these facts was the information related to the MTBs, and specifically the torpedoes used.

> According to Rear Admiral Benjamin "Biny" Telem, the commander in chief of the Israel Navy during its most successful period of operations, the 1973 war, the torpedoes on MTB 203 and MTB 204 were German-made 19-inch torpedoes, acquired by the Israel Navy as part of their worldwide shopping efforts. The torpedoes on MTB 206 were 18-inch torpedoes purchased from Italy. All of the torpedoes were originally aircraft torpedoes that had been converted for use by Israel navy surface ships. The only launch of any of these torpedoes that ever actually hit a target was the one that hit the *Liberty*. According to

Telem, over a period of several years prior to the attack on the *Liberty* and including the five torpedoes launched against the *Liberty*, the Israel Navy had launched about 50 torpedoes, mostly in training exercises; 48 of these torpedoes missed their targets. Of the remaining two, a few years before 1967 one torpedo ran hot and circled back to hit the Israeli ship that had launched it. The other one hit the *Liberty*.

So while Captain McGonagle was hailed as a military genius for evading four torpedoes, the truth may be that the torpedoes themselves did the evading.

Another area of concern is the conflicting testimony Captain McGonagle gave after the attack during the "investigation" for the Court of Inquiry. As James Scott reveals in *The Attack on the Liberty*, McGonagle's testimony seemed to contradict everyone else's.

McGonagle testified that he observed the first reconnaissance flight at 10:30 A.M. followed by others at roughly half-hour intervals. Other witnesses told the court that reconnaissance flights began as early as 5:15 A.M. and that planes reconned the ship at least eight times, a figure the State Department later adopted in its report.

The skipper also said that the fighter jet attack lasted only five to six minutes, much less time than his men recalled. [Lloyd] Painter, who testified immediately after McGonagle, told the court that the jets pounded the ship for at least 20 minutes. CPO Harold Thompson also testified that the air attack lasted between 20 minutes and a half hour.

Other witnesses including Lucas, Lamkin, and Kiepfer described fighting fires, rescuing the injured, and even performing surgery as the fighters strafed the *Liberty*, impossible actions to accomplish in the brief time the skipper recalled.

The skipper also stated that he never issued an order to prepare to abandon ship. His men again refuted him. Painter recalled the order and said he ran out on deck to prepare life rafts for the wounded. Scott testified that he torched confidential messages and publications in a wastebasket. Kiepfer mobilized an evacuation of the wounded from the mess deck and CPO Wayne Smith burned radio authentication codes. Petty Officer Second Class Charles Cocnavitch, whose testimony was not included in the transcript, told Kidd that he heard the order passed over the sound-powered phones. Someone eventually produced a handwritten copy of the *Liberty*'s Combat Information Center log—entered as exhibit 14— showing that at 2:33 P.M. the demolition bill was set, an order that often means to destroy classified materials, set explosive charges, and open valves to scuttle a ship.

McGonagle and Lucas, who stood just feet apart during much of the attack, offered contradictory views on vital events. McGonagle testified that Francis Brown, who was on the helm during the attack, died before the torpedo strike. Lucas took Brown's place at the helm upon his death. He told the court that Brown died after the torpedo hit as the patrol boats strafed the ship with cannons and machineguns. Cocnavitch pulled Brown's body off the bridge seconds after he was killed. Though not asked by the court, Cocnavitch later confirmed Lucas's account. Lucas and the skipper also clashed on the issue of when the Israelis signaled the *Liberty*. McGonagle testified that he believed the signaling occurred before the torpedo attack. Lucas again disagreed. "This was definitely after the torpedo attack," he told the court.

The officers also differed on the *Liberty*'s machine-gunning of the torpedo boats. McGonagle testified that a *Liberty* sailor accurately fired on the Israeli boats and that the Israelis likely believed the spy ship had fired on them. Lucas told the court that he investigated the gunfire and found only ammunition cooking off in a blaze. Thompson also testified that ammunition exploded in the fire. Had the court called Dale Larkins, its members would have heard another witness with a clear view of the bridge's guntub fire. Larkins, who likely fired the *Liberty*'s only effective defensive round during the entire assault, watched the machinegun ammunition cook off. The mounted gun barrel never rose. "The barrel basically was laying on the edge of the tub," Larkins recalled. "I'm sure there wasn't anybody there."

The crewmembers even painted opposing pictures of McGonagle during the attack and immediate aftermath. Lucas testified that while the skipper bled profusely, he continued to bark orders and "insisted on being everywhere that he could." Painter said one of the quartermasters summoned him to the bridge immediately after the attack to take over for the injured skipper. He arrived to find McGonagle unconscious on a stretcher, his leg soaked with blood. Painter photographed the captain on his back, life jacket cinched tightly around him, bathed in sunlight with his eyes closed, a photo the court never saw. Kiepfer's testimony corroborated Painter. The doctor told the court that shortly after the attack he found the captain sweating, having difficulty standing, and showing excessive anxiety, all signs of shock.

Though it is common for witnesses to remember events differently, none of these significant discrepancies prompted the court to recall any of the officers or crewmembers other than McGonagle. Even with the skipper the court members failed to address any of the contradictions. Rather the court asked McGonagle to submit various records, including a timeline of the attack, a breakdown of the projectile hits, and the chart that showed the *Liberty*'s projected track. Kidd appeared more interested in McGonagle's account of guiding the ship that night by the North Star. He asked the skipper to recount the story as the court members listened in silence. The court's final report relied almost exclusively on the testimony of McGonagle, who according to some of his men had passed out from blood loss and shock.

Doc Kiepfer voiced his views about Captain McGonagle, when he responded to a question asked about the "investigation": How could the deck log, which documents the hours during the attack, be so neatly written and list all the dead and wounded in alphabetical order within the hours of 12 P.M. to 4 P.M., but make no mention of the many Israeli overflights that occurred during the morning before the attack?

> The deck log was not written during the attack. Captain McGonagle signed off on the log and that makes it legal, but not authentic. McGonagle was concerned that he would be blamed for the *Liberty* being in troubled waters. I told him, "Over my dead fucking body!'"

> Israel did identify the ship six hours before the attack. Israel did know that the ship was American and admitted to our government that they knew the ship was American; Israel claims only that the attacking forces failed to get the word.

> Modern diplomacy simply does not permit one to embarrass a "friendly" nation, even when that nation is caught red-handed with its torpedo in one's ship!

> McGonagle was tormented by the idea that he was somehow responsible for the agony his ship and crew suffered. One top level theory holds that someone in the Israeli armed forces ordered the *Liberty* sunk because he suspected that it had taken down messages showing that Israel started the fighting during the Six-Day War.

> Typical of Israel's casual attitude toward the episode, an attitude which suggested from the beginning that it was really our fault for being there—in international waters— in the first place.

Messages from Israel directly charged that a share of the blame was McGonagle's. *The Times* of Shreveport [La.] suggested that our government was involved in a cover-up and that the attack itself may have been conducted to prevent the ship and the United States from detecting the pending invasion of Syria which had been scheduled for June 8th but implemented on June 9th.

McGonagle may have misremembered or may have not reported the over a dozen Israeli overflights that morning because he may have thought he should have abandoned our mission—which was to listen in on all communications. My opinion as a civilian is that the Court of Inquiry—which was to determine if the Navy was at fault—should have inquired why he didn't get the *Liberty* out of the area since we could see the smoke from [El] Arish in [the Sinai].

Perhaps the most damning critique of Captain McGonagle's behavior after the attack came from Dave Lewis. A now-deceased *Liberty* officer told Dave some startling information.

I had heard that Captain McGonagle was less than honorable in all of his dealings. He rewrote the deck logs to say what he wanted them to say rather than the OOD doing it. He also, when he was in his cups—drunk—told one of the members of the crew that he had been promised a fourth stripe, a command of his own, and the Medal of Honor if he'd go along with them.

I don't think it would be anything at all remiss if someone were to point out the fact that he must've had some motivation for behaving the way he did.

I don't think you really have to incriminate him [the person who told Dave] to say that it seems odd that the deck logs were changed, and immediately after the court [of inquiry] he got a promotion and a new command.

He made a deal with the devil.

Captain William Loren McGonagle wearing his Medal of Honor

Guilt by Association corroborated Dave's claims about McGonagle.

> McGonagle's daughter later conceded to a fellow veteran that her father admitted he was pressured to fabricate a pro-Israeli account of the assault.

No matter what one wants to think about Captain McGonagle, there are some additional things that must be said, especially the way he was treated leading up to and during his medal ceremony, after the USN had nominated him for the Medal of Honor.

As reported in the obituary pages of the *Los Angeles Times* on March 11, 1999, someone—or something—made sure the ceremony would be out of the way, so as not to draw any attention to it.

> When Navy Capt. William L. McGonagle received his Medal of Honor, it was not bestowed on him by the

president, as is customary, or even presented at the White House. McGonagle, who died last week at 73, was given his award in the relative seclusion of a shipyard near Washington by the Navy secretary.

The Attack on the Liberty provides the most in-depth review of this national disgrace, one of many where the attack on my ship is concerned.

The Medal of Honor often is awarded posthumously because of the extraordinary criteria required to earn it. Those service members fortunate enough to survive combat traditionally are invited to the White House, where the president presents the medal. President Johnson often performed the ceremony, personally placing the medal around the neck of each recipient. Johnson presented at least nine Medals of Honor during the first half of 1968. He had dined with the parents of a deceased recipient in March. Less than a month before McGonagle's ceremony, the president presented medals to four servicemen simultaneously—one from each branch of the military— at the dedication of the Pentagon's new Hall of Heroes.

A review of Israel's involvement in McGonagle's June 11, 1968— almost exactly a year after the massacre—medal ceremony should have every American concerned, as detailed in *The Attack on the Liberty*.

Israeli embassy spokesman Dan Patir wrote that the Pentagon summary chronicled the attack in detail and exonerated McGonagle of wrongdoing. More importantly, Patir wrote that the report might prove politically damaging for Israel. "This announcement includes denunciation of the Israeli attack, that is defined as a 'rash act.' It insists that the incident took place in international waters, and that the *Liberty* had the right to be in them," Patir wrote. "It notes that Israeli airplanes were seen circling above the ship about 6 hours before the attack itself. It assumes with certainty that these aircraft had identified the *Liberty* immediately and had communicated this observation to the headquarters in Tel Aviv."

Israel's U.S. policy-shaping machine swung into action, targeting the highest office in the land.

McGonagle would not be so fortunate [to have the medal presented by Johnson]. The *Liberty* remained too politically sensitive for the administration even a year later and after Johnson's announcement that he would not run for reelection. James Cross, the president's senior military aide, delivered McGonagle's citation and a Presidential Unit Citation for the rest of the crew to the president for his signature on May 15. Cross urged Johnson not to present either award in person. The president signed both citations that afternoon, then followed Cross's advice. "Due to the nature and sensitivity of these awards, Defense and State officials recommend that both be returned to Defense for presentation, and that no press release regarding them be made by the White House."

The president instead visited former president Dwight Eisenhower, Supreme Court Justice William Douglas, and Senator Richard Russell at the Walter Reed Army Hospital the morning of McGonagle's ceremony. During his 10-minute visit with Russell, Johnson presented the Georgia Democrat with a signed copy of his speeches, *To Heal and to Build*, scribbling inside: "To my friend Dick Russell with appreciation." The president returned to the White House afterward, less than four miles from the Washington Navy Yard, where he presided over the graduation ceremony of the Capitol Page School in the East Room. Too concerned about domestic politics to present the nation's highest award for heroism, the commander in chief instead handed out diplomas to high school students.

"Like the vaguely worded tombstone in Arlington that marked the mass grave of *Liberty* sailors," *The Attack on the Liberty* writes, "McGonagle's citation never mentioned Israel, nor was the Jewish state identified as the attacker in the ceremony."

> For conspicuous gallantry and intrepidity at the risk of his life above and beyond the call of duty. Sailing in international waters, the *Liberty* was attacked without warning by jet fighter aircraft and motor torpedo boats which inflicted many casualties among the crew and caused extreme damage to the ship. Although severely wounded during the first air attack, Capt. McGonagle remained at his battle station on the badly damaged bridge and, with full knowledge of the seriousness of his wounds, subordinated his own welfare to the safety and survival of his command. Steadfastly refusing any treatment which would take him away from his post, he calmly continued to exercise firm command of his ship. Despite continuous exposure to fire, he maneuvered his ship, directed its defense, supervised the control of flooding and fire, and saw to the care of the casualties. Capt. McGonagle's extraordinary valor under these conditions inspired the surviving members of the *Liberty*'s crew, many of them seriously wounded, to heroic efforts to overcome the battle damage and keep the ship afloat. Subsequent to the attack, although in great pain and weak from the loss of blood, Captain McGonagle remained at his battle station and continued to command his ship for more than 17 hours. It was only after rendezvous with a U.S. destroyer that he relinquished personal control of the *Liberty* and permitted himself to be removed from the bridge. Even then, he refused much needed medical attention until convinced that the seriously wounded among his crew had been treated. Capt. McGonagle's superb professionalism, courageous fighting spirit, and valiant leadership saved his ship and many lives. His actions sustain and enhance the finest traditions of the U.S. Naval Service.

Admiral Moorer was none too happy with McGonagle's treatment, calling it a "back-handed slap." "I'm surprised they didn't just hand it to him under the 14th Street Bridge," he said.

To add insult to injury, all that was mustered across this once-great nation to honor this man was a health clinic in Virginia, officially the CAPT William L. McGonagle Branch Medical/Dental Clinic.

"The people in the Arlington National Cemetery Welcome Center had never heard of the USS *Liberty*. My wife and I got the location of Captain McGonagle's gravesite, and we looked for about an hour, but couldn't find the Captain's location and gave up for the day. Nowhere will you find anything about who attacked the *Liberty*."

—USS *Liberty* supporter James "Jim" Beardsley

37

Norfolk

There is only one way in and out of the Western Mediterranean, which is through the Strait of Gibraltar lying between Spain and Africa, and that was exactly where we were headed. We didn't push the ship too hard, as she had been patched up only superficially and we didn't want to risk opening up old wounds that could wind up being fatal for us all.

For many of us, the biggest fear as we hit the open seas was not Mother Nature and what she might throw our direction, but rather another attack and cover-up by the Tel Aviv and Washington D.C. Was there a submarine out there with a Star of David painted on the side—like the MTB—just waiting for the right moment to finish us off? After all, I personally had gotten a death threat from Admiral Kidd, so why then would they not rid themselves of their troubles by sinking us once and for all, thus putting an end to any worries they might have about us staying quiet?

At the same time however, we welcomed putting as much distance possible between ourselves and Israel. Every mile, every foot, every inch of distance we put between ourselves and our "ally" was like music to our troubled souls. We wanted to be as far away from those murdering bastards as possible. We trusted them just as much as sheep would trust the friendship of wolves that had not eaten in a few days.

The days at sea were uneventful. I did my normal routine of Sounding and Security watches. One of my duties was to check the CT spaces for any leaks or signs of future trouble.

I would go down there alone, and it was one of the more difficult things I have ever had to do in my life. Every time I descended into this silent grave—this killing field where so many of my shipmates had been murdered—I could feel the eyes of them upon me as I moved. I felt they could read my every thought and I could almost hear their voices crying to my spirit, "Do not let what happened to us be forgotten, Tourney."

It was not just a one-time occurrence. This was something that happened every hour-on-the-hour when I was on watch. I talked to Rick, Dulio, and others who were also on Sounding and Security, and they said they had experienced the same thing. How was this possible that we all felt the same thing and heard the same voices within our hearts and heads? It was the same horror for them as it was for me. Even now, 50 years later, it is still with me.

Since we had only a skeleton crew bringing the ship back home, we were all forced to take on jobs we normally didn't do, which for me included conning the ship's wheel. I was surprised at how quickly and comfortably I stepped into my new responsibility. It didn't take long for me to learn just how far off course you could get by only a degree or two. Normally, if the guy conning the ship got her off course, the OOD would shit a brick and chew your head off. Now, however, after everything we had been through, he would just calmly say, "Bring us back on course" and that would be it.

As the days and weeks passed, life was quiet, and so were we. We were glad to be alive and heading home to our loved ones, for those of us who had any. We expected, as would normally be the case, that there would be a welcoming ceremony waiting for us.

Just as before, it was in the mess decks where we assembled, like a family room back home. Now, however, sitting there in the same room that had been used as a hospital ward where men had cried out in agony—and where I had given our XO his last cigarette—is something that leaves a strong impression on you. Now, eating in there was not the enjoyable event it used to be, not the least of which was due to the smell of death, as much burned into the walls and floors as it was into our memories. When it was chow time we had to gag down our food as quickly as possible and then get the hell out of there as soon as we were finished, if we wanted to keep it in our stomachs.

One thing we did discuss was the massacre itself. Now, with as much as a month having passed, we could think more clearly. One of the things that amazed us all was the ferocity of it. We recollected how many times each of us should have bought it that day, but because of the grace of God, had not.

We were a band of brothers, especially those of us in engineering. Before the attack, we had all trusted each other to the hilt. Now, after what Kidd had put us through, there was a definite, measurable disquiet amongst us. We didn't distrust each other now, but there was this element of justifiable paranoia that each of us privately nursed for reasons of our own self-preservation. And although we didn't distrust one another, we began to mistrust the officers, due to their sudden and subtle change of attitude toward the enlisted ranks.

Even more heartbreaking though was the change in affections we had for Captain McGonagle. Kidd left his stench of treason all over the ship and we saw how it changed McGonagle. He was for all intents and purposes dead to us, gone, not the same man we had known before the massacre. Before, he had been our hero, like a favorite uncle, always affectionate and concerned with our well-being, but willing to kick our butts if we got out of line.

Now we wondered where his outrage was. It was like getting pounced on by five guys who beat the hell out of you and then you catch a glance of your dad who's watching it all and doing nothing.

After all, lying is a punishable offense in the Navy. Lying—or in this case, staying silent about an act of war against your own country—would get you into hot water in a New York minute. The thought of staying quiet about something like this was not an option, and if McGonagle had stood by us and let us know he was with us to the ends of the Earth, we would have disobeyed the silence Kidd imposed upon us, even if it meant going up against the President himself.

As we approached America's coast, we got to work getting things spiffed up. We didn't want to pull into port—to what we assumed would be a big welcoming committee—looking like a bunch of sorry SOBs.

We made sure our uniforms were clean and pressed, shoes spit-shined, dress-whites spotless, haircuts, shaved faces, sparkling teeth, clean fingernails—the whole nine yards. The only thing we could not gussy-up was our eyes, which had aged 100 years in just a few days.

With the sun coming up behind us at last, we saw the same shoreline our forefathers had seen when they came here hundreds of years ago. Our hearts pounded in anticipation as we got closer and closer to home. We were met by tug boats who pulled us in to what we thought would be a heroes' welcome. It was a Saturday afternoon on July 29.

To our great, devastating shock, we did not arrive in our home port of Norfolk, as we assumed we would. Instead, we landed at Naval Amphibious Base, Little Creek, Virginia, which, as its name implies, was small and very much out of the way, particularly to curious eyes.

It was to be a parade of disappointments, for as we got closer we could see the assembled crowd was quite small. We didn't expect to be treated like George Washington and his men after they had won the American Revolution, but the reception we got was no better than someone would get upon returning from a pleasure cruise. No appreciation for the fact we had gone through an unimaginable massacre or that we had lost 34 men with 174 maimed.

Families and dignitaries awaiting Liberty

Waiting for *Liberty*'s return

Yes, there were signs reading, "WELCOME HOME, USS *LIBERTY*." There were families there with tears in their eyes. But in general, the mood did not fit with what had just taken place. There was no respect, no solemnity; no honor, either for the dead or the living.

But then, what more should we have expected? This was why we were rushed to dry dock and patched up and painted in a hurry. They wanted to make sure there were no gasps from the assembled crowd in whichever port it was we landed when we got home. The traitors who covered up this act of war—and the many war crimes— committed against us and the nation as a whole, and protected our attackers, wanted that ship shiny and pretty when it got home so that no one would know anything about what happened.

Steve gave his recollections of the homecoming.

> A few of my friends came to greet us when we arrived. It was a strange sight on the pier—not the huge welcome you would expect for a ship that went through so much. It seemed like a letdown, but I was sure happy to see my friends.

The Attack on the Liberty described the scene:

> Commander McGonagle guided the *Liberty* into the Little Creek Naval Amphibious Base near Norfolk on Saturday afternoon, July 29. Anxious sailors in crisp white uniforms lined the rails as the *Liberty*—still accompanied by the tugboat *Papago*—tied up alongside pier 17 at 5 P.M. A helicopter buzzed high overhead.
>
> McGonagle likely felt a mix of relief and sadness as he observed the families gathered on the concrete pier below, many waving signs welcoming the crew home. When the *Liberty* had sailed from Virginia 88 days earlier for its top-secret mission to Africa, the skipper believed his career had stagnated, and he obsessed over inconsequential matters. He now returned with 34 of his men dead and

303

nearly 200 more injured. His spy ship, which no one was supposed to know existed, had briefly dominated the news that summer.

The roughly 300 wives, children, parents, and reporters gathered could see no outward scars of the attack that had left 821 shell holes and a huge gash in *Liberty*'s side. The only remnants of that violent afternoon sat zipped inside 168 canvas bags under guard in a locked compartment belowdecks, a waterlogged mix of classified records, flesh, and bone fragments. The absence of scars did little to ease the pain for families of the dead, many of whom traveled to Norfolk and climbed the gangway.

As we eased up to the dock, I searched the few faces there for my wife. As it turned out, she was there with her parents, whom I loved dearly. They came aboard, and I got a warm embrace from both my in-laws. I wanted to open up to them about what happened, but then Kidd's words came back to haunt me.

Liberty returns to Little Creek

USS *Liberty* docking at Naval Amphibious Base, Little Creek, Virginia

In the course of our initial conversation, I found out they'd already been told about the attack. In fact, the info that had been given was that I'd been killed. For over a week, this was what they thought until the report had been updated to say I was alive but that I had been wounded.

Many parents were not as fortunate as mine.

On June 11, a USN officer brought the news to a shipmate's parents.

According to the June 15 edition of the local newspaper, the *North Vernon Plain Dealer*, Jerry Lee Goss's parents got the news informing them their son was one of the 34 victims of Israel's murderous rampage.

Goss, who just turned 26-years-old a week before he was murdered, was a Third Class CT, at his GQ, in the research spaces with the 24 other young men who lost their lives when Israel's torpedo blew a 40-foot hole in the side of my ship.

Jerry Lee Goss

The officer told Mr. and Mrs. Harry Goss that their son had drowned in a flooded compartment, or his body was washed out to sea. Basically, he had no idea what happened to one of their five children. He told them that final information would be available after *Liberty* docked in Malta. A few weeks later they received a promised telegram, from the man responsible for covering up their son's murder: Lyndon Johnson.

The telegram, stamped June 29, 1967, was brief, and incredibly insulting to those who knew the truth.

> Mr. and Mrs. Harry Herschel Goss
> 38 Oakwood Drive
> North Vernon Indiana
> Dear Mr. and Mrs. Goss:
>
> I was deeply grieved to learn of the death of your son, Petty Officer Jerry Lee Goss, at sea.
>
> Words are inadequate to express my heartache in this tragedy. I want you to know that all our people share my pride in your son's service. His dedication contributed directly to maintaining the freedom our Nation supports throughout the world.
>
> May God, in his infinite wisdom, bring comfort to you and your loved ones.
>
> Sincerely,
> LYNDON B. JOHNSON

This form letter, without even knowing or caring about the Goss family's loss, incredibly had the gall to insert God's infinite wisdom. LBJ was the cause of their son's murder and cover-up, along with his other buddies, McNamara and Admiral McCain.

Jerry lies in a mass grave in Arlington National Cemetery with five other patriots. There's no way to even know if any of Jerry's—or the other four's—remains are in that grave.

EXECUTIVE
ND 9-2-2/ G4

JUN 29 1967

Dear Mr. and Mrs. Goss:

I was deeply grieved to learn of the death of your son,
Petty Officer Jerry Lee Goss, at sea.

Words are inadequate to express my heartache in this
tragedy. I want you to know that all our people share
my pride in your son's service. His dedication
contributed directly to maintaining the freedom our
Nation supports throughout the world.

May God, in His infinite wisdom, bring comfort to you
and your loved ones.

Sincerely,

LYNDON B. JOHNSON

Mr. and Mrs. Harry Herschel Goss
Thirty-eight Oakwood Drive
North Vernon, Indiana

A letter from the President . . .

IN REPLY REFER TO NAVAL PERSONNEL, DEPARTMENT OF THE NAVY, WASHINGTON, D. C. 20370

| REPORT OF CASUALTY | 100323-A-34-27 | Final | DATE PREPARED 15 Jun 1967 |

1. SERVICE IDENTIFICATION

GOSS, Jerry Lee, 773 61 55, CT3, USNR

1st Enl: 12 Feb 1964
DUSTA: NSGA FT MEADE

2. CASUALTY STATUS ☐ BATTLE ☒ NON-BATTLE   MEDITERRANEAN   6442

MISSING TO REPORTED DEAD   - Died 8 June 1967 as a result of drowning when the USS

LIBERTY (AGTR-5) was accidentally attacked by Israeli Forces in the Eastern
Mediterranean Sea.
Missing report received 9 Jun 1967; Report of death received 11 Jun 1967

3. DATE AND PLACE OF BIRTH, RACE, RELIGIOUS PREFERENCE
30 May 1941; North Vernon, Indiana; Cauc; Protestant

4. DATE AND PLACE OF LAST ENTRY ON ACTIVE DUTY IN CURRENT STATUS AND HOME OF RECORD AT TIME
29 June 1965; Long Beach, California   Los Angeles, Los Angeles, California

5. SOCIAL SECURITY NUMBER, PAY GRADE, LENGTH OF SERVICE FOR PAY, BASIC PAY, INCENTIVE PAY   CHECK IF APPLICABLE
311 42 9952; E-4 Over 3 Yrs; $222.90   ☐ CREW ☐ NON-CREW

6. DUTY STATUS
Active Duty

7. INTERESTED PERSONS (NAME, ADDRESS, RELATIONSHIP)

Harry Herschel Goss	38 Oakwood Drive, North Vernon, Indiana 47265	Father
Ida Estelle Goss	Same	Mother
Jane Carole Goss	Same	Sister

8. REPORT FOR VA TO FOLLOW   ☐ YES ☒ NO
9. REPORTING COMMAND AND DATE REPORT RECEIVED IN DEPARTMENT
USS LIBERTY (AGTR-5)   082202Z (MISSING)
USS LIBERTY (AGTR-5)   101230Z (DEATH)

10. SELECTIVE SERVICE NUMBER, LOCAL BOARD, AND LOCATION (If unknown, enter date and place of first entry in Armed Services)
12 38 41 54; #38, North Vernon, Indiana

11. PRIOR SERVICE DATA   ☐ YES ☒ NO

12. REMARKS

FOOTNOTES
1 Adult next of kin.
2 Beneficiary for gratuity pay in event there is no surviving wife or child - as designated on record of emergency data.
3 Beneficiary for unpaid pay and allowances - as designated on record of emergency data.

13. DISTRIBUTION
7-9RD

14.   (SIGNATURE ELEMENT)
Certified to be a true Certification of Casualty.

By direction of Chief of Naval Personnel

DD FORM 1 MAR 60 1300

"Accidentally attacked by Israeli forces..."

History will reveal the duplicity this government is involved in with the free pass they gave Israel to murder Americans on the high seas and cover it up for the last 50 years.

Shame on all of them.

There was a small reception on the dock for us. No band, no media, no bigwig naval officers or politicians. The party, if it can be called that, was over shortly after it began.

Had it been any other country that attacked us—including the USSR, and especially if it had been an Arab country—the celebration would have gone on for days. Every media outlet in the world would have been there, as well as all the Navy brass, members of Congress and possibly even the president himself.

As it was though, because it was Israel who attacked us, the only noise to be heard was the water sloshing on the side of the ship. Prisoners coming off of Devil's Island would have received a warmer reception than we did. You'd have thought we were a ship of lepers for all the welcome we received. It was as if the boys in D.C., save only a few, would rather have had a mourning party, grieving over the fact we'd come home alive rather than being sunk to the bottom of the sea as they and their friends in Israel had hoped.

It was somewhat of an embarrassment to show my in-laws around, because the reports they received were that we had been shot up badly. Now, here we were, for all intents and purposes, a brand new ship looking like the worst she had been through was being hit with a rock from a sling shot.

My father-in-law would ask me questions about the attack and my response was always the same: "Can't say." To change the subject I encouraged him to walk around the ship and look for patches where there had originally been holes made by either rocket or cannon fire. I told him to look carefully, because if he didn't look closely he would miss them.

The tour lasted for about an hour and then we decided it was time to go. I got my sea bag and pass and exited the ship with 72 hours liberty.

On the almost 300-mile drive home, the questions kept coming about the attack. Just as before, I had to give them the stock answer that most people give when they know that telling the truth is a liability—"No comment." Soon, they realized they were getting nowhere and the questions stopped.

Arriving at their home, I welcomed the feelings of safety and security that pervaded everything. My mother-in-law was a great cook, and I was so relieved to be able to walk into a kitchen that carried the smell of good, home-cooked food rather than the odor of fuel oil and the rotting bodies of my shipmates.

The weekend passed quickly. Before I knew it, I was in my red 1966 Galaxy 500 headed back to Little Creek. I arrived at the naval base and started making my way towards *Liberty*. Surprisingly, as I approached her, I did not feel any of the dread I had expected.

The general talk of the town was that we had been through something pretty damned bad out there. As a result, wearing a USS *Liberty* patch earned you a certain amount of respect from the folks there.

I walked up the gangplank, saluted the flag and then asked permission to come aboard.

For the next week, I got to work doing my regular duties in shipfitting instead of Sounding and Security and Damage Control, since we were not at sea. There were always repairs of some sort to be made.

Around the middle of August, Lieutenant Golden asked me if I would rather do shore patrol duties, and that sounded more appealing to me, since being tasked with throwing drunks in jail meant more money and more excitement. I worked with one other guy from another ship, black and funny to be around but whose name I can't remember anymore. Armed only with billy clubs, we would walk into various bars and make sure that anyone in a U.S. uniform was conducting himself in a manner befitting a member of the U.S. Armed Forces.

Once in a while, we would get someone who felt like mouthing off, so we would drag him back to the paddy wagon and take him to the jail on base where he was given a few days to cool off and reconsider his outlook on things. Some of the hard cases who remained uninfluenced by their stay would get the firehose with the suicide nozzle on it. They were bounced around like a pinball until they cried uncle and decided to play nice. After they broke down, we would hand them a mop and bucket and make them clean up all the water used in washing away their bad attitude.

After dealing with drunks in bars for about three months, I decided to take some leave. Less than a week into my 14-day leave, the phone rang and it was one of the yeomen aboard the *Liberty*. A Yeoman performs administrative and clerical duties, kind of like a secretary. He called to try to convince me to re-up, but he also said if I wanted to, I could get an early out. We spent about 30 minutes on the phone, most of the time with him trying to get me to stay in the Navy.

I immediately decided to cut my leave short, so I hopped in my Galaxy and drove the 300 miles to the ship. After being aboard for about three days, all the "lifers"—those who make the Navy their career—came up to me to make their pitch for my reenlistment. They offered me a $10,000 bonus—around $73,000 in 2017—to stay in.

By then, I had time to reflect about what had been done to me as well as my shipmates. There was no way in hell I was going to reenlist after what my government had put us all through. As I mentioned earlier, I did not trust authority any further than I could throw an elephant with one arm. What was next in their black bag of dirty tricks against me? Send me out to sea and throw me overboard into shark-infested waters? They could have offered me any amount of money and it wouldn't have been enough. On top of this, my wife had given birth to our first child, a girl.

I would still have to remain on the ship for a while because of the paperwork involved, but I wanted to be off it yesterday. I went to the same yeoman to see how soon I was getting off, and he motioned toward a stack of papers a mile high, indicating there was no way for him to go through all that just to find out when I was going to be freed from what was—for me at least—a prison of sorts. I threw $25 on the table.

"When am I scheduled to leave?" I asked him again.

His response was quick, as he shoved the money into his pocket.

"Tomorrow."

On December 12, I walked down the gangplank, left the *Liberty* and never looked back at her.

Almost 50 years later, some more disturbing evidence was delivered to me about the U.S. government's cover-up of the attack on my ship, proving that they knew all along when we were attacked and who attacked us.

I was contacted via email on May 24, 2016 by Colin M. Jones, a retired USN captain. Captain Jones was a 31-year-old Fleet Electronics Officer for the Atlantic Fleet from the fall of 1965 until the fall of 1967.

> I went there from the *Sampson* where I'd been chief engineer, and I was selected for lieutenant commander while I was on the *Sampson*.

USS *Sampson* (DDG-10) was a guided missile destroyer that played a part in the *Liberty* massacre.

Sampson was assigned to the *America* carrier task group, which, along with *Saratoga*, was conducting war games off the coast of Crete while my shipmates were being slaughtered. *Sampson* was also one of the ships that steamed to rendezvous with the *Liberty*, when our treasonous government allowed us to get some aid.

> I was on the staff of COMNAVSURFLANT [Commander, Naval Surface Force, Atlantic].

COMNAVSURFLANT is a post within the U.S. Fleet Forces Command headquartered at Naval Station Norfolk. COMNAVSURFLANT supervises all surface ships based on the Eastern and Gulf Coast of the U.S.

> I reported to COMNAVSURFLANT and also to Admiral Moorer who was CINCLANTFLT [Commander-in-Chief Atlantic Fleet].

> We knew that morning in Norfolk, we knew for sure that the ship had been attacked and who it had been attacked by, and we were pretty sure that morning that they knew who the hell they were attacking. I don't think there was ever any doubt about that.

Unfortunately I cannot now recall what the hour was when we first learned of the attack, but it was sometime that morning in Norfolk. My recollection is that I sent Lieutenant JG Ray Levesque, an LDO [limited duty officer] who worked for me and had all those ships out there that day. Levesque had specific responsibility for the *Liberty* and all of those ships. When he arrived I don't now recall. I also am sure we were told to say nothing, and all of us who were in the business were sensitive to that. Of course by the time we got the word it was long over.

I am now in my 80s, in very poor health, and probably in the process of crossing that last river, but it has always amazed me that the full story has not ever been told. I have memories of the engine room on the *Liberty*, as you must. Know I visited the ship several times in Norfolk and elsewhere.

38

Dayan

In September, 2013, the aforementioned Dr. Tony Wells wrote a paper entitled "Moshe Dayan and the Attack on the United States Ship *Liberty*—June 8, 1967," where he points the blame for the massacre squarely on the shoulders of this man.

Dayan was born in 1915 in what was then Ottoman Syria within the Ottoman Empire, his parents Ukrainian Jewish immigrants. At 14, he joined the Zionist group Haganah, the Jewish paramilitary organization which became the Israel Defense Forces (IDF). He was appointed as the Defense Minister of Israel—responsible for defending the State of Israel from internal and external military threats and overseeing most of the Israeli security forces, like the IDF—on the first day of the Six-Day War.

6

7.2000 9:27nM   NO. 4cu
                                                                    PROC

INFORMATION REPORT INFORMATION REPORT

1 NOV 1967   **CENTRAL INTELLIGENCE AGENCY**

This material contains information affecting the National Defense of the United States within the meaning of the Espionage Laws, Title 18, U.S.C. Secs. 793 and 794, the transmission or revelation of which in any manner to an unauthorized person is prohibited by Law.

CONTROLLED DISSEM	C-O-N-F-I-D-E-N-T-I-A-L	NO DISSEM ABROAD

COUNTRY	Israel	REPORT NO. B-321/33403-67
SUBJECT	Prospects for Political Ambitions of Moshe Dayan/Attack on USS Liberty Ordered by Dayan	DATE DISTR. 9 Nov 67
		NO. PAGES 1
		REFERENCES.

(b)(1)
(b)(3)

16735-46

DATE OF INFO. Oct 67

PLACE & DATE ACQ. Tel Aviv -- 1967

THIS IS UNEVALUATED INFORMATION

(b)(1)
(b)(3)

SOURCE   US citizen,_____ who frequently visits Israel
                          /Source is normally available should this
report generate requirements./

(b)(1)
(b)(3)

1. I recently returned from Tel Aviv where I visited with
    friends_____ for whom I have
    high regard. Our discussions included the future political role
    of Moshe Dayan. These people said that the longer Israel waits
    for elections, the less chance Dayan has of becoming Prime Minister.
    They recognize that Dayan's appointment as Minister of Defense
    provided impetus to the Israel war effort. Since the war, respon-
    sible Israelis have given and continue to give less credit to Dayan
    and more credit to Gneral Rabin. My Israeli friends also are
    emphatic in saying that there will never be a negotiated peace with
    the Arabs so long as Dayan is Defense Minister.

2. My friends commented on the sinking of the US communications ship,
    Liberty. They said that Dayan personally ordered the attack on the
    ship and that one of his generals adamantly opposed the action and
    said, "This is pure murder." One of the admirals who was present
    also disapproved the action, and it was he who ordered it stopped
    and not Dayan. My friends believe that the attack against the US
    vessel is also detrimental to any political ambition Dayan may have.

-end-

FULL TEXT COPY DO NOT RELEASE

INFORMATION REPORT INFORMATION REPORT

U	NO	C-O-N-F-I-D-E-N-T-I-A-L		S	NO

The dissemination of this document is limited to civilian employees and some duty military personnel within the intelligence components of the USIB member agencies, and to those senior officials of the member agencies who must act upon the information. However, unless specifically restricted in accordance with paragraph 8 of DCID 1/7, it may be released to those components of the departments and agencies of the U.S. Government participating in the production of National Intelligence. IT SHALL NOT BE DISSEMINATED TO CONTRACTORS. It shall not be disseminated to organizations or personnel, including consultants, under a contractual relationship to the U.S. Government without the written permission of the originator.

INFORMATION REPORT Nov 1967 , Central Intelligence
Agency (full text overleaf)

INFORMATION REPORT   Nov 1967
Central Intelligence Agency

This material contains information affecting the National Defense of the United States within the meaning of the Espionage Laws, Title 18, U.S.S. Secs 7903 and 794, the Transmission or revelation of which in any manner by an unauthorized person is prohibited by law.

CONTROLLED DISSEM
C-O-N-F-I-D-E-N-T-I-A-L
NO DISSEM ABROAD

COUNTRY   Israel   REPORT NO   B-321/33403-67
SUBJECT Prospects for Political Ambitions of Moshe Dayan/Attack on USS Libery [sic] Ordered by Dayan
DATE DISTR. 9 No 67
NO. PAGES   1
REFERENCES   16835-46 [written]
DATE OF INFO Oct 67
PLACE & DATE ACQ.   Tel Aviv -- 1967
THIS IS UNEVALUATED INFORMATION
SOURCE

US citizen, [redacted] who frequently visits Israel
Source is normally available should this report generate requirements.

1. I recently returned from Tel Aviv where I visited with [redacted] friends [redacted] for who I have high regard. Our discussions included the future political role of Moshe Dayan. These people said that the longer Israel waits for elections, the less chance Dayan has of becoming Prime Minister.

They recognize that Dayan's appointment as Minister of Defense provided impetus to the Israel war effort. Since the war, responsible Israelis have given and continue to give less credit to Dayan and more credit to General Rabin. My Israeli friends also are emphatic in saying that there will never be a negotiations peace with the Arabs as long as Dayan is Defense Minister.

2. My friends commented on the sinking of the US communications ship, Liberty. The said that Dayan personally ordered the attack on the ship, and that one of his generals adamantly opposed the action and said, "This is pure murder." One of the admirals who was present also disapproved the action, and it was he who ordered it stopped and not Dayan. My friends believe that the attack against the US vessel is also detrimental to any political ambition Dayan may have.

-end-

FULL TEXT COPY NOT RELEASE

INFORMATION REPORT INFORMATION REPORT

Approved for Release 2015/10/19 C01286836

Below is Dr. Wells's paper, which makes for interesting reading, and sheds some light on why the massacre took place aboard my ship.

The background and key reasons for the Israeli attack on the United States Ship *Liberty* on June 8, 1967 rest squarely on the Israeli Minister of Defense, Moshe Dayan. The latter's character and record prior to Dayan becoming Minister of Defense on June 5, 1967 shows a person who was a supreme risk taker and one who had demonstrated on several occasions a capacity to make reckless decisions that led to failure and controversy. Dayan was a self-willed man who never failed to either take charge or make a command decision when the situation demanded. His recklessness was equaled by indefatigable courage and determination, and a fighting spirit that took him to the top of the Israeli Army as Chief of the General Staff. His impetuous and poor judgments may have been the chief reasons for his failure to secure the highest office, Prime Minister of Israel.

Moshe Dayan had a strategic goal to seize the Golan Heights and, if the situation demanded and the opportunity permitted, invade Syria and take Damascus. The reasons were to provide a key security barrier for Israel. There may also have been additional reasons related to the acquisition of more agricultural land. There remain some disagreements about this latter point. Dayan later regretted his impetuous decision to take the Golan Heights. The Syrians were not a serious threat to Israel and the Israelis had provoked far more border clashes with the Syrians than the Syrians had with Israel.

The most significant point of all is that Dayan made a unilateral decision to take the Golan Heights. He did not consult either the Israeli Prime Minister or the Chief of Staff of the Israeli Army. He went ahead and gave specific orders without any consultation.

In 1976-1977 I interviewed the U.S. Secretary of State in 1967, Dean Rusk, on three occasions. Secretary Rusk was totally open and he provided insights and facts that revealed why he had gone on record as saying that the attack on the USS *Liberty* was not an accident, but deliberate. He made it very clear to me that the culprit was the renegade Minister of Defense, Moshe Dayan, who had in effect taken the law into his own hands and ordered the attack on Syria.

Dayan was very much aware of the role, missions, and likely location of the *Liberty* and that she was undoubtedly collecting key SIGINT against Israel and the other protagonists. Rusk was adamant—the Prime Minister and the other key Israeli leaders had no role at all in the decision to attack Syria and the USS *Liberty*. Dayan wanted his actions totally unmonitored during the crucial day of June 8, 1967 when Dayan ordered the attack on Syria. Dayan was gambling on both surprise and decisive military action while silencing the one intelligence asset that he assessed could monitor his every move—the USS *Liberty*.

He wanted to achieve a massive military victory on the Golan Heights before anyone could react—a fait accompli by occupation that the Syrians and Russians would not be able to reverse. The last thing Dayan wanted was U.S. intervention with his Prime Minister to say stop right now and do not even contemplate such aggression against Syrian territory and an attack on a U.S. warship. *Liberty* held the keys to unravelling his plans and reporting them instantly to Washington. There were several other intelligence assets in place and in the region of which Dayan was totally unaware. The notion that Dayan wanted to draw the U.S. into the conflict in the event that Egypt was accused of attacking and destroying the *Liberty*, thereby invoking U.S. retaliation, is not supported by any known evidence.

Dayan had no desire or motivation in bringing the U.S. into the war because he was confident that Israel would achieve alone all her military and strategic objectives. Indeed the U.S. would remain the countervailing power to the Soviet Union and its Middle East client states. The calls between the White House and Moscow in which Secretary Rusk was the centerpiece with the President did indeed lead to Israel ceasing its advance beyond the Golan Heights and brought the conflict to a conclusion.

Dayan had, therefore, achieved his strategic objectives, none of which would have been approved by his own leadership if he had been consultative and sought prior authority to act.

For Dean Rusk and President Johnson the attack on Syria was the most frightening event in the Middle East conflict and an event that would trigger Soviet support for its ally, Syria. A potential disaster was in the making. Dean Rusk told me that for him June 8, 1967 represented the worst day for American security since the climatic day during the Cuban Missile crisis when the Soviet Union backed down.

In effect, Moshe Dayan was taking the West to the brink with the Soviet Union by attacking Syria. Dayan's personal decision and order to attack the U.S. spy ship listening to his communications was not just egregious in the extreme, it could, potentially, along with the attack on Syria, have taken the Soviet Union over the edge if the U.S. had mistaken the perpetrator and taken action against, for example, Egypt. Dean Rusk and I discussed in detail the events of that day and the subsequent exchanges with Moscow and the urgent need to deter the Soviet Union from air lifting into Syria a large force that would confront Israel—a disaster in the making both for Israel and U.S. national security.

The CIA has released a sensitive HUMINT report from Tel Aviv that confirms Secretary Rusk's very sensitive statements to me in my interviews with him and his more general comments that he made public about the attack on *Liberty* as being deliberate.

The Director of the CIA in June 1967, Richard Helms, a career CIA officer of great distinction, made similar general statements in his lifetime about the attack on *Liberty* being deliberate, but he never provided any detail for very clear security reasons relating to sources and methods inside Israel and other parts of the Middle East, plus collateral HUMINT intelligence from the British, and the whole panoply of hugely sensitive SIGINT and ELINT from both the National Security Agency and its cousin, GCHQ in the UK.

The latter had longstanding very special sources and methods in the region. However, no asset was better placed than USS *Liberty*. Moshe Dayan knew this and wanted zero collection of Israeli communications. Furthermore he wanted *Liberty* destroyed without trace with no survivors to testify against the attackers. Hence the multiple attacks from the air and torpedo boats with numerous weapon systems that were intended to sink *Liberty* and obliterate her crew.

On June 8, 1967 Moshe Dayan made two hugely ill-considered and monstrous decisions irrespective of the consequences for the U.S.and its allies, and most of all for Israel itself.

It is clear that once the facts became known to Secretary Rusk and President Johnson, with abject apologies from the Israeli Prime Minister, that they were left with a major dilemma, knowing that Dayan was the perpetrator and that the rest of the Israeli leadership had no part in the decision to attack the USS *Liberty*.

However, any notion that the attack had ever been a tragic mistake of identity is totally inaccurate. To compound Dayan's egregious actions another worst aspect of this series of events was the failure by President Johnson and his Secretary of Defense to support the Sixth Fleet Commander's and his Carrier Battlegroup Commander's decision to continue the flight of U.S. carrier based aircraft dispatched in prompt response to the attack on *Liberty*.

The direct intervention from Washington and recall of these aircraft will always remain a very sad blight on the records of both Lyndon Johnson and Robert McNamara.

Those senior U.S. Naval personnel involved in the rescue attempt on *Liberty* have for good reason found it difficult to ever accept the decision of the President and his Secretary of Defense to recall those aircraft outbound to assist a U.S. warship not only under attack but in grave distress.

By any standards of international law the attack on the *Liberty* constituted a war crime.

The CIA report also reflects Israeli harsh criticism of Dayan's decision to order the attack. The Prime Minister and other key Israeli leaders cannot be held accountable for the actions of Moshe Dayan. The CIA document in the USS *Liberty* Document Center collection supports the other public records regarding the deliberate Israeli attack on USS *Liberty*.

It should be noted that the U.S. and its major ally, the United Kingdom, do not for very good reasons release highly sensitive intelligence documents even over 46 years after the events of June, 1967. There are several reasons—the most important of which is sources and methods that are still in place today in the region, and which if exposed would reveal the complexity, high quality and location of crucial assets.

With regard to HUMINT neither the CIA nor MI6 will ever reveal documents that may be used to trace not just various tradecraft skills, tactics, techniques and procedures, but which also can reveal HUMINT network architectures and likely workings that are still in place today.

Moshe Dayan was not just a great Israeli patriot and leader, he was also personally courageous and gave of his all for his country. The tragedy of Moshe Dayan is that his determination and fearsome patriotism blinded his judgment on several occasions during his career. The events of June 8, 1967 remain not merely a terribly egregious blight on his otherwise fine patriotic record, but a testament to how recklessly misplaced patriotism can take a country, indeed the world, to the brink of disaster.

For the brave men of the crew of the USS *Liberty* who never knew of Moshe Dayan and his dire actions, or have been privileged to know a great American like Secretary of State Dean Rusk, there always remained the *Why rather than the What and When and By Whom*. It is intended that this short and precise analysis goes someway to explaining the *Why*.

What does remain totally uncontested, and will always remain an enduring beacon for future generations of the U.S. Navy is the indomitable courage, fortitude and sheer resilience and bravery of the men of the USS *Liberty*— their deeds will long outlive the controversy surrounding the circumstances of the attack on their ship. They remain the most highly decorated ship in the history of the United States Navy, and their courage will endure.

Dangerous Liaison: The Inside Story of the U.S.-Israeli Covert Relationship, which details the long-lasting relationship between the American CIA and Israel's national intelligence agency, Mossad, lends more insight into the Dayan connection to the massacre aboard my ship.

There is a body of opinion within the American intelligence community that [James Jesus] Angleton [chief of CIA Counterintelligence from 1954 to 1975 and a great friend of the Zionist state] had played a leading part in orchestrating the events leading up to the June 1967 war.

One long-serving official at the CIA's ancient rival, the code-breaking National Security Agency, states flatly that "Jim Angleton and the Israelis spent a year cooking up the '67 war. It was a CIA operation, designed to get Nasser." Such a verdict, from a source inside an agency that had inclination and the facilities to monitor both the CIA and the Israelis, must carry some weight.

Why, for example, did the Israelis attack the American intelligence ship *Liberty* off the coast of Sinai on June 8? It is clear that the Israelis knew that they were attacking a vessel of the U.S. Navy, especially as it was flying a large Stars and Stripes at the time. The fact that they spent six hours reconnoitering and executing the attack, which included machine-gunning lifeboats, attests to the deadly intent of the operation.

The fact that the U.S. government, then and since, has done its best to cover up the circumstances of an attack in which 34 Americans died suggests that the two countries share some very guilty secrets indeed. However, it is still unexplained why the Israelis did it. It has been suggested that they wanted to prevent the U.S. from discovering, through military traffic intercepted by the *Liberty*, that despite the cease-fire they were going to open another front against Syria. But the U.S. was by no means as solicitous of the alleged Soviet proxies in Damascus as it had been of King Hussein. Furthermore, while Dayan had only to give the go-ahead for the IDF northern commander, David Elazar, to swing into action on the Golan, the assault on the *Liberty* involved coordination with the air force and navy. Since Dayan did not consult Rabin about ordering the Syrian attack, could he have told the general staff to attack the Americans without explaining why he was doing it?

For whatever reason, the Americans on the *Liberty* were regarded as expendable, and Washington accepted the results of the June war with entire satisfaction.

39

Israel

A lot has been said and written about the power Israel and Jews have over the United States. I'm not here to make that case, but to simply present the evidence of how events unfolded in relation to the massacre on my ship and to let the reader decide.

As news of the attack spread through the corridors of power in Washington, D.C., good intentions turned to political expediency when the 800-pound gorilla—Israel—was in the room.

The few officials in D.C. who attempted to call Israel on the carpet didn't stand a chance.

As James Scott detailed in *The Attack on the Liberty*, the power of Israel and American Jews was just too much for most to compete with, especially when they tried to do the right thing.

> Rather than openly confront Israel, the United States moved to protect it from possible public relations fallout, the same rationale that had prompted some senior officials to previously suggest sinking the *Liberty* at sea to prevent reporters from photographing it.
>
> Many American Jews, already angry over the neutrality blunder, would blame the administration for stirring up anti-Israel sentiment. The beleaguered president, anxious to retain Jewish support and refocus on Vietnam, couldn't afford the domestic political controversy.
>
> "It was no help if you had a lot of people getting angry at the Israelis," recalled [U.S. Under Secretary of State Nicholas deBelleville "Nick"] Katzenbach. "If the Israelis

326

screw up the relations, then the Jewish groups are going to bail out the Israelis. It ends up with you having a more difficult situation than you would have otherwise."

In his 2008 memoir, *Some of It Was Fun: Working with RFK and LBJ*, Katzenbach recalled his involvement with the *Liberty* massacre.

Back in Washington, I was briefed on the Mideast crisis by Ben Read and Larry Eagleburger and read a bunch of cables and intelligence memos. There was a real risk of war breaking out, although all the intelligence assessments concluded that Nasser and his Syrian allies would be no match for the Israelis (even with the help of a reluctant Jordan) should the Arabs launch an attack. The other possibility was that Israel would use the buildup of troops on its borders as a reason to attack first in alleged self-defense.

The secretary was seeking to mediate, and with the Egyptian vice president coming to Washington at LBJ's request, he was fairly optimistic about getting an agreement. The Israeli Foreign Minister, Abba Eban, was already in Washington, seeking American support to open up the Gulf of Aqaba as, he urged, we and the British were obligated to do by treaty. Nasser, having gotten the UN forces out of the Sinai, continued to mass his troops and threaten to eliminate Israel, though nobody thought he really wanted a war he was unlikely to win.

I went to Gene Rostow's office, where, in my absence, he had been working to persuade various NATO nations to send warships to the straits and open up the gulf to shipping. At this point only the British had agreed to join us. It was clear the Israelis wanted us to act on their behalf, just as it was clear that the Arabs would resent it. Gene had put together a crisis team, and it was obvious that he was thoroughly enjoying working with his brother Walt, the national security advisor, in the White House.

My role would clearly be marginal.

Given the optimism over settlement, coupled with the intelligence about Israeli strength, LBJ was reluctant to send warships into the gulf. President Johnson used the hotline to the Soviet Union to insure that the Russians were not pressing for an attack on Israel. The Egyptian vice president arrived in Washington, but before any mediation could take place, the Israelis attacked as a matter of self-defense.

Rusk was furious, and so, perhaps to a lesser degree, was LBJ. The Israeli attack was brilliantly conceived and carried out by defense minister Moshe Dayan and Chief of Staff Yitzhak Rabin. Air attacks neutralized the Egyptian air force from day one. With absolute air superiority, Israeli ground forces were punishing the Jordanian, Egyptian, and Syrian armies mercilessly. Thus began the Six-Day War.

One of the reasons the Israeli smashing victory was not as brilliant as many ascribe it to be is due to the fact that the Zionist state had many agents who had infiltrated the various countries that hosted them, but which they did not consider their homes. Their allegiance was, as Jews, to Israel.

The most notable example of this can be found in the story of Eliyahu Ben-Shaul Cohen, commonly known as Eli Cohen.

This Israeli spy is best known for the espionage work he did from 1961–1965 in Syria, where he "developed close relationships with the political and military hierarchy and became the Chief Adviser to the Minister of Defense."

Cohen's scheme was eventually uncovered, and he was captured, convicted, and sentenced to death. His exploits—while spying for a foreign country, Israel—against his native Egypt—is what allowed Israel's victory in the Six-Day War to be referred to as brilliant. While spying in Syria for Israel, Cohen provided the IDF an "extensive range of intelligence" from '61–'65, via radio, secret letters, and three secret trips to Israel.

His best bit of spying for a foreign government was when he toured the Golan Heights to uncover Syrian fortifications there.

Pretending to be concerned for the soldiers exposed to the sun, Cohen had trees planted—ostensibly for shade—at important positions. These trees were then "used as targeting markers by the Israeli military during the Six-Day War and enabled Israel to capture the Golan Heights in two days with relative ease."

Cohen also learned of a Syrian secret plan to create three bunker lines with mortars, when the IDF would have expected to encounter just one bunker, thus helping Israel in its "brilliant" victory.

Examples similar to Cohen's are legion, although perhaps not as successful.

In 1965, almost exactly two years before the Six-Day War, Cohen was publicly hanged as a traitor, but has become a national hero in Israel, like U.S. Navy analyst Jonathan Pollard. Many streets and neighborhoods are named after Cohen, a memorial stone was erected in Jerusalem honoring him, and his son's 1977 bar mitzvah was attended by "Prime Minister Menachem Begin, Defense Minister Ezer Weizmann, Chief of Staff Mordechai Gur, and several Mossad operatives."

Katzenbach then discussed the Liberty massacre.

Apart from the war itself, which the United States would have liked to avoid despite Nasser's inexcusable provocation, there were two unfortunate incidents. First, the State Department issued a statement of neutrality that was both unnecessary and unwise. It irritated the Israelis and angered the American Jewish community, including some of LBJ's most loyal supporters.

How it happened, I have no idea. Second, the Israelis attacked an American naval intelligence vessel, the USS *Liberty*, in international waters, killing more than 30 sailors and wounding more than 100. The Israeli government quickly apologized and said it was an accident, a case of mistaken identity. That explanation was hard to accept, given the fine weather, the large American flag, and the clearly visible ship's markings. The Navy did not believe it, nor did most American officials, but it seemed inconceivable that such an attack would have been ordered by senior Israeli officials.

LBJ demonstrated his political finesse by accepting the Israelis' apology but insisting that they do more than simply say it was a mistake. He called me and told me to tell the Israelis that they should not only pay for the *Liberty* but should offer generous compensation to the families of the victims.

I spoke to the minister in charge of the Israeli embassy and deliver the message, but the Israelis insisted that the whole thing was an unhappy accident and said that they did not wish to assume any additional responsibility. I pushed hard on them from the outset and on subsequent occasions, arguing that it was clearly in their best interest to do so. Eventually Israel came up with some $13 million in compensation. But the incident angered many, and to this day the Israeli explanation remains questionable in the view of many people, including me.

As various officials, even LBJ, attempted to exact some sort of penance out of Israel, Israelis and American Jews teamed up to embarrass and muzzle the president, displaying the incredible influence they had—and no doubt still have—over the American political machinery and mainstream media.

Ephraim Evron, the Israeli Embassy's second in command, accused the administration of politicizing the *Liberty*. He wrote in a confidential memo that the news leaks were designed to dampen enthusiasm for Israel that only days earlier had sparked thousands to rally in American streets and raised millions in donations. If the administration could marginalize Israel's political influence it would have greater freedom to take positions contrary to Israeli interests, dangerous ground for the Jewish state as it prepared to negotiate a peace deal that would involve controversial issues, such as territorial gains and refugees.

"We can assume that the U.S. Department of State and the White House are both party to this decision, each for its own reasons. The U.S. Department of State, and especially Rusk, who had tried throughout the crisis to create the impression of not identifying with us, are attempting to use the incident to create a bridge to the Arab countries," Evron wrote. "The President has been showing in the past few days special sensitivity and dissatisfaction with respect to Jewish pressures on him. He thinks that an information-based treatment of the matter of the ship in the aforesaid manner will lead to weakening of the pro-Israeli pressure that envelopes many circles, even outside the Jewish public."

The Israeli Embassy now countered with its own spin campaign. "We are facing a clear and deliberate attempt to turn public opinion against us," Evron cabled Jerusalem. "Our informative process must avoid confrontation with the United States Government, since it is clear that the American public, if faced with a direct argument, will accept its government's version."

Silencing President Johnson was the top priority. Evron suggested the embassy remind the president "of the dangers facing him personally if the public learns that he was party to the distribution of the story that is on the verge of being blood libel." The embassy turned to Supreme Court justice Abe Fortas, a close friend of Johnson's, and Washington lawyer David Ginsburg— referred to in Israeli documents as "Ilan" and "Harari," respectively—for advice and to help pressure the president. Fortas and Ginsburg urged the embassy to publicly propose a joint U.S.-Israeli commission to investigate the attack. America would reject the proposal, because that would expose the *Liberty*'s officers to interrogation by Israel. But diplomats recognized that even the rejection would "improve our position in public opinion" as Israel would appear more cooperative and open than America.

Embassy staffers hammered the media to kill critical stories and slant others in favor of Israel. Before *Newsweek*'s story appeared, embassy spokesman Dan Patir had reviewed an advance copy of the article. He successfully pressured editors to run a "toned down" version. Editors added a question mark to the headline and deleted the words "deliberate attack." The magazine also killed an accompanying commentary that said the leak was designed to free American leaders from pro-Israel pressure.

When *Newsweek*'s story broke, embassy officials pounced, labeling the allegations "malicious" in competing newspapers. "Such stories are untrue and without foundation whatever," an unnamed embassy spokesman told reporters. "It was an unfortunate and tragic accident which occurred in an area where fierce land and air fighting took place in recent days." Patir derailed another story about a House Armed Services Committee member under pressure from constituents to launch a congressional investigation: "We have made sure that the journalistic source will refrain from writing about this for now." Israel's spin frustrated American officials, who increasingly bore the media's hostility. Phil Goulding later accused Israel of "floating one self-serving rumor after another" with the mission "to make this tragedy the fault of the United States instead of the fault of the Israeli government."

Here is the "story" in *Newsweek*—really just a paragraph—that caused such an uproar:

THE PERISCOPE

Newsweek, June 19, 1967

AHEAD OF THE NEWS

Sinking the Liberty: Accident or Design?

The Israeli attack on the naval communications ship U.S.S. Liberty has left a wake of bitterness and political charges of the most serious sort. First of all, the Liberty was no ordinary vessel but an intelligence-gathering ship on a "ferret" mission. It carried elaborate gear to locate both Israeli and Egyptian radio and radar and to monitor and tap all military messages sent from command posts to the battlefield. Although Israel's apologies were officially accepted, some high Washington officials believe the Israelis knew the Liberty's capabilities and suspect that the attack might not have been accidental. One top-level theory holds that someone in the Israeli armed forces ordered the Liberty sunk because he suspected it had taken down messages showing that Israel started the fighting. (A Pentagon official has already tried to shoot down the Israeli claim of "pilot error.") Not everyone in Washington is buying this theory, but some top Administration officials will not be satisfied until fuller and more convincing explanations of the attack on a clearly marked ship in international waters are forthcoming.

Newsweek, June 19, 1967, page 21

THE PERISCOPE

The Attack on the Liberty detailed how Israel attempted to place the blame on my ship for their massacre!

Rumors evolved into deception. Israeli officials told the press that the day the war began, the Jewish state contacted the American Embassy in Tel Aviv and asked if the United States planned to operate any ships off the Sinai Peninsula in the east ern Mediterranean. Israel claimed that the American Embassy failed to answer, so it was left to assume that no American ships steamed nearby. The implication was clear: America was to blame. When the story appeared in *The Washington Post*, Rusk fumed. The only request Israel had made about American ships came after its forces torpedoed the *Liberty*. The secretary of state telegrammed the American Embassy in Tel Aviv, demanding "urgent confirmation" that no prior inquiry was made. Ambassador Walworth Barbour confirmed Israel's story was bogus. "No request for info on U.S. ships operating off Sinai was made until after *Liberty* incident," Barbour cabled back. "Had Israelis made such an inquiry it would have been forwarded immediately to the chief of naval operations and other high naval commands and repeated to dept."

After the Israelis conducted their own sham "investigation," which even had the gall to blame the attack on the U.S., they applied pressure to Washington to make sure it got minimal exposure.

Sixteen days after the *Liberty* tied up in Virginia, Ephraim Evron delivered a copy of Israel's final report on the attack to Eugene Rostow at the State Department. Israeli diplomats urged American officials to downplay the 19-page report now that the attack had faded from the headlines. American leaders agreed and limited distribution largely to members of Congress and senior officers at the Pentagon. "I made clear that the document is secret and added that in our opinion, it is best not to re-evoke the matter now that it is being forgotten," Evron cabled to Jerusalem. "Rostow responded that confidentiality will be guaranteed."

The Israeli "investigation" angered some U.S. officials.

NSA deputy director Louis Tordella went further. Tordella, who previously told members of the House Appropriations Committee in a closed-door meeting that he believed Israel intentionally targeted the *Liberty*, was outraged by [Lieutenant Colonel Yeshayahu] Yerushalmi's findings. He made his feelings clear in a handwritten note. "A nice whitewash for a group of ignorant, stupid and inept xxx," he wrote, substituting the letter x for his true beliefs. "If the attackers had not been Hebrew there would have been quite a commotion. Such crass stupidity—30 knots, warship, 2 guns, etc., does not even do credit to the Nigerian Navy."

Louis W. Tordella, the longest serving deputy director of the NSA, when he was informed by the deputy director of the Joint Reconnaissance Center that "consideration was then being given by some unnamed Washington authorities to sink the *Liberty* in order that newspaper men would be unable to photograph her and thus inflame public opinion against the Israelis," made an "impolite" comment about the plan to murder those who had survived the massacre, wrote a memo of the conversation for the record, and stored it away.

To add insult to injury, when it was time for Israel to pay for their attack on my ship, they haggled and fought tooth and nail, further dishonoring the memory of those who died and those who were—and are—still suffering. A team of Israelis and American Jews fought hard to pay almost nothing.

At 10:30 A.M. on March 25, 1968—more than nine months after the attack—Israeli Ambassador to the United States Yitzhak Rabin arrived in the seventh-floor office of Nicholas Katzenbach, the State Department's second in command. After serving as the chief of staff of the Israel Defense Forces during the Six-Day War, Rabin had replaced Avraham Harman as ambassador to the U.S. in February 1968. Many Israelis believed that Rabin "incarnated the narrative of Israel's courageous fight for independence."

State Department lawyers sensed trouble with Rabin's visit. Washington lawyer David Ginsburg accompanied him. Throughout the summer and fall of 1967, U.S.-government lawyers had calculated claims on behalf of the wives, children, and parents of the 34 men killed on the *Liberty*. The American Embassy in Tel Aviv had presented the Israeli government with a bill for $3.3 million on December 29. In its accompanying note, the State Department urged Israel to promptly pay in "view of the substantial economic hardship suffered by these claimants." Israel responded by hiring Ginsburg.

Deputy State Department legal adviser Carl Salans, who drafted the earlier analysis highlighting the myriad discrepancies between the reports of the Israeli and American investigations, dashed off a memo to Katzenbach days before the meeting with Rabin. Salans was blunt. "We clearly do not want to encourage a protracted nit-picking and haggling exercise. An extended 'negotiation' over the death claims would result in considerable delay and added hardship for the claimants and would, we think, be severely criticized in Congress," he advised Katzenbach. "We should again urge the Israelis to proceed expeditiously with payment of the death claims."

Rabin began by stating that Israel "accepted in principle the obligation to pay the claims, but that more than half the compensation claimed related to shock and emotional anguish." Rabin said the Israeli government wanted to know how the United States quantified emotional anguish. Ginsburg then elaborated. The veteran lawyer said Israel was willing to pay $1.54 million for loss of support, but described shock and mental anguish as an "arbitrary figure." He also pointed out that Israel still faced claims for the injured and the *Liberty* repairs, figures the American government had not yet calculated.

Katzenbach responded "that the death claims had been presented first out of humanitarian considerations." Some of the families, the undersecretary said, had a "genuine financial need." The remaining claims for the injured demanded more time to compile. The government still did not know the full extent of the injuries in some cases or did not have long-term medical care estimates. Katzenbach again "urged that the Government of Israel not hold up the death claims." Congress was concerned most, he warned, with compensation for the families of the dead.

If Israel agreed to pay an "arbitrary figure" for emotional anguish, Rabin said he feared it might set a precedent forcing it to "accept other arbitrary figures, such as that for pain and suffering in the personal injury cases." Ginsburg said he wanted details of how the United States determined the figures for emotional anguish in the death cases and asked for the formula the government planned to use for the personal injury cases and an estimate of the *Liberty* repair bill. The embassy's lawyer added that federal statutes don't recognize payments for emotional anguish in claims against the United States. Why should Israel have to pay?

Katzenbach again emphasized that Israel should pay the death claims immediately rather than wait for the other claims. State Department officials warned Rabin after the meeting that any delays would spark victims to "redouble efforts through congressional and other channels to insure their claims not being sidetracked. This could seriously agitate issue of *Liberty* attack at time when it has generally subsided." The threat didn't sway Rabin, who "seemed unimpressed by political risks involved."

337

State Department lawyers outlined on several occasions in the following weeks how the United States calculated the $3.3 million claim. Israel still waffled. As the one-year anniversary of the attack approached, the Jewish state proposed a compromise. Israel wanted to use the same formula the American government used to pay death claims for service members. State Department lawyers calculated that Israel's proposal slashed its total compensation to $1.25 million. The proposal would hit the parents of unmarried sailors the hardest, cutting payments from $20,000 each to $5,000 each.

State Department officials fumed. The *Liberty* men didn't die in a combat zone or a war in which the United States was involved. The *Liberty* sailed in international waters with an American flag on a clear day. *Liberty* sailors had a reasonable expectation of safety. "We think this proposal entirely misconceives the legal situation," the State Department's top lawyer wrote in a memo to Katzenbach. "The payments provided for in United States legislation are in no way related to liability of another government under international law to pay compensation for wrongful death."

Some in the State Department advocated that if necessary, the United States could have a "public airing" of Israel's refusal to pay. Pressure mounted as the days passed and the first anniversary of the attack approached. The public and members of Congress continued to harass the State Department, demanding to know if Israel had paid its reparations. On May 27—354 days after its pilots and skippers strafed and torpedoed the *Liberty*—Israel relented and wrote a check to the United States treasurer for $3,323,500. The two-paragraph press release issued at noon the next day stated that as soon as the check was deposited in the treasury, families would be paid.

On July 3 the United States billed Israel $7,644,146 for the *Liberty*'s repairs. Lawyers still calculated injury claims.

The Israeli newspaper *Haaretz* ran an article stating that Israel expected America to reconsider whether it owed further reparations since the Pentagon had failed to order the *Liberty* farther from shore. "It has become clear that the U.S. Naval Command realized that a ship that is virtually in the midst of a battle zone endangers herself and therefore the order was given to the ship to get away," the article read. "It is believed in Jerusalem that the U.S. is likely to take that fact into account when she submits further claims to Israel."

The article, immediately translated and forwarded to the State Department, foreshadowed Israel's new legal theory to avoid claims, a theory it formally presented two weeks later in a note to the American Embassy in Tel Aviv. Israel now stated that various investigations of the attack exonerated the Jewish state of any liability. The previous $3.3 million payment to the families of the dead, Israel now claimed, "was motivated by humanitarian considerations relating to the economic hardship suffered by the families of the deceased."

Israel's posture outraged Rusk, who called it "totally unacceptable." The United States refused to accept Israel's claim that it was "not legally liable for death and material damage resulting from attack." Furthermore, Rusk wrote that no evidence had arisen in any inquiry exonerating Israel from paying. The secretary of state threatened that the United States would release Israel's note to the press. "We have not made either fact of receipt or contents known to public or to Congress," he warned. "If necessary, we will respond formally."

Israel backtracked. Its Foreign Ministry asked that the note be returned and forgotten. In March 1969 the United States presented claims on behalf of injured sailors. Israel paid the full $3,566,457 a month later, a figure that included $92,437 to reimburse the government for medical care and $21,745 to pay for ruined personal property. Awards ranged from a few hundred dollars for sailors with minor wounds to some in excess of $100,000 for more severe injuries, which included brain damage in one case and the loss of a kidney in another. Then the United States returned to the $7,644,146 bill for the *Liberty*'s repairs.

Israel ignored it.

Various memos and telegrams reveal the frustration the State Department faced, describing Israel as "evasive" and "petulant." A telegram to the American Embassy in Tel Aviv urged the diplomats to remind Israel that its "unresponsive attitude towards this claim will not lead to its being forgotten." In August 1971, Israel secretly offered the United States the token sum of $100,000, about 1.5¢ on the dollar. Walworth Barbour, the American ambassador to Israel, urged that the United States accept the deal.

Others disagreed. Israel's lowball offer was an insult. "The suggested sum is so small as to call clearly for a courteous rejection out of hand," wrote Heywood Stackhouse, then the State Department's country director for Israel and Arab-Israel affairs. "We think it better to keep the claim outstanding than to make a settlement unsatisfactory in so many ways. It would not be a serious irritant in our relations, and it would be a continuing reminder we are not that easy a mark."

The issue dragged on for years. Lawmakers and the press finally began asking questions in 1977 when the *Liberty* repair bill showed up as outstanding debt on the annual claims report of money owed by foreign governments submitted to Congress. The State Department hustled to come up with a deal, but negotiations stalled again as the United States soon focused on the Camp David peace process. By 1980, Israel's bill had climbed to $17,132,709, a figure that included $9,488,563 in interest. Democratic senator Adlai Stevenson of Illinois, chairman of the Senate select subcommittee on the collection and production of intelligence, threatened a congressional investigation. "Since this ship was on an intelligence mission, I intend to use the subcommittee as a means of looking into this matter further, to try to determine belatedly what the truth is," he told a reporter. "Those sailors who were wounded, who were eyewitnesses, have not been heard from by the American public."

Former Senator Adlai Stevenson III—now a spry 87-years-old, told Dave Gahary and me his views on the attack, his attempt to investigate the massacre and the ruin it brought to his career.

Although his father was a tough act to follow—who received the Democrat Party's nomination for president in 1952 and 1956—Adlai III was certainly no slouch. In 1952 he was commissioned as a lieutenant in the U.S. Marine Corps and served in the Korean War until he was discharged from active duty in 1954, then discharged from the Marine Reserves in 1961 as a captain. During that time—in 1957—he received a law degree from Harvard, and in 1964 served as an Illinois state representative, and then as Illinois's treasurer from 1967 to 1970. Stevenson then served in the U.S. Senate from 1970 to 1981, racking up a series of significant accomplishments, including authoring the International Banking Act of 1978 (which brought all U.S. foreign bank branches and agencies under the jurisdiction of U.S. banking regulations), the Stevenson Wydler-Technology Innovation Act of 1980 (the first major U.S. technology transfer law), the Bayh-Dole Act of 1980 (the Patent and Trademark Law Amendments Act), as well as conducting "the first in-depth congressional study of terrorism," which led to the introduction of the Comprehensive Counter Terrorism Act of 1971. It was while serving as Chairman of the Subcommittee on the Collection and Production of Intelligence that Stevenson discovered where modern terrorism had its roots: Israel, due primarily to their illegal land grab during the Six-Day War, the same time the massacre aboard my ship occurred.

This was not a mistake or was ascribed at the time an accident. Even Dean Rusk, the then-secretary of state,

341

later acknowledged that it was not an accident. The flag was flying, the *Liberty*'s name was inscribed; it was obviously an American ship. And I think I recall hearing that Israeli pilots had been overheard identifying this ship as American before they attacked. The fact that it was deliberate and not accidental is not and never has been in doubt.

I was chairman of the Senate Subcommittee on the Collection and Production of Intelligence, and since this was an intelligence-gathering mission by the *Liberty*, I suggested to my colleagues in that subcommittee and the full Intelligence Committee of the Unites States Senate, that we had a duty to investigate. But nobody would go along; they refused to investigate. They were all complicit, which tells you something about the influence of the Israeli lobby in our politics. And it continued. It was very frustrating for me. I tried to halt the Israeli aggressive settlement of the West Bank and the Golan Heights after the Likud came into power, and I paid a pretty high price for that effort.

Ironically, Stevenson, a great supporter of Israel, sponsored a pro-Israel bill, only to find out about the ruthless, unforgiving nature of the American Israel Public Affairs Committee (AIPAC).

As chief sponsor of the bill that became law that amended the Export Administration Act of 1969, Stevenson stood up for the Zionist state.

I was a friend of Israel, in fact I wrote the Arab anti-boycott law, which made it unlawful for U.S. companies to participate in the Arab boycott of Israel. Boy, was that easy to pass! I never got a bill passed so easily as that bill. It sailed through the Congress.

From Stevenson's terrorism analysis background, he knew from where the problem generated.

After the Likud had come to power and begun its aggressive settlements policy—and having been there I could foresee the results and the possibilities of terrorism—I offered an amendment on the Senate floor suggesting that U.S. funding for Israel be cut by $200 million a year—a small part of what we were spending on Israel—until such time as the president could certify that Israel's settlement policy was consistent with U.S. policy. Well, my amendment got seven votes.

After the amendment went down in flames, a colleague offered Stevenson some advice.

"One senator, he was from Montana—not exactly a citadel of Jewish [power]—he came up and just said, "Well, sorry Adlai, but I'm up for reelection." Money went far.

I support Israel. But I also support the United States and peace! And I do not support deceiving the American people.

Stevenson elaborated on what happened in Congress when trying to pursue the interests of the country he was elected to serve, and the fallout from opposing AIPAC.

I tried to halt the Israeli aggressive settlements of the West Bank and the Golan Heights after the Likud came into power, and I paid a pretty high price for that effort. I experienced the wrath of AIPAC and the Lobby on several occasions.

They'll go after you no matter what office you run for, and make a lesson of you if you dare to represent the United States, and if in fact you dare represent Israel, and its best interests. It's almost treasonable. But who can complain? You get punished if you do.

Stevenson touched upon some colleagues who had also dared oppose AIPAC.

> My dear friend and colleague Senator Charles Percy of Illinois, they got him! And all he did was support certain arms sales to Saudi Arabia, which were disapproved by AIPAC at the time. Look what happened to Pete McCloskey and Paul Findley, first-rate American and public servants.
>
> They have very successfully intimidated the American politicians, and Israel is paying a high price for it, and so are we. The whole Middle East is destabilized, and at the root of it is [the] aggressive settlements policy and the occupation of the West Bank and the Golan Heights, and the continued oppression of the Palestinian people.
>
> And many Israelis, many American Jews agree. In fact, it's much easier to stand up in the Knesset than in the U.S. Congress for peace in the Middle East, and an end to this aggressive, right-wing settlements policy of the Likud.

One such American Jew was a big supporter of Stevenson.

> Phil Klutznick, the former president of the World Jewish Congress, former Department of Commerce secretary, and a former ambassador, with some experience in the world and some standing in the Jewish community, he agreed with me completely, and contributed generously to one of my subsequent campaigns for governor when the Israeli Lobby came after me and finally got me by one vote in the Illinois Supreme Court, which denied us a recount.

Stevenson was alluding to his 1982 Illinois gubernatorial campaign where he was literally robbed of the prize, revealing here how that happened. Although the initial vote count had him winning, the final official count recorded Stevenson losing by .14%. Petitioning the Illinois Supreme Court for a recount while presenting "evidence of widespread election irregularities, including evidence of a failed punch card system for tabulation of votes," he was denied the recount by a one-vote margin, three days before the gubernatorial inauguration.

> This one judge was Jewish—nothing wrong with that—and he was a Democrat, and he went over and voted with the Republican judges, to deny us a recount, even though we had proof that I had won the election. And this one judge told a mutual friend—who's still living—who later confided to me that that judge told him that he had voted as he did because of "just one word," Israel.

Although Stevenson was shattered by the loss, he shared his feelings on who the real losers were.

> What hurt was the fact that the people of Illinois had been deprived of their choice for governor, and in favor of somebody who deserved to lose. That hurts; it's a sad commentary on our politics. And maybe I'm responsible. I'm an example of what happens if you stand up to The Lobby. [That's why] nobody does.

The Attack on the Liberty detailed the perversity of the final settlement from the massacre of my ship.

> Israel offered to settle for $6 million, payable in three annual installments of $2 million. The final offer was less than the original bill for damages. The United States, weary of the negotiations, accepted the deal in December 1980. Thirteen years had passed since the attack and nearly eight years since President Johnson had died of a heart attack at his Texas ranch. *The New York Times* wrote in a front-page story that the United States and Israel

"had finally closed the book on one of the most divisive issues between the two countries." Stevenson dropped his proposed investigation.

Former secretary of state Rusk challenged the idea that the issue was dead in a 1981 letter to one of the *Liberty*'s officers. Rusk wrote that he believed the attack "was and remains a genuine outrage." Despite the years of negotiations, he added that he felt Israel did not pay enough to the families of the men killed or the survivors. Rusk was pragmatic. The bill for the ship was the least important: "It was not a major point because, in light of our aid programs for Israel, we would, in effect, be paying ourselves."

40
Spotlight

One day, sometime in the mid-1980s after being elected president of the LVA, I got a phone call from a reporter writing for a Washington D.C.-based newspaper called *The Spotlight*. Her name was Trisha Katson, and she wanted to know everything about what happened to the USS *Liberty*.

The Spotlight was a populist, "anti-elitist," nationalist, pro-American, "America First" Washington, D.C.-based weekly newspaper that began in 1975 until it was driven out of business in 2001 by various globalist groups who were not fond of newspapers, groups or individuals promoting an America-First agenda or having the guts to question certain historical events such as the "Holocaust." It was branded a "Holocaust denial" publication for daring to examine the official narrative of that part of WW2 history, and labeled "anti-Semitic," as well as other slurs that are used by the powers-that-be to silence any criticism of any sacred cow.

At its peak it had a circulation of nearly 400,000, counting John Wayne and Eddie Albert amoing its subscribers.

Trisha and I talked every day for a month, sometimes as long as three hours at a time. In the meantime, she was running weekly stories based on our conversations concerning the attack.

Then one day she called and asked if I would be willing to come to D.C. to speak at a conference the paper was sponsoring. She read off the list of some of the others scheduled to be there.

When I heard that the nightly news anchor, Tom Brokaw was one of them—he was a no-show—I knew I had to go. This was the best opportunity to get our story out that had ever come along. The next thing I knew, I was on an airplane headed for our nation's capital.

I was very nervous because I had never spoken in front of a large crowd before and from what I had been told it would be large. I was greeted at the airport by Trisha, and on the way to the hotel, we talked about the conference taking place the next night, discussing when I would be speaking and for how long and all that.

The next night came and the conference with it. My nerves were just about as bad as they were the day we were attacked. Before I knew it, I was up there in front of a big crowd.

This was going to be one of the first, if not the first public talk ever given concerning the attack on our ship. I had written out notes to try and keep everything straight, but as soon as I looked out at the sea of people staring at me, I froze.

I looked down at my notes, trying to follow them but in the process, I just ended up stumbling through my words. At last, realizing the gravity of what was taking place, I put the note cards down, took a deep breath and just started to speak to them, one-on-one, as a survivor of the *Liberty*, to his fellow countrymen. I told them everything that happened.

I described the savagery of the attack, or as best as I could remember it at that time. I looked around at the audience and noted that all those in attendance spanned every generation, young and old.

And when I saw before me a cross-section of America, I used language I never used before.

> Ladies and gentlemen, this attack was not just an attack on my ship, it was an attack on you, your children, your grandchildren and all Americans. It was an act of war no different than the attack on Pearl Harbor.
>
> I am not here to be a Jew-hater. If that's how it appears, then I'm sorry, but they did this to themselves. My reason for being here is to let them, you and the world know that no one—no one—should be allowed to get away with premeditated, cold-blooded murder, not even Israel.

The applause was as loud as a hurricane. It made me feel good, if for no other reason than I felt I had done something for my shipmates, both living and dead, but more so for the dead, because this was something they could not do for themselves.

As I came down off the podium, I was swarmed with well-wishers reaching out for me, shaking my hands, slapping me on the shoulder and telling me their names. Willis Carto, the brains behind the whole *Spotlight* operation, came up and thanked me for my speech. This was the first time since the massacre that someone actually wanted to hear about what happened to us.

In my lifetime, I have never met a more distinguished and honorable man than Willis A. Carto, who gave all he could give, financially and in print, to get the real truth out about the savage attack on our ship. Sadly, Willis Carto passed away October 26, 2015 at the age of 89.

41

Library

In the October 19, 1987 edition of *The Spotlight*—a week after I had spoken at the conference—there was a picture of yours truly right on the front page and a story about my speech.

That date, whether you believe in coincidences or not, was also Black Monday, when the world's stock markets crashed.

Within a few days of that paper hitting the streets, I got a phone call from Willis who informed me he had a letter of great interest he needed to forward to me, and a few days later, it was in my hands.

> Dear Mr. Tourney,
>
> Congratulations on your courage in your interview in *Spotlight* of October 19, 1987. My brother Ted and I made a substantial contribution to build a new library in Grafton, Wisconsin, which entitles us to name the library.
>
> Instead of naming it the "Grob Library" as suggested, we would like to call it "The USS *Liberty* Memorial Public Library." Before doing this, we would like to have the reaction of the families of the murdered as well as the survivors.
>
> Very Truly Yours,
> Benjamin Grob

After reading the letter, I had to sit down and gather my thoughts. I didn't know who to call first. I was elated and overwhelmed with emotion over the idea that my words had touched so many different individuals, one of whom wanted to dedicate a library in honor of our ship.

I contacted Ben Grob at the address on the letter and in the following weeks, after some back-and-forth with the U.S. postal system, I got to be good friends with both him and his brother Ted. Ben and Ted had emigrated to the U.S. from Sweden many years earlier, and the mass murder of 34 American servicemen had a great impact on them.

I was soon informed that when certain members of the rather large Jewish community in Milwaukee—of which I was unaware—had heard that a library was going to be named after and dedicated to a USN ship, the USS *Liberty*, they went ballistic.

One of the many hundreds of articles liberally splayed across the pages of Wisconsin newspapers, like this one, "Jew Seek to Change Library's Name," from *The Milwaukee Journal* (5/8/88)

This in the Unites States of America of all places, where freedom of speech is enshrined in the First Amendment of the Bill of Rights to the U.S. Constitution.

Demands came pouring into the mayor's office and the newspapers. Like the machinegun bullets I had to dodge over 20 years earlier, complaints and accusations of "anti-Semitism" were rained down upon the whole project and everyone associated with it.

Jim Grant, the mayor of Grafton, along with John Dickman, a prominent local businessman, stood shoulder-to-shoulder against the assault.

Where is the outrage in Grafton?

Is it possible, as Grafton Village President James Grant seems to suggest, that village residents are in lockstep over the controversial name chosen for the new public library? Why is there no outcry over a decision that has clear anti-Semitic overtones?

To their credit, members of the Milwaukee Jewish Council met with Grant this week in an unsuccessful effort to persuade village officials to reconsider the name. As things now stand, Grafton's new library will be called the USS Liberty Memorial Public Library, after a US ship attacked by Israel more than 20 years ago.

Israel explained the incident as a tragic case of mistaken identity and paid reparations to the United States, but a number of people — especially on the extreme right of the political spectrum — believe the attack was deliberate. What's most unfortunate is that anti-Semitic organizations have seized upon the Liberty case as justification for their hate-mongering against Jews and Israel.

Against that backdrop, it's not so difficult to understand why Jews here might find the

AROUND THE REGION
An opinion of The Journal Editorial Conference

library name offensive, for it seems to imply anti-Semitism. Grant argues that the name was chosen only to honor the 34 American sailors who died in the attack, but he can't credibly ignore what the Liberty case has come to represent. Moreover, a friend of Grant was wounded in the Liberty attack, so the village president's perspective might be somewhat jaundiced.

Were the library naming the only blunder Grafton officials have made with respect to the Liberty case, that might be the end of it. But village officials have also designated June 8 as "USS Liberty Memorial Day."

Surely not all residents of Grafton are comfortable with the anti-Semitic message their elected officials seem to be sending. Won't the citizens who have doubts please break the silence?

Another attack on the name which would honor *Liberty* by the mainstream media, in this "opinion piece," "Where is the Outrage in Grafton?" in *The Milwaukee Journal* (5/13/88)

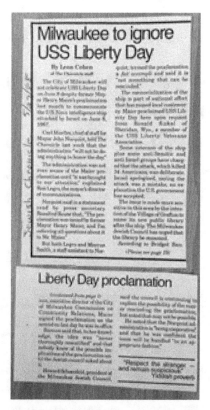

Over a year before the dedication, Jewish groups had applied enough pressure to Milwaukee's politicians to force them "ignore" a day set aside to honor the sacrifices the crew of *Liberty* suffered through the day of the massacre, crowed about in this article entitled "Milwaukee to Ignore USS *Liberty* Day," in *The Wisconsin Jewish Chronicle*

One day I got a phone call from Ted Grob who told me there was a "crack in the dam." The crack he was talking about was an upcoming vote on the town council on whether or not the public library would be named after *Liberty*.

He told me he called every one of the council members and told them that if they voted against naming the library after *Liberty*, all the money which he and his brother had promised—$250,000—would be withdrawn and every penny of it would be given to the LVA. All of the sudden, the crack that was there yesterday was shored up like the bulkheads in the belly of *Liberty* had been over 20 years earlier. The new library would be built and named after the ship.

Grafton group urges residents to speak out

This June 6, 1988 article reports on a group encouraging Grafton's residents to oppose the proposed name for the library, because it is "offensive to all who oppose bigotry and racial prejudice in our country."

I was getting regular updates on the project, complete with photos of the library as it was being built, and the date of the dedication was approaching quickly.

Persons of note were contacted and asked if they would be willing to travel to Grafton to speak on behalf of the library and the survivors. One of the speakers included California Congressman Paul Norton

"Pete" McCloskey, Jr., who gave one of the more heartfelt speeches of his life.

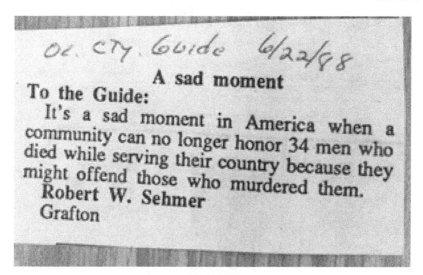

Ok. Cty. Guide 6/22/98

A sad moment

To the Guide:

It's a sad moment in America when a community can no longer honor 34 men who died while serving their country because they might offend those who murdered them.

Robert W. Sehmer
Grafton

One of the few messages of support for the library name, allowed to be printed in the papers, which summed up the situation nicely

Incredibly, what was even more dramatic than the speeches given that day were the steps that had to be taken to ensure our safety. As many as 40 police officers from several different departments were out in force. There were SWAT teams on rooftops with sniper rifles and bomb-sniffing dogs. Their police handlers were patrolling the area, and the town was cordoned off to prevent vehicles from going places they weren't supposed to be on that day.

The reason for this enormous police presence in what was a very small Wisconsin town—population 9,000—was that several threats on the lives of *Liberty* survivors had been made. We don't need Sherlock Holmes or his friend Watson to figure out who made these threats and why. Why certain American Jews would choose Israel over their own country is why the term dual loyalty exists, and here, in Grafton, it was on full display.

When the dedication ceremony took place on June 10, 1989— attended by 60 *Liberty* survivors—I had the honor of sitting in the front row right next to Ted and Ben Grob, the persons responsible for this wonderful testimony to all whose lives were immeasurably changed on June 8, 1967. To make the event even more memorable, Ted Grob extended the offer to my wife, Lisa, and I to stay at his home.

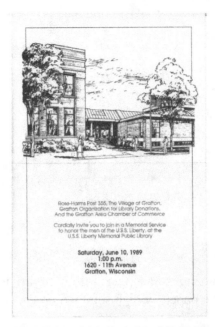

Rose-Harms Post 355, The Village of Grafton,
Grafton Organization for Library Donations,
And the Grafton Area Chamber of Commerce

Cordially invite you to join in a Memorial Service
to honor the men of the U.S.S. Liberty, at the
U.S.S. Liberty Memorial Public Library

Saturday, June 10, 1989
1:00 p.m.
1620 - 11th Avenue
Grafton, Wisconsin

Invitation to USS *Liberty* Memorial Public Library dedication
ceremony in Grafton, Wisconsin, June 10, 1989

The dedication ceremony was not without drama, and insult.

As a final gesture to the pro-Israeli interests who were outraged over the dedication, someone on the library's board of directors had slyly made sure that the huge silver letters on the outside wall of the library announcing its name, had "USS *Liberty* Memorial" in small letters, while the words "Public Library" were in huge letters.

As proof that they were intent upon seeing this thing through to the end, the Grob brothers had a new sign made where the name "USS *Liberty* Memorial" was prominently displayed, for the "paltry sum" of an additional $50,000.

After it was all over, I received the following letter from Ted Grob, thanking me for all I had done in helping to bring this about.

Dear Phil,

It amazes me how much publicity we receive due to the new USS *Liberty* Memorial Public Library in Grafton.

Just a few days ago, a lady phoned and made an appointment to meet Ben and me. As Ben is still in Florida, I put it off for a few weeks until Ben is here again. The lady's husband is in the Navy and read about it in their Navy publication. They also want to see us and see the articles.

Even though the name of our library made us some enemies, more important is it made us some friends. Which reminds me to thank you for your part, because without you, the name of the new Grafton Library would not be USS *Liberty* Memorial Public Library. Of course, credit is due to many, and each played a part in the name to be born and to be adapted. This was *The Spotlight* with an article of your speech at one of their meetings. Without your speech, we would not have known that there was a USS *Liberty* Veterans Association. My brother, Ben, got the idea to name the new library USS *Liberty* Memorial after reading your courageous speech. Credit also goes to Jim Ennes Jr. for writing the book *Assault on the Liberty* from which we knew what it was all about. Then, the name would have never stuck if it was not for the village president, James Grant and others like John Dickman.

To you and all those others, our heartfelt thanks.

Sincerely, your friend,
Ted Grob

50 years later, the attacks and threats still come . . .

42

Threats

My undying desire to get the story of the massacre on my ship out there didn't—and doesn't—come without peril. Just for wanting to tell the story of the massacre that took place aboard my ship I have been called every name in the book, from "Nazi," to "Jew hater," to "anti-Semite;" you name it.

My wonderful wife, Lisa, remembered when the attacks began.

> Around 1984, we were living in an apartment complex in Lakewood, Colorado, when one morning we woke up to find our 1978 turquoise Mercury Cougar spray-painted with swastikas. We tried to scrub them off but portions still remained. The mirrors were beaten off and hanging off the doors.
>
> Phil called the local police department. They came out and took an incident report. Nothing ever came of the case. They just ignored it and swept it under the rug. We didn't have any of our children then.

The article in *The Spotlight* and news of the library renaming also had an impact on our safety.

Another encounter with threats made towards me and my family was after I was interviewed for a full-page article about the *Liberty* in the [Fort Collins] *Coloradoan* in 1988. After that, I started getting threatening and hang-up phone calls, and a swastika was painted on my garage door. When we moved to Cedaredge, Colorado in 1990, the phone calls disappeared because it was an unlisted number, and

I thought it was all behind me. I became even more active writing newspapers articles and speaking to anybody who would listen.

Then around 1994, when our daughter was in the 3rd or 4th grade, we received a one minute phone call threatening to harm to her by name.

"We know where your daughter is, and we're gonna get [her]. You better quit talking about the *Liberty* or it's gonna get worse," he said before I hung up the phone.

I called the school and told them about the call and asked them to please bring all three of our children to the office so we could pick them up. After that, I called the police and filed a complaint. Of course, they took down all the info we gave them, but not surprisingly, nothing ever came of that threat either.

In 2006, their verbal threats and harassment turned real.

I was going down the highway—the speed limit—and my pickup truck began to swerve. I got it to the side of the road and got out and checked the front end, and on the left side there were a few lug nuts remaining on the left and on the right side there was only one.

On another occasion I was in my son's truck, a Ford F-150, and we were doing at least 70 mph, and the same thing happened. The right, front wheel had all the lug nuts removed. The tire fell off and totaled the truck by twisting the front frame.

A few years after that, those intent on keeping the story of the *Liberty* massacre under wraps tried a new strategy, as Lisa explained.

> Towards the end of October, 2009, Phil, myself, and my mother were in San Diego staying at a Holiday Inn. We had been at activities all day, so Phil—with his *Liberty* jacket and hat on—and I decided to have a couple of drinks in the hotel bar.

> We sat down at the bar on the end closest to where we came in. There were three seats on that end, and there were a few people in the bar besides us. We sat on the two seats to the left. Around 15 minutes after we sat down a man sat next to Phil in the empty seat to his right. He knew Phil's name. Phil and this guy started polite conversation.

Phil asked him what he did for a living, and he replied that he was a doctor. Phil asked him for his business card and he stated he had none.

He went to the bathroom and Phil asked the bartender about him and she said he had been coming in the previous several nights and nursing a glass of white wine and appeared to be waiting for someone to arrive. By this time Phil knew exactly who/what he was. He appeared in his early-or-mid-40s, was tall, had curly hair, a large nose, and spoke with an Israeli accent.

After he came back, Phil told him—after a bit more small talk—that he knew he was a *sayan* or Mossad agent. The agent was wearing a huge gold watch on his left wrist and kept shoving it in Phil's face. Phil continuously told him to "get that damn watch out of my face." The two of them sidled up close to one another and continued talking in hushed tones. I could barely make out their conversation.

Sayanim—Hebrew for helpers or assistants—is a term popularized by former Mossad agent Victor Ostrovsky's 1990 book, *By Way of Deception: The Making and Unmaking of a Mossad Officer*. Outside of Israel, *sayanim* provide assistance to Mossad officers including money, logistics, medical care, and oftentimes overt intelligence gathering.

"They can be judges, court clerks, expert witnesses, child protective service workers, assistant district attorneys, police officers, or anyone with a great degree of power over people's lives, and will do anything at the behest of Mossad case officers for the State of Israel against its enemies or those perceived to be unfavorable politically to Israeli policy."

It is estimated *sayanims* number in the hundreds of thousands worldwide.

The agent said something like "It was a terrible mistake; you were in a war zone."

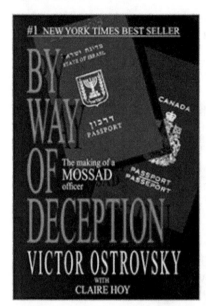

By Way of Deception: The Making and Unmaking of a Mossad Officer

Phil knew he was a Mossad agent and that he was trying to talk him out of speaking out about the *Liberty* by threatening him with his life, which I did hear. Phil asked the agent when Phil was scheduled to die. The "doctor" said when Iran gets attacked.

I couldn't believe this was actually happening. It was the first time I had heard the actual threatening tactics of the Zionists. Phil had told me of the several times he and our family had been threatened that I hadn't previously been aware of. I was completely freaked out and had a hard time calming down. I finally asked Phil if this guy was for real. Phil told me he was. I got up from my seat and walked around Phil to where the doctor was sitting. I had to say something. By this time I was seething with anger and really just wanted to kill him.

I asked him if he know what he had done to my family; like he would really care. I intentionally kept my questions to a minimum volume. I told him he was the beast and he was going to go straight to hell. He replied to me with an emphasis on being loud saying he was sorry over and over and louder and louder trying to draw attention to me, like I was a nut and accosting him. I kept telling him he was not sorry and that his kind was the beast and all going to hell. I had to go outside at that point because I was having a severe panic attack.

After putting up with this for around 30 minutes, Phil called security over and asked them to escort us back to our room, because he thought we needed help. Security followed us all the way to our room.

When we got back home, Phil contacted the local police, the California Bureau of Investigation, and the FBI. As with every other report filed, nothing ever came of it.

43

Cristol

In 2002, a Jewish man named Ahron Jay Cristol wrote the book *The Liberty Incident: The 1967 Israeli Attack on the U.S. Navy Spy Ship*, which attempted to prove that the attack was all a case of mistaken identity.

Cristol, currently the Chief Judge Emeritus of the U.S. Bankruptcy Court in for the Southern District of Florida, is perhaps most notable for awarding the rights of O.J. Simpson's book to the family of Ronald Goldman for the wrongful death judgment against the former football star.

He was born in 1929, joined the Navy in 1951, flew noncombat missions after the Korean War, and a few years later, left active duty for the Naval Reserve. In 1958 he received a B.A. degree from the University of Miami, and the next year he received a J.D. degree from the same institution's law school. Afterwards, he graduated from Naval Justice School and served as a Judge Advocate General Corps Navy lawyer (JAG) for 20 years. Cristol enrolled in the University of Miami School of Law's Graduate School of International Studies and spent 10 years researching the *Liberty* massacre, writing his dissertation on it, and earning his Ph.D. in 1997.

In his thesis, entitled *The Liberty Incident*, Cristol analyzed the "official" investigations—there has never been an official investigation—conducted almost 500 interviews, filed Freedom of Information Act (FOIA) requests for declassified reports, 22 hot line messages, 22 NSA documents and 31 National Security Council documents, and even classified Israeli documents.

Following the thesis, he sued the NSA under FOIA, who released audio tapes collected by the spy agency aboard the previously mentioned EC-121 Warning Star aircraft flying above when the massacre took place. He published his book afterwards, claiming the tapes proved the attack was a case of mistaken identity.

All it took, however, to dispel the myths and mistaken conclusions that Cristol had labored for decades on to exonerate Israel, was an October 2, 2007, *Chicago Tribune* special report on the attack, entitled "New Revelations in Attack on American Spy Ship," which contained numerous previously unreported quotes from former military personnel with first-hand knowledge of the massacre.

Ahron Jay Cristol

Of course all Cristol had to do, but he dared not, was to interview *Liberty* survivors, who would have told him what they thought of his conclusions.

Bob Hamel had a run in with Cristol, who had contacted him for his whitewash of Israel's massacre. Bob explained what happened.

> I was contacted by an author who was extremely aggressive and anti to my position. He was writing a book to disprove everything and to say it was a lie.
>
> I said, "How dare you accuse me of lying?" He tried to tear me apart, as of course being anti-Semitic. And I said, "You insult me with your racist comments. I was there.

As a naval officer I pride myself on always telling the truth, and I have no axes to grind, and I'm repeating to you what these dying men said to me and what I saw. So how can you possibly impugn me, my motives or my honesty?"

And I got quite upset and we did not part on good terms. I felt like I was in a stand being grilled by some defense attorney on some evidence that I had produced in court.

Not surprisingly, the book was endorsed by Senator John S. McCain, III, son of the same Admiral John S. McCain, Jr. responsible for orchestrating the cover-up of the massacre. I heard that every member of Congress was provided a free copy of the book as "reference" if and when they received correspondence from their constituents regarding Israel's deliberate, murderous attack on our ship.

44

Boston

Immediately after Cristol's apologia for Israel was released for public consumption, Captain Ward Boston, Jr., the Navy's Chief Legal Counsel for the Court of Inquiry looking into the massacre 35 years earlier, was so outraged over Cristol's attempt at re-writing history in Israel's favor, that he was "pushed . . . to speak out."

Boston, born June 21, 1923, served in WW2 as a Navy fighter pilot aboard the carrier USS *Yorktown* (CV-10) and worked as a special agent for the Federal Bureau of Investigation prior to his assignment to the Navy's JAG Corps. He passed away June 12, 2008.

Ward Boston, Jr.

On June 26, 2002, Boston told a *Marine Corps Times* reporter the attack was deliberate and that the Court of Inquiry was a politicized sham with conclusions preordained to exonerate Israel.

The story, published in the *Navy Times* in July 2002, is reproduced below.

Conflicting Comments Rekindle *Liberty* Dispute

Key investigators express belief that Israel deliberately attacked U.S. ship

By Bryant Jordan

Thirty-five years after Israeli air and naval forces attacked a lightly armed U.S. Navy spy ship during the Arab-Israeli Six- Day War, the CIA director at the time and the legal counsel to the Navy's court of inquiry say the attack was deliberate.

"It was no accident," former CIA director Richard Helms said May 29, bucking that agency's June 13, 1967, report that indicated the incident could have been a mistake.

Retired Navy legal counsel Capt. Ward Boston says he and the court's president, the late Rear Adm. Isaac "Ike" Kidd, always believed Israeli forces knowingly attacked the *Liberty*.

"I feel the Israelis knew what they were doing. They knew they were shooting at a U.S. Navy ship," said Boston, who lives in Coronado, Calif. "That's the bottom line. I don't care how they tried to get out of it."

The attack killed 34 men and wounded 172 others, and sparked a long-running controversy: Did Israel knowingly try to sink the American ship or did it believe the ship was an Egyptian vessel?

Officially, the Navy exonerated Israel on June 18, 1967— 10 days after the attack—when the Navy court of inquiry found that available evidence indicated the attack was a case of mistaken identity.

The Court of Inquiry

Boston said Kidd told him he believed the attack was deliberate and that the Israelis knew the ship was American. That flies in the face of the findings of Kidd's court, and also what the author of a new book on the *Liberty* says Kidd told him in interviews in the early 1990s.

A. Jay Cristol, a federal judge in Florida and retired Navy aviator who also served in the service's Judge Advocate General's Corps, is the author of the upcoming "The Liberty Incident."

"Kidd told me an entirely different story," said Cristol, whose new book is dedicated to Kidd, who died in 1999.

Cristol said that during one interview with Kidd in December 1990, Kidd related that when he brought the court's report to then-Chief of Naval Operations Adm. David Lamar McDonald, the CNO asked him, "Ike, was it intentional?"

"Ike said, 'No, Admiral,'" Cristol recalled. But Boston remembers that when Kidd returned from Washington, he said officials were not interested in hearing the truth.

"In military life, you accept the fact that if you're told to shut up, you shut up. We did what we were told," Boston said.

He explained that he is willing to talk now because "every one else is shooting their mouth off."

Boston said he does not know whether his beliefs were shared by the other members of the court, Capts. Bert M. Atkinson, Jr. and Bernard J. Lauff.

Lauff could not be located for comment. Atkinson died in 1999.

But Boston's statements do put him now in the camp of retired Adm. Merlin Staring, who as a captain and staff legal officer in London was initially told to review the court's report.

Staring said . . . the report was taken from him before he finished his review, but based on what he had seen, the evidence did not support the contention that the attack was an accident.

Staring concedes he still has not read the entire report.

Staring, who went on to become the Navy's top JAG officer, is now part of a newly formed Liberty Alliance, which includes former CNO and Joint Chiefs of Staff chairman Thomas Moorer and two Marine Medal of Honor recipients, Gen. Ray Davis and Col. Mitchell Paige.

The group wants a full congressional investigation into the attack and is lobbying military organizations, including the Veterans of Foreign Wars and the American Legion, hoping to garner support among their members, said Tito Howard, the group's executive director.

Survivors Allege Conspiracy

Many *Liberty* survivors and their supporters long have maintained that the attack was deliberate and that the Kidd report excluded testimony from crewmembers that would have shown that.

Boston recalled that testimony was taken from crewmembers who said the Israelis fired on life rafts when they were put into the water.

The court's report includes testimony indicating the shooting of the life rafts was incidental, occurring when the ship was strafed by Israeli jets.

Some allege Israel wanted the spy ship sunk to ensure it did not pick up communications showing Israel was planning to seize the Golan Heights from Syria. Others say it was to prevent *Liberty* from intercepting communications dealing with an alleged Israeli massacre of Egyptian POWs in the Sinai.

Some *Liberty* survivors and supporters claim the U.S. government covered up the incident to avoid a conflict with Israel that could have cost the Johnson administration support among Jewish voters and supporters. Subsequent administrations and Congresses have avoided a thorough airing of the incident for the same reasons, they say.

But Cristol says there have been 10 U.S. investigations, ranging from the court of inquiry and the CIA's report to several conducted by House and Senate committees.

Five drew no conclusions regarding Israel, according to a list compiled by Cristol, while others accepted that it was an accident.

The most recent official look at the incident was in 1991, when the House Armed Services subcommittee on investigations found no evidence to support the *Liberty* survivors' claim that Israel attacked the ship deliberately.

Reports and Recollections

The CIA's report, the earliest of those assembled, held open the possibility that the attack was a case of mistaken identity— the finding that the Kidd court went on to make five days later— though it did not present that as a conclusion.

In the June 13, 1967, report, the CIA stated that "an overzealous pilot" could have mistaken the *Liberty* for an Egyptian ship, the *El Quesir*. Helms, the former CIA director, declined to discuss the incident at length.

"I've done all I can. I don't want to spend the rest of my life in court" testifying about the incident, he said.

Mike Weeks, a naval aviation writer and amateur historian who studied the official Navy communications that occurred during and after the attack and believes it was an accident, said there is more information on the *Liberty* still classified and believes the government should release all of it.

"Just put it out there and see how it flows," he said. "The bottom line, all this stuff ought to be let loose, for heaven's sake."

Bryant Jordan is a staff writer for *Marine Corps Times*.

Captain Boston revealed that the Court was ordered by LBJ himself to conclude the attack was a case of mistaken identity. Boston also stated that the Court of Inquiry transcript released to the public was not the same one he certified and sent to D.C. Also, he stated that Cristol flat-out lied when recounting a telephone conversation he had with him.

In early 2004, Boston repeated the revelation before a State Department conference about the Six-Day War.

In a January 8, 2004 signed four-page affidavit—reproduced below—he stated that LBJ and McNamara ordered Admiral Kidd to rule "that the attack was a case of mistaken identity" despite "overwhelming evidence to the contrary."

DECLARATION OF WARD BOSTON, JR., CAPTAIN, JAGC, USN (RET.)

I, Ward Boston, Jr. do declare that the following statement is true and complete:

1. For more than 30 years, I have remained silent on the topic of USS *Liberty*. I am a military man and when orders come in from the Secretary of Defense and President of the United States, I follow them.

2. However, recent attempts to rewrite history compel me to share the truth.

3. In June of 1967, while serving as a Captain in the Judge Advocate General Corps, Department of the Navy, I was assigned as senior legal counsel for the Navy's Court of Inquiry into the brutal attack on USS *Liberty*, which had occurred on June 8th.

4. The late Admiral Isaac C. Kidd, president of the Court, and I were given only one week to gather evidence for the Navy's official investigation into the attack, despite the fact that we both had estimated that a proper Court of Inquiry into an attack of this magnitude would take at least six months to conduct.

5. Admiral John S. McCain, Jr., then Commander-in-chief, Naval Forces Europe (CINCUSNAVEUR), at his headquarters in London, had charged Admiral Kidd (in a letter dated June 10, 1967) to "inquire into all the pertinent facts and circumstances leading to and connected with the armed attack; damage resulting therefrom; and deaths of and injuries to Naval personnel."

6. Despite the short amount of time we were given, we gathered a vast amount of evidence, including hours of heartbreaking testimony from the young survivors.

7. The evidence was clear. Both Admiral Kidd and I believed with certainty that this attack, which killed 34 American sailors and injured 172 others, was a deliberate effort to sink an American ship and murder its entire crew. Each evening, after hearing testimony all day, we often spoke our private thoughts concerning what we

had seen and heard. I recall Admiral Kidd repeatedly referring to the Israeli forces responsible for the attack as "murderous bastards." It was our shared belief, based on the documentary evidence and testimony we received first hand, that the Israeli attack was planned and deliberate, and could not possibly have been an accident.

8. I am certain that the Israeli pilots that undertook the attack, as well as their superiors, who had ordered the attack, were well aware that the ship was American.

9. I saw the flag, which had visibly identified the ship as American, riddled with bullet holes, and heard testimony that made it clear that the Israelis intended there be no survivors.

10. Not only did the Israelis attack the ship with napalm, gunfire, and missiles, Israeli torpedo boats machinegunned three lifeboats that had been launched in an attempt by the crew to save the most seriously wounded—a war crime.

11. Admiral Kidd and I both felt it necessary to travel to Israel to interview the Israelis who took part in the attack. Admiral Kidd telephoned Admiral McCain to discuss making arrangements. Admiral Kidd later told me that Admiral McCain was adamant that we were not to travel to Israel or contact the Israelis concerning this matter.

12. Regrettably, we did not receive into evidence and the Court did not consider any of the more than 60 witness declarations from men who had been hospitalized and were unable to testify in person.

13. I am outraged at the efforts of the apologists for Israel in this country to claim that this attack was a case of "mistaken identity."

14. In particular, the recent publication of Jay Cristol's book, *The Liberty Incident*, twists the facts and

misrepresents the views of those of us who investigated the attack.

15. It is Cristol's insidious attempt to whitewash the facts that has pushed me to speak out.

16. I know from personal conversations I had with Admiral Kidd that President Lyndon Johnson and Secretary of Defense Robert McNamara ordered him to conclude that the attack was a case of "mistaken identity" despite overwhelming evidence to the contrary.

17. Admiral Kidd told me, after returning from Washington, D.C. that he had been ordered to sit down with two civilians from either the White House or the Defense Department, and rewrite portions of the court's findings.

18. Admiral Kidd also told me that he had been ordered to "put the lid" on everything having to do with the attack on USS *Liberty*. We were never to speak of it and we were to caution everyone else involved that they could never speak of it again.

19. I have no reason to doubt the accuracy of that statement as I know that the Court of Inquiry transcript that has been released to the public is not the same one that I certified and sent off to Washington.

20. I know this because it was necessary, due to the exigencies of time, to hand correct and initial a substantial number of pages. I have examined the released version of the transcript and I did not see any pages that bore my hand corrections and initials.

Also, the original did not have any deliberately blank pages, as the released version does. Finally, the testimony of Lt. Painter concerning the deliberate machinegunning of the life rafts by the Israeli torpedo boat crews, which

I distinctly recall being given at the Court of Inquiry and included in the original transcript, is now missing and has been excised.

21. Following the conclusion of the Court of Inquiry, Admiral Kidd and I remained in contact. Though we never spoke of the attack in public, we did discuss it between ourselves, on occasion. Every time we discussed the attack, Admiral Kidd was adamant that it was a deliberate, planned attack on an American ship.

22. In 1990, I received a telephone call from Jay Cristol, who wanted to interview me concerning the functioning of the Court of Inquiry. I told him that I would not speak to him on that subject and prepared to hang up the telephone. Cristol then began asking me about my personal background and other, non-Court of Inquiry related matters. I endeavored to answer these questions and politely extricate myself from the conversation. Cristol continued to return to the subject of the Court of Inquiry, which I refused to discuss with him. Finally, I suggested that he contact Admiral Kidd and ask him about the Court of Inquiry.

23. Shortly after my conversation with Cristol, I received a telephone call from Admiral Kidd, inquiring about Cristol and what he was up to. The Admiral spoke of Cristol in disparaging terms and even opined that "Cristol must be an Israeli agent." I don't know if he meant that literally or it was his way of expressing his disgust for Cristol's highly partisan, pro-Israeli approach to questions involving USS *Liberty*.

24. At no time did I ever hear Admiral Kidd speak of Cristol other than in highly disparaging terms. I find Cristol's claims of a "close friendship" with Admiral Kidd to be utterly incredible. I also find it impossible to believe the statements he attributes to Admiral Kidd, concerning the attack on USS *Liberty*.

25. Several years later, I received a letter from Cristol that contained what he purported to be his notes of our prior conversation. These "notes" were grossly incorrect and bore no resemblance in reality to that discussion. I find it hard to believe that these "notes" were the product of a mistake, rather than an attempt to deceive. I informed Cristol that I disagreed with his recollection of our conversation and that he was wrong. Cristol made several attempts to arrange for the two of us to meet in person and talk but I always found ways to avoid doing this. I did not wish to meet with Cristol as we had nothing in common and I did not trust him.

26. Contrary to the misinformation presented by Cristol and others, it is important for the American people to know that it is clear that Israel is responsible for deliberately attacking an American ship and murdering American sailors, whose bereaved shipmates have lived with this egregious conclusion for many years.

Dated: January 8, 2004 at Coronado, California

Ward Boston, Jr., Captain, JAGC, USN (Ret.)

Senior Counsel to the USS *Liberty* Court of Inquiry

The Attack on the Liberty reveals how the "investigation" affected Boston.

The graphic testimony bothered the court members, who also explored the damaged ship. Captain Boston watched men haul bodies out of the torpedoed spaces during a recess. He spotted a sailor emerge from the hole, crying and vomiting after finding a headless body. These sights, coupled with the testimony of the crew, led Boston to conclude the attack must have been deliberate. The excessive damage, the pre-attack reconnaissance, and the sustained and violent assault ruled out friendly fire, he believed. Alone in a stateroom at night, Kidd confided in his lawyer that he agreed, describing the attackers as "murderous bastards." Boston, who would not voice his opinions publicly for 35 years, hinted at his true beliefs in his summation. "After living intimately with the facts of this case for the past week, I have become more and more appalled that such a tragedy should have ever occurred," he told the court. "No matter what conclusions are reached as to the cause of the incident, the horrendous impact of the effect should disturb even the most impassioned."

45

Moorer

Just three-and-a-half short months before he passed on, Tom Moorer, a great American patriot I came to personally know and love, released a report into the massacre on my ship.

Alabama born and raised Thomas Hinman "Tom" Moorer rose through the ranks in the USN as a naval aviator to become an admiral, the CNO—the highest you can go in the USN—from '67 to '70, and the Chairman of the JCS—the highest-ranking and senior-most military officer in the entire U.S. Armed Forces—from '70 to '74.

According to Arlington National Cemetery's website, Admiral Moorer "was promoted to Rear Admiral in 1958, reportedly becoming at age 45 the youngest officer at the time selected for that rank. He made Vice Admiral in 1962 and full Admiral two years later. *Time* magazine called him "America's fastest-rising sailor."

Admiral Thomas Hinman "Tom" Moorer, taken a few months after the massacre

Prior to his 2003 report, Tom issued a statement on the 30th anniversary of the massacre, still furious about how my ship and its crew had been treated after three decades, produced in part below:

MEMORANDUM:

From: Admiral Thomas H. Moorer

Subject: Attack on the USS *Liberty* June 8, 1967

Date: June 8, 1997

I have never believed that the attack on the USS *Liberty* was a case of mistaken identity. That is ridiculous. I have flown over the Atlantic and Pacific oceans, thousands of hours, searching for ships and identifying all types of ships at sea. The *Liberty* was the ugliest, strangest looking ship in the U.S. Navy. As a communications intelligence ship, it was sprouting every kind of antenna. It looked like a lobster with all those projections moving every which way.

Israel knew perfectly well that the ship was American. After all, the *Liberty*'s American flag and markings were in full view in perfect visibility for the Israeli aircraft that overflew the ship eight times over a period of nearly eight hours prior to the attack. I am confident that Israel knew the *Liberty* could intercept radio messages from all parties and potential parties to the ongoing war, then in its fourth day, and that Israel was preparing to seize the Golan Heights from Syria despite President Johnson's known opposition to such a move. I think they realized that if we learned in advance of their plan, there would be a tremendous amount of negotiating between Tel Aviv and Washington.

And I believe Moshe Dayan concluded that he could prevent Washington from becoming aware of what Israel was up to by destroying the primary source of acquiring that information: the USS *Liberty*. The result was a wanton sneak attack that left 34 American sailors dead and 171 seriously injured. What is so chilling and cold-blooded, of course, is that they could kill as many Americans as they did in confidence that Washington would cooperate in quelling any public outcry.

I have to conclude that it was Israel's intent to sink the *Liberty* and leave as few survivors as possible. Up to the point where the torpedo boats were sent in, you could speculate on that point. You have to remember that the *Liberty* was an intelligence ship, not a fighting ship, and its only defensive weapons were a pair of .50 caliber machineguns both aft and on the forecastle. There was little the men could do to fight off the air assault from Israeli jets that pounded the *Liberty* with bombs, rockets, napalm and machinegun fire for 25 minutes.

With the *Liberty* riddled with holes, fires burning, and scores of casualties, three Israeli torpedo boats closed in for the kill. The second of three torpedoes ripped through a compartment at amidships, drowning 25 of the men in that section. Then the torpedo boats closed to within 100 feet of the *Liberty* to continue the attack with cannons and machineguns, resulting in further casualties. It is telling—with respect to whether total annihilation was the intent—that the *Liberty* crew has reported that the torpedo boats' machineguns also were turned on life rafts that were deployed into the Mediterranean as well as those few on deck that had escaped damage.

As we know now, if the rescue aircraft from U.S. carriers had not been recalled, they would have arrived at the *Liberty* before the torpedo attack, reducing the death toll by 25. The torpedo boat commanders could not be certain that Sixth Fleet aircraft were not on the way and this might have led to their breaking off the attack after 40 minutes rather than remaining to send the *Liberty* and its crew of 294 to the bottom. Congress to this day has failed to hold formal hearings for the record on the *Liberty* affair. This is unprecedented and a national disgrace. I spent hours on the Hill giving testimony after the USS *Pueblo*, a sister ship to the *Liberty*, was seized by North Korea. I was asked every imaginable question, including why a carrier in the area failed to dispatch aircraft to aid the *Pueblo*. In the *Liberty* case, fighters were put in the air not once, but twice. They were ordered to stand down by Secretary of Defense McNamara and President Johnson for reasons the American public deserves to know.

The captain and crew of the *Liberty*, rather than being widely acclaimed as the heroes they most certainly are, have been silenced, ignored, honored belatedly and away from the cameras, and denied a history that accurately reflects their ordeal. I was appalled that six of the dead from the *Liberty* lay under a tombstone at Arlington Cemetery that described them as having "died in the eastern Mediterranean," as if disease rather than Israeli intent had caused their deaths. The Naval Academy failed to record the name of Lt. Stephen Toth in Memorial Hall on the grounds that he had not been killed in battle. I intervened and was able to reverse the apparent idea that dying in a cowardly, one-sided attack by a supposed ally is somehow not the same as being killed by an avowed enemy.

Commander McGonagle's story is the stuff of naval tradition. Badly wounded in the first air attack, lying on the deck and losing blood, he refused any treatment that would take him from his battle station on the bridge. He continued to direct the ship's defense, the control of flooding and fire, and by his own example inspired the survivors to heroic efforts to save the ship. He did not relinquish his post until hours later, after having directed the crippled ship's navigation to a rendezvous with a U.S. destroyer and final arrival in Malta.

I must have gone to the White House 15 times or more to watch the President personally award the Congressional Medal of Honor to Americans of special valor. So it irked the hell out of me when McGonagle's ceremony was relegated to the obscurity of the Washington Navy Yard and the medal was presented by the Secretary of the Navy. This was a back-handed slap. Everyone else received their medal at the White House. President Johnson must have been concerned about the reaction of the Israeli lobby.

A little over six years after this memorandum, Tom released— with several other noted patriots—"The Moorer Report," officially entitled "Findings of the Independent Commission of Inquiry into the Israeli Attack on USS *Liberty*, the Recall of Military Rescue Support Aircraft while the Ship was Under Attack, and the Subsequent Cover-up by the United States Government."

The entire report, reproduced below, was published in the Congressional Record by Congressman John Conyers on October 7, 2004:

Capitol Hill, Washington, D.C.

October 22, 2003

Admiral Thomas H. Moorer, USN, (Ret.)
Former Chairman, Joint Chiefs of Staff

General Raymond G. Davis, USMC, (MOH)
Former Assistant Commandant of the Marine Corps

Rear Admiral Merlin Staring, USN, (Ret.)
Former Judge Advocate General of the Navy

Ambassador James Akins, (Ret.)
Former U.S. Ambassador to Saudi Arabia

We, the undersigned, having undertaken an independent investigation of Israel's attack on USS *Liberty*, including eyewitness testimony from surviving crewmembers, a review of naval and other official records, an examination of official statements by the Israeli and American governments, a study of the conclusions of all previous official inquiries, and a consideration of important new evidence and recent statements from individuals having direct knowledge of the attack or the cover-up, hereby find the following:

1. That on June 8, 1967, after eight hours of aerial surveillance, Israel launched a two-hour air and naval attack against USS *Liberty*, the world's most sophisticated intelligence ship, inflicting 34 dead and 173 wounded American servicemen (a casualty rate of 70%, in a crew of 294);

2. That the Israeli air attack lasted approximately 25 minutes, during which time unmarked Israeli aircraft dropped napalm canisters on USS *Liberty*'s bridge, and fired 30 mm cannons and rockets into our ship, causing 821 holes, more than 100 of which were rocket-size; survivors estimate 30 or more sorties were flown over the ship by a minimum of 12 attacking Israeli planes which were jamming all five American emergency radio channels;

3. That the torpedo boat attack involved not only the firing of torpedoes, but the machine-gunning of *Liberty*'s firefighters and stretcher-bearers as they struggled to save their ship and crew; the Israeli torpedo boats later returned to machine-gun at close range three of the *Liberty*'s life rafts that had been lowered into the water by survivors to rescue the most seriously wounded;

4. That there is compelling evidence that Israel's attack was a deliberate attempt to destroy an American ship and kill her entire crew; evidence of such intent is supported by statements from Secretary of State Dean Rusk, Undersecretary of State George Ball, former CIA director Richard Helms, former NSA directors Lieutenant General William Odom, USA (Ret.), Admiral Bobby Ray

Inman, USN (Ret.), and Marshal Carter; former NSA deputy directors Oliver Kirby and Major General John Morrison, USAF (Ret.); and former Ambassador Dwight Porter, U.S. Ambassador to Lebanon in 1967;

5. That in attacking USS *Liberty*, Israel committed acts of murder against American servicemen and an act of war against the United States;

6. That fearing conflict with Israel, the White House deliberately prevented the U.S. Navy from coming to the defense of USS *Liberty* by recalling Sixth Fleet military rescue support while the ship was under attack; evidence of the recall of rescue aircraft is supported by statements of Captain Joe Tully, Commanding Officer of the aircraft carrier USS *Saratoga*, and Rear Admiral Lawrence Geis, the Sixth Fleet carrier division commander, at the time of the attack; never before in American naval history has a rescue mission been cancelled when an American ship was under attack;

7. That although *Liberty* was saved from almost certain destruction through the heroic efforts of the ship's Captain, William L. McGonagle (MOH), and his brave crew, surviving crewmembers were later threatened with "court-martial, imprisonment or worse" if they exposed the truth; and were abandoned by their own government;

8. That due to the influence of Israel's powerful supporters in the United States, the White House deliberately covered up the facts of this attack from the American people;

9. That due to continuing pressure by the pro-Israel lobby in the United States, this attack remains the only serious naval incident that has never been thoroughly investigated by Congress; to this day, no surviving crewmember has been permitted to officially and publicly testify about the attack;

10. That there has been an official cover-up without precedent in American naval history; the existence of such a cover-up is now supported by statements of Rear Admiral Merlin Staring, USN (Ret.), former Judge Advocate General of the Navy; and Captain Ward Boston, USN, (Ret.), the chief counsel to the Navy's 1967 Court of Inquiry of *Liberty* attack;

11. That the truth about Israel's attack and subsequent White House cover-up continues to be officially concealed from the American people to the present day and is a national disgrace;

12. That a danger to our national security exists whenever our elected officials are willing to subordinate American interests to those of any foreign nation, and specifically are unwilling to challenge Israel's interests when they conflict with American interests; this policy, evidenced by the failure to defend USS *Liberty* and the subsequent official cover-up of the Israeli attack, endangers the safety of Americans and the security of the United States.

WHEREUPON, we, the undersigned, in order to fulfill our duty to the brave crew of USS *Liberty* and to all Americans who are asked to serve in our Armed Forces, hereby call upon the Department of the Navy, the Congress of the United States and the American people to immediately take the following actions:

FIRST: That a new Court of Inquiry be convened by the Department of the Navy, operating with Congressional oversight, to take public testimony from surviving crewmembers; and to thoroughly investigate the circumstances of the attack on the USS *Liberty*, with full cooperation from the National Security Agency, the Central Intelligence Agency and the military intelligence services, and to determine Israel's possible motive in launching said attack on a U.S. naval vessel;

SECOND: That every appropriate committee of the Congress of the United States investigate the actions of the White House and Defense Department that prevented the rescue of the USS *Liberty*, thereafter threatened her surviving officers and men if they exposed the truth, and covered up the true circumstances of the attack from the American people; and

THIRD: That the eighth day of June of every year be proclaimed to be hereafter known as

USS *LIBERTY* REMEMBRANCE DAY, in order to commemorate USS *Liberty*'s heroic crew; and to educate the American people of the danger to our national security inherent in any passionate attachment of our elected officials for any foreign nation.

We, the undersigned, hereby affix our hands and seals, this 22nd day of October, 2003.

Thomas H. Moorer
Raymond G. Davis
Merlin Staring
James Akins

And what did the U.S. Congress and the mainstream media do after the findings of this study were released? You could still hear the crickets chirping.

46

Symposium

B oston's revelations were a bombshell, and that is putting it mildly. Here we had someone who was on the inside of the cover-up and who had witnessed everything on a firsthand basis admitting what we *Liberty* survivors had been asserting all this time.

Therefore, in the interests of throwing a bucket of water on what could easily have become an out-of-control fire as far as the *Liberty* cover-up went, busy little bees went into action.

It was decided that a "symposium" would take place at the U.S. State Department to "discuss" the event. D.C. hadn't suddenly come down with an attack of patriotism; the reason for doing this was not a fact-finding mission but rather to further bury the truth.

It was just another kangaroo court of sorts, not unlike a guy being on trial for raping a girl where the judge, prosecuting attorney and jury are all members of her immediate family.

In 2004, I stood outside the U.S. State Department building with my friend Matthew Balic, a long-time *Liberty* supporter who arranged for me to be there. Standing with us in the cold January weather was Pat Blue, widow of the aforementioned Alan Blue, the NSA linguist blown to bits from the torpedo blast that hit the CT spaces, as well as former CT Joe Lentini, who only barely survived.

Matt also paid $18,000 for two full-page announcements of my letter to President George W. Bush to appear in *The Washington Times* when I was president of the LVA.

The letter was a personal account of what I saw that day as our ship was attacked as well as the subsequent cover-up and a plea for him to do his duty as President in fixing what was unquestionably an act of war against America.

U.S. Department of State 2201 C Street NW Washington, D.C.

As the symposium was the closest thing we ever had to telling our story to an official body in Washington D.C., we all thought that perhaps this was "it," and that after we told our story, heads would start to roll.

Before entering the room we had to provide our IDs and names, which were written down and given to the "proper authorities," meaning the individuals overseeing the event.

We sat down and waited for our day in court. I was in the second row from the front.

Once the show began, Marc J. Susser, head moderator of the symposium and the State Department's "official" historian, stood and gave an almost 45-minute speech which was clearly meant to poison the water. It was obvious that he was totally on the side of Israel and her insulting "mistaken identity" story. He constantly referred in glowing terms and slavish demeanor to Cristol, who sat up on an elevated podium at a long table, smiling like a mob lawyer who knew his client was about to get an acquittal because the judge and jury had been bribed.

Before Susser's speech, the *Liberty* survivors present were introduced to the audience, so they certainly knew who we were ahead of time.

As the symposium began, it was obvious from the beginning that it was going to be yet another whitewash.

389

Besides Cristol, there was Michael B. Oren—born Michael Scott Bornstein—an American-born Israeli who was former Israeli Ambassador to the U.S. (2009-2013) and is currently a member of the Knesset, Israel's parliament, as well as a close personal friend of Benjamin "Bibi" Netanyahu, the same man who characterized the 9/11 attacks as "good" because they would generate "immediate sympathy" for Israel.

In the final tally, James Bamford was the only one out of the seven up there who wasn't part of Susser's crooked jury.

Bamford, a former Naval Intelligence Analyst and best-selling author on matters dealing with the NSA—who has always been a supporter and friend of the *Liberty*—read aloud Boston's affidavit.

They bantered about for around an hour, debating small items about the massacre that day but never mentioning the cover-up that followed. Cristol's book was used over and over again as the "definitive source" in refuting any evidence revealing Israel's culpability.

Not just the panel, but the audience as well was packed with Israeli supporters. You could see it in their demeanor, as their arrogance and hostility towards us was obvious. They smiled, chuckled, snickered and in general showed their approval for anything Cristol or anyone else said in perpetuating the "big lie." In general, the entire thing was just as much a defamation of not only the dead, but the survivors as well, as the original "investigation" had been almost 37 years earlier.

After the panel finished with what was, for all intents and purposes, one big jabber-jawing session in favor of Israel, Susser gave yet another painfully long speech about how the matter was settled and we should all just go back to thinking Israel is America's best buddy in the universe. He then opened up a question and answer session from the audience.

Joe was physically closer to the microphone than I was, so he got there before I did and spoke for a few minutes without addressing any of the lies in Cristol's book, only saying that he was not friends with Cristol, as Cristol had alleged during interviews with him.

As soon as he finished I prepared for my turn, since I was standing at the other microphone. When they saw that it was yours truly, Susser hastily announced the symposium was over—immediately. My microphone was cut off so that no one could hear anything I said.

Several people in the audience, including my friend Matt shouted out loud, "LET HIM SPEAK!" several times, but to no avail.

The reason they cut my microphone off so quick was no mystery—the symposium was being covered by C-SPAN—Cable-Satellite Public Affairs Network—which meant it would be broadcast across the nation.

I was so angry I was shaking and ready to explode. The USS *Liberty* had just been torpedoed again, only this time instead of Israel doing it off the coast of the Sinai, it was done within the walls of our very own State Department.

Not that I should have been particularly surprised at this. After all, just a short distance away you could go to Arlington National Cemetery and view the headstones of those killed in the attack on our ship, and not one of them mentions it was Israel who did the killing. Furthermore, out of the 200-plus decorated vets from the *Liberty* awarded Purple Hearts, Bronze Stars, Silver Stars and everything else you can imagine, there had never been one word discussed about why those awards were handed out. In fact, *Liberty* is arguably the most decorated ship in the annals of naval history in a single engagement. There isn't a single case in the history of our country, going all the way back to the American Revolution, of someone being killed in action with no mention being made of how it happened, except ours.

Matt and I left the building and got on the tram for the hotel, not saying a word the whole time, as we were so upset.

Later that day I got on a plane wearing the same outfit I wear everywhere I go—my Purple Heart USS *Liberty* jacket and my blue USS *Liberty* hat. I had a two-hour wait at the airport, so in utter disbelief and yet believing it all, I sat at the bar and had a beer, hoping the medicine in the bottle would help calm me down and dampen my fury.

I boarded the plane, got to my seat, leaned back as far as I could and prepared myself for what would be one of the longest flights I had ever taken. Despite everything I had been through up to that point, if someone had told me ahead of time I would see what I just saw, I would never have believed them.

As soon as I got home, I wrote a letter to Secretary of State Colin Powell demanding that he fire Susser for the disrespect he personally showed my 34 dead shipmates and the rest of the crew. I further categorized what had just taken place within the walls of the State Department as being every bit as diabolical as the attack itself. I sent the letter certified—not just one copy but several—and never received a reply.

Significantly, around five years later, the Jewish Susser was "reassigned after an inspector general's investigation found 'serious mismanagement for which the director must be held accountable.'"

NSA Headquarters Fort Meade Maryland

Dave Gahary and I found out while writing this book that the dishonor showed the crew of *Liberty*—living and dead—wasn't just confined to the halls of "Foggy Bottom"—a nickname for the U.S. Department of State when its headquarters moved to the Harry S. Truman Building in 1947, where the office of the U.S. Secretary of State now resides.

The aforementioned filmmaker and author Richard Belfield experienced something strikingly similar at the NSA, jokingly referred to by some as No Such Agency.

Every two years the NSA does a conference on historical cryptography, and I wrote a [2008] book about six unsolved codes, *The Six Unsolved Ciphers: Inside the Mysterious Codes That Have Confounded the World's Greatest Cryptographers.*

In 2009 I did a talk at the NSA about an unsolved code about an English stately home, and there was a session on the *Liberty*. And the way the NSA behaved was disgraceful, because the day before there was a session on the *Pueblo*, and the *Pueblo* crew were up on the stage and were feted, and all these people from the NSA were groveling around them and telling them what heroes they were.

And the next day there's a session on the *Liberty*, and James [Scott] had 20 minutes and then there were three Israeli apologists, and when James was 18 minutes in, the moderator from the NSA was telling James he had to wrap up. And then we had these three Israeli propagandists really, including that judge [Cristol] who's written that ridiculous book. They were all allowed to go over on time, and so at the end there was virtually no time for debate.

And the crew were all in the audience, and the crew stood up, and said, "How come the *Pueblo* were treated like heroes, and we're just treated with contempt?" And Jim Bamford stood up and said this was the most disgraceful thing he'd ever seen the NSA ever do.

Richard knew why *Liberty* was—and still is—allowed to be treated like dirt.

That's the pressure of the Lobby.

47

Warcrimes

On June 8, 2005, the 38th anniversary of the massacre on the *Liberty*, a 28-page war crimes report was submitted to the Secretary of the Army for crimes committed against U.S. military personnel. It was filed by the LVA on behalf of the surviving crewmembers of USS *Liberty*.

The "CONCLUSION" states in part:

> The USS *Liberty* Veterans Association has established, *prima facie* [at first appearance], the commission of war crimes by the state of Israel against U.S. military personnel and civilians. These Americans volunteered to serve their country. They followed all orders given to them. In the course of following those orders, they were suddenly and deliberately attacked by naval and air forces of the state of Israel and their country did absolutely nothing to protect them or seek justice on their behalf.
>
> The failure of the United States government to undertake a complete investigation of the Israeli attack on USS *Liberty* has resulted in grievous harm to the surviving victims, as well as to the families of all crewmembers. Equally serious, this failure has resulted in an indelible stain upon the honor of the United States of America. It has sent a signal to America's serving men and women that their welfare is always subordinate to the interests of a foreign state. The only conceivable reason for this failure is the political decision to put the interests of Israel

ahead of those of American servicemen, employees, and veterans.

Finally, the fact that the Israeli government and its surrogates in the United States have worked so long and hard to prevent an inquiry itself speaks volumes as to what such an inquiry would find.

James Ronald Gotcher III was the attorney who filed the report, along with the LVA's board, and although he was not on *Liberty*, nor in the USN, he felt compelled to do his part to set the record straight.

Ron explained how he got involved with *Liberty*.

I was sitting in Vietnam in June of '67 when *Liberty* was attacked, and I saw clear evidence that it was a deliberate attack and nothing was ever done about it, and I was furious about that. And then in January, the USS *Pueblo* got taken, and nothing was done about that. And then a few months later, a Navy EC-121 flying over the Sea of Japan got shot down by the North Koreans, and nothing was ever done about that. And it bothered me; it really, really bothered me.

Ron was a 20-year-old analyst and weapons controller in the Air Force Security Service assigned to the 6924th Security Squadron in Vietnam.

As he detailed in a declaration he signed May 17, 2004:

During the early evening (local time) of June 8, 1967 we received a CRITIC [Critical Intelligence Communications] message, informing us that USS *Liberty* was under attack by Israeli aircraft. Shortly thereafter, we began receiving rough translations of the Israeli air-to-air and air-to-ground communications.

The next day, we received the final translations of the intercepts. There was virtually no difference between the two versions.

While I have a clear recollection of reading transcripts of conversations between pilots and controllers, I do not recall ever reading anything similar to the transcripts recently released by the National Security Agency concerning Israeli helicopter pilots.

It was clear from the explicit statements made about "the American ship" by both the aircraft crews and the controllers that the aircraft were flying a planned mission to find and sink USS *Liberty*.

My understanding of what I read led me to conclude that the Israeli pilots were making every effort possible to sink USS *Liberty* and were very frustrated by their inability to do so.

Approximately 10 days to two weeks later, we received an internal NSA report summarizing the Agency's findings. The report stated, in no uncertain terms, that the attack was planned in advance and deliberately executed. The mission was to sink USS *Liberty*.

A few days after the report arrived, another message came through directing the document control officer to gather and destroy all copies of both the rough and final intercept translations, as well as the subsequently issued report.

After the destruction of those documents, I saw nothing further on this subject. I have read the translated transcripts, released by the Israeli government, which purport to be actual transcripts of the air-to-ground communications between the controllers and the attacking aircraft. I know this document to be a fabrication because I have read the actual intercepts and they were nothing like this. It is not possible that the differences could be due to different translations being used.

If called upon to testify, I am competent to testify to all of the foregoing on the basis of direct observation and personal knowledge.

Ron explained why the war crimes report was filed.

Just frustration with not being able to get anything done and we thought this would provoke something.

I read Jim Ennes's book and I was more upset than ever, but I couldn't really do anything about it. Then I had occasion to get to know Jim toward the end of the '90s and we became very close friends, in fact, we talked every day. And I started getting more and more involved in *Liberty* matters. And as that progressed, I started talking to different guys and talking about what could be done, and we were brainstorming ideas. I think that Joe Meadors came up with the idea of the war crimes report.

Ron explained the rationale behind the war crimes report, entitled "A Report: War Crimes Committed Against U.S. Military Personnel, June 8, 1967."

Federal law provides that any reported war crimes by members of the U.S. military or against members of military must be reported to the Secretary of the Army— who acts as a screener for the Secretary of Defense—who then takes it under advisement and decides what needs to be done.

What we decided to do, and by "we" I mean the LVA board and I—as well as a bunch of other LVA members who weren't part of the board at that time—was put together a very carefully drafted war crimes report. Being a lawyer, that became my job, so I drafted it. The writing's all mine, and any mistakes in there are mine, although I don't think there are any.

And what I decided to do, tactically, was only use undisputed facts. And by undisputed facts I mean statements made by the Israelis, officially, and statements made by the United States and others that were never contradicted or otherwise controverted by the Israelis.

So for example, Jim Ennes made log entries concerning seven overflights by Israeli aircraft during the morning before the attack, where an Israeli aircraft would fly out, circle them, and then fly back. And he put those in the ship's log, which we still have. The Israelis did not dispute that. The speed of the ship just before they came under attack, according to the ship's log, they were making turns for about five knots, but they were going into a five knot current, so they were basically standing still. And that really wasn't disputed by anyone. The Israelis alleged that a pilot said that the ship was moving at high speed at 25 knots or whatever, which I didn't have a problem dealing with that because on the one hand you have an official ship's log from a United States Navy ship and on the other you have an unauthenticated allegation by an alleged pilot about a ship that was only operating one boiler at the time and when both boilers were operating could do no more than 20 knots.

There were things like that that just didn't make sense, but for the most part we took statements from the official Israeli reports like the naval observer who came back to air force headquarters at 11 A.M., or in the hour between 11 and 12, and then opened up a copy of *Janes* [*Fighting Ships*] and pointed to the ship that he saw earlier that morning, which was USS *Liberty*, it was a photo of USS *Liberty*, and he said, "Yeah, that's what it was." He admitted that. So, an hour before the attack they knew the identity, the specific identity of the ship.

It's very heavily footnoted. Every allegation of fact is footnoted. We put all of this together and reached a conclusion.

Essentially, what we argued was, both the U.S. and Israel were signatories to the Geneva Conventions, and all of it, various protocols, The Hague Convention on Naval Warfare, The London Convention on Naval Warfare overall, those were all incorporated up into the Geneva Conventions, and they dictate how belligerents must behave during war.

No one disputes that USS *Liberty* was about 21 miles off the coast of Egypt [then the United Arab Republic]. Israel claimed, at that time, a three-mile territorial limit. The Egyptians claimed a 12-mile limit. Immediately prior to the attack, Lloyd Painter triangulated two objects on the shore and determined that they were, I think, 21.6 miles from the coast. So they were clearly in international waters.

International law requires a belligerent to identify a target before attacking it. You can't just go out and start shooting up everything under the sun. They had an affirmative legal obligation to identify the target. And the way they were supposed to proceed under international law was that they were required to direct the unknown ship to heave to so that they could come aboard and inspect their paperwork.

Now, obviously if they had done that they would have been told this was a U.S. Navy ship in international waters, get the hell out of here. But they made no attempt to have the vessel heave to. No one was firing at them, no one was shooting at them, the ship didn't pose any danger to them. So there was absolutely no excuse for attacking; no legal justification whatsoever. They attacked a neutral ship in international waters. That's a war crime.

Putting aside the international definition that it's a war crime, under the U.S. Code, assaulting a member of the U.S. government, which includes people in the military, is a federal crime. And killing someone, killing an American particularly, a military person, overseas in a situation like this on the high seas, constitutes murder. There is no statute of limitations on murder, so there were 34 murders committed. The assaults on the other people, while the statutes of limitations had passed, the murders are still there and this was murder. You cannot lash out and attack someone without knowing who they are, without suffering consequences.

Imagine you're a homeowner, you hear somebody out in the street and you think maybe they're going to burgle your house, but they're out in the middle of the street, you can't quite see them. So you take a gun and you shoot them. That's murder. They're not on your property, they're not posing any kind of threat, but you've killed them. So that's pretty much the case.

We made a case that if you look at the undisputed facts: Liberty was a neutral ship, in international waters, the Israelis made no effort to identify it, and they attacked it, that's a war crime. But we don't have to go to The Hague for it because they also committed crimes under the U.S. Criminal Code.

And so what we wanted the Secretary of the Army to do was recommend to the Secretary of Defense that the matter be referred to the Department of Justice and that the criminals responsible for these acts be extradited to stand trial in the U.S.

As it turned out they said, "Nope, we don't find any basis for proceeding."

The answer was the next closest thing to being ignored.

Ron didn't think the report would ever be honored, because it was Israel who committed the crime.

Ron also explained that although the U.S. Constitution's Article 1 Section 8 is a law "to define and punish piracies and felonies committed on the high seas and offenses against the law of nations," and would apply to the attack on *Liberty*, it doesn't force Congress to act.

> That would work. It gives Congress plenary power to do that, but it doesn't mandate that Congress must. That's one of the big problems with agency law. You argue that Congress must do this, and the courts say, "No, don't think so."

What about a full congressional investigation?

> It isn't legally required. Decency requires it. It's the only attack with that kind of loss of life that hasn't involved an investigation.

Although many claim that *Liberty* is the most decorated ship in the U.S. Navy for a single action, the Naval History and Heritage Command (NHHC), which is "responsible for the preservation, analysis, and dissemination of U.S. naval history and heritage," disagrees, stating in an email that "NHHC has not recognized any ship's claim to be the most decorated, primarily because there is disagreement about what defines a decoration."

Ron thinks that has more to do with who attacked *Liberty*.

> I would think that nobody else comes close. You have a Medal of Honor, a Navy Cross, several Silver Stars, Bronze Stars, 208 Purple Hearts. I can't imagine any unit getting more awards than that. I just can't imagine anybody, any ship or Air Force squadron, or Army or Marine unit getting more awards than that for a single action.

Then why won't they recognize *Liberty*?

They're afraid of Israel.

48

Billboards

A recent event that occurred in the early part of 2016 painfully illustrates how difficult it has been for USS *Liberty* survivors and supporters to get our story out to the American people, or anyone else in the world for that matter. It also shows how groups and individuals use money, or the threat of withholding it, to pressure businesses to comply with their demands.

One sole billboard was taken out by the group "Friends of the *Liberty*," which refers to itself as "a bipartisan association of friends, supporters, and USS *Liberty* family members, including Senator Adlai Stevenson III, Senator James Abourezk, Congressman Pete McCloskey, retired Brigadier General James J. David, and former high level CIA officer Raymond McGovern."

Billboard, in West Haven, Connecticut, on Interstate 95

And the billboard in question, what did it say to so offend American Jews and Israel partisans in this country? Eight words that speak the truth and that no one can deny:

"Help the USS *Liberty* Survivors," and below those words, "Attacked by Israel."

Apparently it's OK to ask the public to help all members of the U.S. Armed Forces except those who were attacked by Israel.

And why might that be? Well, because it's anti-Israel, ant-Jewish and anti-Semitic, according to those whose desire is to keep the true story of the massacre on the USS *Liberty* under wraps.

The billboard, in West Haven, Connecticut, on Interstate 95 "is sparking outrage from a local lawyer and criticism from the Anti-Defamation League [ADL] for what they say is its anti-Israel message," reported the *New Haven Register* on March 25, 2016.

"Inoffensive to southbound drivers but highly offensive to north bound drivers," said Max Buxbaum, an attorney who lives and works in New York but grew up in New Haven and has a home in East Haven.

"It's one of those conspiracy theories that are kept alive by the same sort of people who say that Jews are responsible for everything from Pearl Harbor to 9/11," he wrote in an email to the newspaper. "Considering that my father's entire family was wiped out in the Holocaust, it was particularly troubling to me on a personal level."

OK, Max, so what happened to me and my shipmates on June 8, 1967, is a conspiracy theory? You mean Israel attacking our ship and murdering 34 of my shipmates and wounding 174 others—including me—really didn't happen?

Steve Ginsburg, the regional director of the ADL-Connecticut, said while the words themselves are not anti-Semitic, "the misleading ad targets Israel and that can have an anti-Semitic impact."

"It is clearly anti-Semitic in its conspiracy theory (against Israel) that has been proven wrong," he said.

Proven wrong, Steve?

The co-owner of the billboard company said he received a phone call about the billboard and sent his sales staff to check it out and he personally went to the website and clicked the links "to determine whether there was hateful language against Israel by the group or its supporters."

"I found nothing that appears to be anti-Semitic," Bruce Barrett said.

"Friends of the Liberty" placed a few billboards across the country, and, well, you can guess what happened.

The reaction to one in the Keystone State is indicative of Israel's power over our so-called representatives. No less than 14 Pennsylvania House of Representatives members (read: traitors) from South Central Pennsylvania wrote a letter to "Friends of the Liberty" demanding the billboard's removal. Forget the First Amendment, especially where Israel is concerned.

Several billboards across the U.S. were taken down because they were offensive to some American Jews, who were—and are— uncomfortable with the fact that a foreign country, a country that limits citizenship to race—Israel—attacked a U.S. ship, and would prefer that this fact was erased from history.

Sorry, Charlie, it ain't gonna happen.

49

Fallout

As self-important as it may sound, the attack on my ship and its aftermath had and continues to have a lasting impact on nearly everyone one of our lives—every inhabitant of planet Earth—from June 8, 1967 to the current day. In fact, the attack on the *Liberty*—perhaps more than any other post-WW2 event—set the stage for how our world has unfolded. The ways this is manifested are many, but the consequences of allowing Israel to fulfill and maintain its illegal land grab—and to suffer no punishment for its slaughter of innocent Americans on the high seas in international waters—has certainly not moved the world on a peaceful path.

In the book *Blind Spot: The Secret History of American Counterterrorism*, Timothy Naftali makes very clear where the origins of modern-day terrorism spring from: the Six-Day War and Israel's illegal—not to mention immoral—land grab.

Naftali, a Canadian-American historian and author, was the director of the Richard Nixon Presidential Library and Museum from 2007 to 2011. Before that, his area of focus was the history of counterterrorism and the Cold War. He was an associate professor at the University of Virginia, and taught at Yale—his alma mater—and the University of Hawaii. He holds graduate degrees from Harvard and Johns Hopkins.

While serving as a consultant to the 9/11 Commission, he was commissioned to write an unclassified history of American counterterrorism policy, which was later expanded into *Blind Spot*.

The book traces the history of terrorism on the shores of this once-great nation, and shows Arab terrorists didn't even exist, prior to Israel's land grab.

Soviet terrorism was of even less concern to the FBI in the first decades of the Cold War. What little terrorism there was then in the United States was more the consequence of the Spanish-American War of 1898 than the confrontation with the Kremlin. In the 1950s, radical members of the Puerto Rican independence movement turned to violence and caused a few dramatic terrorist incidents in Washington, D.C. In 1950, two gunmen killed a guard in a failed assassination attempt on President Truman, and four years later some Puerto Rican terrorists opened fire in the House of Representatives from the visitor's gallery, wounding five congressmen. Neither incident caused the FBI or the interested public to treat terrorism as a threat to national security.

The Puerto Rican independence movement operated as a clandestine paramilitary organization whose goal was an independent Puerto Rico. It was responsible for more than 120 bomb attacks on U.S. targets.

Blind Spot pulls no punches identifying who the real culprits are.

Kennedy's successors, Lyndon B. Johnson and Richard Nixon, would be the first American Cold War presidents to have to contend with the problem of international terrorism. As we shall see, the threat involved neither weapons of mass destruction nor the Soviets. Events in the Middle East would be responsible for grabbing Washington's attention and introducing this new threat to the American people.

Again—as was the case when my ship was attacked—Jewish politicians revealed their allegiance to a foreign power, Israel, and not the country of their birth.

Senators Jacob Javitz and Abraham Ribicoff "wanted Congress to be able to dictate to the President which states were sponsors of terror and which, therefore, would have to be punished. It was assumed, for example, that the list would immediately complicate U.S. efforts to facilitate the Arab-Israeli peace process. The two senators had made no secret of their intention to sanction four Arab countries that sponsored Palestinian terrorism."

Naturally these politicians, nor the politicians of today, would ever dare mention the underlying reasons for the terrorism that the entire world has had to live with for over 50 years: Israel's illegal and immoral land grab of June 1967.

Guilt by Association details the consequences of the U.S. government letting Israel get away with premeditated, cold-blooded murder on the high seas of American servicemen, and helping to cover it up.

After President Lyndon Johnson (with the assistance of Admiral John S. McCain, Jr.) covered up Israel's killing of 34 Americans aboard the USS *Liberty* on June 8, 1967, it became clear there was no extreme to which Tel Aviv could go that would endanger White House support. From a game theory perspective, the Six-Day War fulfilled its strategic purpose. It not only rallied moderate Jews who were lukewarm to Colonial Zionism but the success of that territorial expansion also confirmed throughout the Middle East that America was firmly on the side of Israeli expansion, Zionist extremism and fundamentalist Judaism.

The Israeli killing of Americans aboard the USS *Liberty* (a premeditated murder according to Admiral Moorer) marked a strategic milestone for the Jewish state. No one in the Israeli government or military received even a reprimand. Tel Aviv suffered no political repercussions either for its preemptive seizure and continued occupation of Arab lands or for the murder of Americans. Instead, Lyndon Johnson increased U.S. financial military and political support and the Pentagon was directed to include security of the belligerent Zionist state as a strategic objective of U.S. national security.

The failure to prosecute and hold accountable those responsible for the massacre has brought shame on this country.

> The Six-Day War pre-staged today's geopolitics. Following that 1967 conflict, America discredited itself by allowing its values to be associated with Israeli duplicity. By its entangling alliance with a duplicitous state, the U.S. was seen as a partner in the same treachery and deceit for which Israel was already infamous.

The inability to properly punish the murderers also affected U.S. military protocol, whose members—past, present and future—learned Israel comes first, not their own country.

> By advancing the careers of senior naval officers complicit in the cover-up, Johnson signaled future generations of military leaders that they can expect promotions if, following orders, they abandon their tradition of duty and honor. Much as AIPAC intimidated members of Congress by removing from office Paul Findley and others who challenged Israeli policies, LBJ set a precedent for rewarding military commanders who subordinate their honor to Israeli interests.

The free pass given to Israel by the U.S. to murder Americans in international waters has allowed them to punish—day in and day out—the rightful owners of the land they stole.

> Israeli offenses against international law were routinely covered up by U.S. vetoes of UN Security Council resolutions. In the UN General Assembly, American diplomats routinely defended Israeli violations of norms of civilized behavior. As American values of moderation, tolerance and candor became identified with Israeli extremism, racism and deceit, the U.S. emerged guilty

by association. Meanwhile U.S. policymakers continued to deceive themselves that Israel was a democracy and an ally.

With America seen as its defender, Zionist extremists concluded they could ignore international law with impunity. To date, they have been correct, as 39 UN resolutions urged that Israel vacate territories occupied since 1967. With each U.S. veto, the credibility and moral standing of the U.S. declined, along with the authority and effectiveness of the UN as it too became guilty by association.

The failure to address the slaughter had the perverse effect of rewarding the murderers.

Confidential: The Life of Secret Agent Turned Hollywood Tycoon Arnon Milchan, which details Milchan's secret double life—Hollywood heavyweight and Israeli spy—shows how Israel was rewarded shortly after the massacre aboard my ship:

> In late 1967, Israel received its first squadron of McDonnell Douglas A-4 Skyhawks from the United States, which would become its primary ground attack aircraft. A few short years later, on September 5, 1969, it received its first squadron of F-4 Phantoms, also made by McDonnell Douglas.

Guilt by Association added more detail.

> Soon after the Six-Day War, France cancelled an Israeli contract for the delivery of 50 Mirage jet fighters. That led to U.S. negotiations for the delivery to Israel of 50 Phantom F-4 jet fighters beginning in 1969. Within two years of the Six-Day War, the Pentagon was training Israeli pilots on U.S.-made fighter jets. With that step, any future Israeli aggression in the region would be perceived

as enjoying the approval of U.S. foreign policy and the enthusiastic support of Americans.

The refusal to even investigate the vicious assault on my ship has made the entire world a much more dangerous place.

Israel soon emerged as a major arms supplier worldwide as a sizeable portion of its workforce became dependent on the perception of Israel as a weak and vulnerable state under siege by a hostile world of anti-Semites, Jew haters and Holocaust deniers.

Yet it was only after Israel's 1967 land grab that such charges were deployed in the U.S. to intimidate and discredit Americans who criticize Israeli policies.

When Johnson declined to make delivery of nuclear-capable F-4 Phantom jets contingent on Israeli compliance with the Nuclear Non-Proliferation treaty, he not only signaled that the U.S. had no objection to Tel Aviv's nuclear weapons program, he also opened the way for Israeli firms to distribute nuclear components worldwide and signaled the U.S. was not serious about non-proliferation.

50

Movie

The USS *Liberty* is the most decorated United States Naval ship for a single engagement.

But if this is true, why have so few Americans ever heard of the *Liberty*?

The reasons are many, but have everything to do with who attacked the *Liberty* and who covered up the attack, an ongoing and disgraceful cover-up for over 50 years.

Though attempts have been, and continue to be, made, to bring the truth about the massacre on the *Liberty* to a wider audience, those responsible for the attack and the cover-up have many resources available to keep this national tragedy buried.

And the most shocking part of this story, is that the country who attempted to sink the *Liberty* with all those aboard—Israel—on that beautiful, sunny day in the Eastern Mediterranean in June, 1967, not only continues to erase the true history of what happened, but our own country, the United States of America, and those public officials sworn to uphold and defend the U.S. Constitution, initiated the cover-up and continue, to this very second, to dishonor those 34 men viciously slaughtered and the 174 wounded, who are forced to live knowing their own country abandoned them on the altar of political expediency.

The cover-up has been so thorough that this is the only maritime attack in U.S. history not afforded a Congressional investigation. It is a true national disgrace. Based on the new book by *Liberty* survivor Phillip F. Tourney and U.S. Navy veteran David R. Gahary, *Erasing the* Liberty: *The Battle to Keep Alive the Memory of Israel's Massacre on the USS* Liberty, some of the ship's survivors and supporters decided the most effective way to bring the story of the *Liberty* to the widest possible audience was through a full-length feature film.

Liberty survivors are dying off and need to have their story told. They and the American people deserve no less.

Help us make this dream a reality. Donate to the USS *Liberty* film project today.

Visit www.usslibertymovie.com to donate to the film project or order more copies of *Erasing the Liberty* from www.erasingtheliberty. com. All funds received from the sale of the book go towards the film project. Neither Phil nor Dave are compensated from any part of book sales or donations to the film project.

Or send your check or money order to:

Erasing the Liberty LLC
6256 Bullet Drive
Crestview FL 32536

Appendix

Operation Susannah: The Lavon Affair and its
Meaning for the USS *Liberty*

One of the most pressing questions to arise from the attack on the USS *Liberty* remains the question of "why." Why would Israel carry out the attack on an American ship in the first place?

Why would the Israeli air force and navy try its very best to sink the USS *Liberty* at the very height of the Six-Day War, when Israeli troops were marching across the Sinai Desert? What possible purpose could such an attack serve?

The only possible answer to this question lies in an understanding of how the Jewish state has attempted—largely successfully—to manipulate Western governments into intervening in the Middle East on behalf of Israel.

The so-called "Lavon Affair," or to give it its real name, Operation Susannah, provides a perfect example of this strategy, and its meaning cannot be lost on anyone who is familiar with the story of the attack on the USS *Liberty*.

In July 1954, a series of four bombings took place in Egypt. The first explosion, on July 2, 1954, took place at the post office in the port city of Alexandria.

The next few days saw bombings at the U.S. Information Agency in Alexandria, and in Cairo, while a fourth bomb went off at a British-owned theater in Cairo.

The bombs were skilfully assembled. Hidden inside books, they were made of nitro-glycerine inserted into cut-out books, and triggered by an acid-based substance which provided a sophisticated time delay mechanism.

The bombings—all aimed at American and British linked establishments—appeared to be the work of Egyptian nationalists, and the Muslim Brotherhood in particular, which already had a long history of antagonism with the British colonial authorities and the Americans, who were, correctly, viewed as proxies for the Israelis.

The background to this antagonism lay with the British occupation of the area around the Suez Canal. In 1936, the two nations had signed the Anglo-Egyptian Treaty in terms of which Britain was granted a lease on the Suez for 20 years.

In 1951, however, the Egyptian government had declared the treaty void, and demanded that Britain withdraw all its troops. The British refused, pointing to the 1936 treaty and beefed up its military presence in the Suez.

The rising hostility with Egyptian nationalists soon erupted into unrest, and in January 1952, an attempt by the British to disarm an Egyptian auxiliary police force in Ismailia led to the deaths of 41 Egyptians.

The deaths in turn resulted in massive anti-Western riots in Cairo. British and American-owned buildings were attacked, and dozens of Westerners were killed, including at least 12 UK nationals.

The unrest in turn led to a military coup by the Egyptian nationalist "Free Officers Movement"—led by Muhammad Neguib and future Egyptian President Gamal Abdel Nasser.

Although Britain—and America—attempted to patch up relations with the new government—most notably by the British withdrawing from its occupation of the Sudan in return for the Egyptians abandoning their claim to the region, and the Americans opening relations with the new government—tensions still remained, and sporadic outbursts of violence occurred.

Thus the bombings of July 1954 came as no surprise—and it was almost immediately condemned as the work of Egyptian nationalists.

Would the British react as expected, and intervene militarily?

Then, at a critical phase, the Egyptian government announced a dramatic development: they had arrested the bombing team.

Instead of Egyptian nationalists, the bombers were Israeli secret service agents, members of a secret cell known as Unit 131.

One of the Unit 131 Jews, agent Avri Elad, provided the key to unravelling the operation.

Sent in to oversee the bombings, Elad had somehow come to the attention of the Egyptian intelligence agency, and this had led them to arresting one of the Jewish saboteurs *in flagrante delicto*—"caught red-handed"—outside the fifth target, the famous Rio Theatre in Alexandria.

The Jew, named Philip Natanson, was arrested outside the building after the bomb he had been carrying accidentally ignited prematurely.

A search of his residence produced further incriminating evidence and the names of other agents involved in the operation.

Several were arrested, including two Egyptian Jews and the undercover Israelis, Yosef Carmon and Israeli Meir Max Bineth. Elad and others however managed to escape and flee back to Israel.

The Jewish terrorists were put on trial and in January 1955, with two of the main accused, Moshe Marzouk and Shmuel Azar, sentenced to death, while most of the others received long prison terms.

Operation Susannah had been a total failure, and the Israel's Minister of Defense Pinhas Lavon—under whose direction the operation had been planned—was forced to resign. For this reason, the operation became known as the "Lavon Affair."

The reason for the operation soon became clear: Israel had attempted, through the use of violence, to incite both Britain and America into a conflict with the new Egyptian government.

Had this plan succeeded—and there was a very real possibility that it would have—the British and Americans might very well have intervened in Egypt, and deposed the new government, which was overtly hostile to Israel.

Undeterred, it was not long before Israel retook the initiative.

In October 1956, Israel simply invaded Egypt, occupied the Sinai desert—and Britain and France dutifully followed up with their own invasion of Egypt, all in an attempt to forcibly remove the new Egyptian government and to regain full control over the Suez Canal.

This was the infamous "Suez Crisis" of 1956, which was nothing more than a continuation of the events which inspired the Lavon Affair.

The meaning of the Lavon Affair for the USS *Liberty* massacre is clear.

Just as the Israelis attacked British and American targets in Egypt in an attempt to incite war against that latter nation by the Western powers, the attack on the USS *Liberty*—which took place at the very height of the 1967 Six-Day War, fought between June 5 and 10, 1967 by Israel and its neighboring states of Egypt, Jordan and Syria—was obviously designed to have the same effect.

That war had been started when Israel invaded Egypt once again.

What better way to drag America into that war—on Israel's side—than to carry out a repeat of the Lavon Affair, this time using a virtually unarmed American ship as the bait?

If the USS *Liberty* could be sunk—without alerting anybody to who its attackers were—then the loss could be blamed on the Egyptians, exactly as had been the plan of the Lavon Affair, with the bombings in Alexandria and Cairo in 1954.

Once the Americans were convinced that Egypt had attacked and sunk one of their vessels, it would have been an easy step to justify intervention in the Six-Day War—on Israel's side.

This plan was only foiled by the failure to sink the *Liberty* and kill all its crew in the first three attempts. The failure of the torpedo attack on the American vessel must have made it clear to the Israelis that their plan was not going to work—because by now, their signal jamming and destruction of *Liberty*'s antennas had been circumvented, and other American forces had been alerted to the attack.

It was another Lavon Affair—and the only way out was to claim that the attack on *Liberty* had been a "mistake."

This provides the only rational explanation why the attack occurred in the first place. It was yet another example of Israeli malfeasance, a tactic which has characterized all of the Jewish state's interactions with its "greatest ally," America, since then.[1]

---

1 The best evidence of this ongoing betrayal can be seen from the list of Jewish spies arrested while betraying America to Israel. Some of the more prominent examples include:
1970: While working for Senator Henry Jackson, the Jew Richard Perle is caught by the FBI giving classified information to Israel. Nothing is done.
1978: Stephen Bryen, then a Senate Foreign Relations Committee staffer,

is overheard in a D.C. hotel offering confidential documents to top Israeli military officials. Bryen obtains a lawyer, Nathan Lewin, and the case heads for the grand jury, but is mysteriously dropped. Bryen later goes to work for Richard Perle.

1985: Jonathan Pollard—described as the "most damaging spy in U.S. history"—delivered over 1,000 classified documents to Israel while working as an intelligence analyst for the U.S. Navy. Included in those documents were the names of over 150 U.S. agents in the Mideast, who were eventually "turned" into agents for Israel. By far the most serious damage done by Pollard was to steal classified documents relating to the U.S. Nuclear Deterrent relative to the USSR and send them to Israel. According to sources in the U.S. State Department, Israel then turned around and traded those stolen nuclear secrets to the USSR in exchange for increased emigration quotas from the USSR to Israel.

1992: *The Wall Street Journal* reports that Israeli agents tried to steal Recon Optical Inc.'s top-secret airborne spy camera system.

1995: The Defense Investigative Service circulates a memo warning U.S. military contractors that "Israel aggressively collects [U.S.] military and industrial technology." The report stated that Israel obtains information using "ethnic targeting, financial aggrandizement, and identification and exploitation of individual frailties" of U.S. citizens.

1996: A General Accounting Office report, "Defense Industrial Security: Weaknesses in U.S. Security Arrangements With Foreign-Owned Defense Contractors," found that according to intelligence sources "Country A" (identified by intelligence sources as Israel, *Washington Times*, 2/22/96) "conducts the most aggressive espionage operation against the United States of any U.S. ally."

1996: An Office of Naval Intelligence document, "Worldwide Challenges to Naval Strike Warfare" reported that "U.S. technology has been acquired [by China] through Israel in the form of the Lavi fighter and possibly SAM [surface-to-air] missile technology."

1997: An Army mechanical engineer, David A. Tenenbaum, "inadvertently" gives classified military information on missile systems and armored vehicles to Israeli officials." (*New York Times*, 2/20/97)

2004: The arrest of Gentile Lawrence A. Franklin (an analyst of Iranian affairs who worked in the Pentagon) revealed an Israeli spy network that involved the passing of "classified information from the mole, to the men at [the American Israel Political Action Committee] AIPAC, and on to the Israelis," according to a CBS report [Israeli Diplomat, Spy Suspect Met, CBS News, 2/11/09]. Franklin passed information to AIPAC policy director Steven Rosen and AIPAC senior Iran analyst Keith Weissman who were both indicted for illegally conspiring to gather and disclose classified

Postscript: The surviving Unit 131 agents were regarded as heroes in Israel, and in March 2005, the Jewish state publicly honored them when Israeli President Moshe Katsav presented each one with a certificate of appreciation for their efforts.

---

national security information to Israel. The charges against those two Jews were mysteriously dropped.

2008: Ben-Ami Kadish, a former U.S. Army mechanical engineer, pleads guilty to being an "unregistered agent for Israel," and admitted to disclosing classified U.S. documents to Israel in the 1980s.

Index

Symbols

Printed in the USA
CPSIA information can be obtained
at www.ICGtesting.com
JSHW011049091123
51673JS00002B/5